John Buchan was born in 1875 in Perth, the son of a minister. Childhood holidays were spent in the Borders, for which he had a great love. His passion for the Scottish countryside is reflected in his writing. He was educated at Glasgow University and Brasenose College, Oxford, where he was President of the Union.

Called to the Bar in 1901, he became Lord Milner's assistant private secretary in South Africa. In 1907 he was a publisher with Nelson's. In World War I he was a *Times* correspondent at the Front, an officer in the Intelligence Corps and adviser to the War Cabinet. He was elected Conservative MP in one of the Scottish Universities' seats in 1927 and was created Baron Tweedsmuir in 1935. From 1935 until his death in 1940 he was Governor General of Canada.

Buchan is most famous for his adventure stories. High in romance, these are peopled by a large cast of characters, of which Richard Hannay is his best known. Hannay appears in *The Thirty-nine Steps.* Alfred Hitchcock adapted it for the screen. A TV series featured actor Robert Powell as Richard Hannay.

BY THE SAME AUTHOR
ALL PUBLISHED BY HOUSE OF STRATUS

Fiction

The Blanket of the Dark
Castle Gay
The Courts of the Morning
The Dancing Floor
The Free Fishers
The Gap in the Curtain
Greenmantle
Grey Weather
The Half-Hearted
The House of the Four Winds
Huntingtower
The Island of Sheep
John Burnet of Barns
The Long Traverse
A Lost Lady of Old Years
Midwinter
The Path of the King
The Power-House
Prester John
A Prince of the Captivity
The Runagates Club
Salute to Adventurers
The Scholar Gipsies
Sick Heart River
The Thirty-nine Steps
The Three Hostages
The Watcher by the Threshold
Witch Wood

Non-fiction

Augustus
Gordon at Khartoum
Julius Caesar
The King's Grace
The Massacre of Glencoe
Montrose
Oliver Cromwell
Sir Walter Raleigh
Sir Walter Scott

JOHN BUCHAN

The Clearing House

First published in 1946

This edition published in 2001 by House of Stratus, an imprint of
Stratus Holdings plc, 24c Old Burlington Street, London, W1X 1RL, UK.
Also at: Suite 210, 1270 Avenue of the Americas, New York, NY 10020, USA

www.houseofstratus.com

Typeset, printed and bound by House of Stratus.

A catalogue record for this book is available from the British Library
and The Library of Congress

ISBN 1-84232-763-1

THE CLEARING HOUSE

A SURVEY OF ONE MAN'S MIND

A SELECTION FROM THE WRITINGS OF JOHN BUCHAN

ARRANGED BY LADY TWEEDSMUIR

WITH A PREFACE BY GILBERT MURRAY, OM

There was a clearing-house in his soul where all impulses were ordered and adjusted, and this repose gave him happiness.

Quoted from John Buchan's biography on Sir Walter Scott.

CONTENTS

PREFACE

Some fifty years ago, at the end of a lecture to my Middle Greek Class at Glasgow University, a boy of seventeen came up to ask a question. That was ordinary enough, but it was not the sort of question one expected. The boy, it appeared, was editing Bacon's Essays for a London publisher, and wanted to know why Bacon quoted the Greek philosopher Democritus in Latin. Where could he have found a Latin translation of Democritus? The passage was no doubt a quotation from Cicero, but such a pupil in the Middle Class was obviously a treasure, and we formed a friendship which lasted through life.

John Buchan at the time seemed absorbed in literature, both literature as romance and literature as the art of words. The two sides showed themselves in two books which he was actually then writing – without neglecting his work as a student – the collection of Essays, *Scholar Gypsies*, and the story *Don Quixote of the Moors*, which he was good enough to dedicate to me. *John Burnet of Barns*, more mature in style, must have been on the stocks about the same time. He would have seemed to be a dreamer of the same type as R L Stevenson were it not for an extreme and resolute industry which made him master effectively all his academic work and took him successfully to Oxford. One might have foreseen the great series of romances that he would write, but no one knowing that clever and sensitive boy, in love with letters and Scottish legends and the memories of the countryside, would have expected for him a career of administration in South Africa, of the management of a great publishing firm, a seat in the House of Commons and then in the House of Lords, and finally a memorable record as Governor General of the Dominion of Canada. The stories which would have been amply enough life-work for an ordinary man of letters seem to have been to Buchan a relaxation and a pastime. Some of the best were written while he was ill in bed, but there is never a trace of slack work about them.

It is an extraordinary career, not for its mere success, but, as Buchan himself might put it, for its "competence." He could do well anything he was called upon to do; yet that is not what is most characteristic about him. Some conservatism is based upon fear; just as some reforming ardour is based upon envy. But Buchan's conservatism was based, I think, on a generous liking and understanding of men and things as they are, and a thorough impatience with the doctrinaires who wanted to alter them because they did not comply with some arbitrary pattern. The real thing was so much more interesting than the abstraction. He had a real liking for the life and world about him, for human beings as they are – especially if they have the good luck to be Scottish or to bear names famous in Scottish history; for his country and its institutions, for the great men who have built it up, for the wonderful adventure of the Empire, for the hills and valleys of Galloway or of Africa or North-western Canada, all of which to him had the charm of historical memories as well as present beauty.

The range of this little anthology is very remarkable, a range both of knowledge and of sympathy. Buchan was a man of wide understanding: "Every man has a creed, but in his soul he knows that that creed has another side, possibly not less logical, which it does not suit him to produce" (page 179). He loved history. He was very little attracted by philosophical abstractions. Doctrines are never much more than half-truths; abstractions are useful as a sort of short-hand but they derive real meaning entirely from the context in which they are preached. *Travail famille*, *patrie* sound just as well as *Liberté*, *Egalité*, *Fraternité*, and every one of them is capable at any time to have plenty of crimes committed in its name. I remember Buchan describing to me the judgement pronounced by Lord Eldon, decreeing that Shelley was obviously unfit to bring up his own children, who must consequently be transferred to other guardians, and the almost bewildered protest of Shelley that such should be the reward of his specially earnest pursuit of virtue. The two men were to Buchan typically the slaves of contrary abstractions, incapable of understanding one another and, as he trenchantly put it, both mad. As against such fanatics "there is a moderation which is itself a fire, where enthusiasm burns as fiercely for the whole truth as it commonly does for half-truths" (page 210). It is a moderation which might he called "realism" had that unhappy word not been perverted into various bad senses, for it is based on understanding of real facts and conditions, not on *a priori* theories about them. It accepts the limitations of human knowledge. It knows that "most of our rules are not eternal truths," and most of the great contests of history have been fought on "narrow margins."

Life, after all, consists in dealing day by day with the real world, and Buchan had little interest in either impracticable saints who would not face the world or in high-principled eccentric failures. One can see from this little collection how he loved "normal" men, like Scott, "moderates" like Montrose, men who knew how to handle a dangerous situation and bring good out of evil, like Julius and Augustus Caesar. Cromwell is among the very few "failures" whom he loves, and it is only by a severe historical judgement that Cromwell's aim can be shown to have failed. His admiration for Calvin reminds me of Gibbon's hatred for the man. In Gibbon's marginal notes, written in French, opposite the account of Calvin's trapping and burning alive of his rival Servetus, is the jotting "Monstre! Cruel!" There are things which Gibbon could never forgive and things which Buchan could never forgive, but they are not at all the same.

PREFACE

This anthology will be worth reading for its large historical range, the thoughtfulness of its judgements, and its resolute abstinence from showiness or paradox, as well as for the picture it leaves of one of the most gifted figures of this generation; story-teller, historian, administrator, statesman, indomitable imaginative worker. He worked always for causes that he loved and died in harness at the height of his powers. Of such a one it may be well said

> "*This is the happy warrior, this is he*
> *Whom every man in arms should wish to be.*"

GILBERT MURRAY.

October 1945

CHAPTER I

THE HISTORIAN

THE HISTORIAN'S TASK
THE GOOD HISTORIAN
MILITARY GENIUS

I can picture Clio with knitted brows, striving to disentangle the why and the wherefore of things. I can picture her with rapt eyes, making epic and drama out of the past. But I can picture her most easily with the puzzled and curious face of a child, staring at the kaleidoscope of the centuries, and laughing – yes laughing – at an inconsequence that defies logic, and whimsicalities too fantastic for art.

Men and Deeds: The Causal and the Casual in History

THE HISTORIAN'S TASK

I

By history I mean the attempt to write in detail the story of a substantial fragment of the past, so that its life is re-created for us, its moods and forms of thought re-constructed, and its figures strongly represented against a background painted in authentic colours. Hence for my argument I exclude memoirs and biographies, which are side-shows in the historical theatre. The historian's task differs from the biographer's, for while the latter produces a miniature, or at best a kit-kat, the former works with a large canvas and a multitude of figures. In history quantities as well as qualities are demanded. As in a novel of Scott or a play of Shakespeare, a great piece of life must be taken, the threads of it distinguished, the motives and causes diagnosed, and the movement of it represented with something of the drama of the original. Some will concern themselves chiefly with the evidence, for unlike fiction history must produce its credentials; some will prefer to dwell on the evolution of ideas and the birth of movements and the contribution of the period to the world's stock of thought; while others will see only the bright colours and the sounding deeds. Each half-view will claim to be the whole, and will label history accordingly as a science, as a philosophy, or as an art. But the truth is, that no more than a drama or a novel can history afford to be only one of these things. It must have science in its structure, and philosophy in its spirit, and art in its presentation.

Homilies and Recreations: The Muse of History

THE GOOD HISTORIAN

II

The historian who rashly proclaims himself a scientist can have only a nodding acquaintance with the character of the physical sciences. Where is the clockwork uniformity which science postulates in its effects and causes? Where are the historical laws of universal validity? The "teaching" of history is as various and contradictory as the theories about the Pentateuch. M Bergson has shown us that half the blunders of philosophy are due to the application of the methods and ideals of physical science to spheres of thought where they are strictly inapplicable. In the kaleidoscope of the past we cannot sort out effects and causes with any precision, nor can we weigh evidence in the scrupulous scales which science demands. Even when causes are reasonably plain, their classification eludes us; we cannot tell which is the *causa causans*, which are proximate or efficient or final. We must be content with generalizations which are only generalizations and not laws, with broad effects and massed colours, like a landscape seen from a far hill-top. The vice of the scientific historian is that he underrates the complexity of human nature. He would turn mankind into automata, motives into a few elementary emotions, and the infinitely varied web of life into a simple geometrical pattern. Order and simplicity are great things, but they must be natural to the subject and not due to the colour-blindness of the historian.

Homilies and Recreations: The Muse of History

III

The good historian, whatever his period, must have in his composition something of the scientist, much of the philosopher, and more of the artist. Perhaps the elements have never yet been perfectly compounded; perhaps, indeed, they are of the nature of incompatibles and can never mix, the scientific impulse striving against the artistic to the end of the chapter. Who among men have come nearest to the perfect harmony? Gibbon, undoubtedly, among the moderns, for in spite of the limitations of his sympathy he understood as no other man has understood the organic continuity of history, and the surge and roll of his great narrative has qualities of art which have not been surpassed. Next to him perhaps stands Mommsen, less of the philosopher, more of the scientist, a little less of the artist, who, according to Mr Gooch, "alone has achieved the complete assimilation and reproduction of a classic civilization."

Homilies and Recreations: The Muse of History

IV

Let us be a little chary about accepting the so-called "streams of inevitable tendency" which are the delight in each generation of simple souls, and give them the opportunity of posing as minor prophets and announcing the "decline of the West" or the "recrudescence of barbarism," or some such journalistic slogan. The historian is wise if, like the Romans of the early Empire, he admits Fortuna and even Sors to a place in his Pantheon, and concedes the eternal presence of the irrational and the inexplicable. It is a recognition which encourages intellectual humility.

I venture to think, too, that our sense of the mystery and variousness of life is enlarged, when we realise that the very great may spring from the very small. How does Edmund Burke put it? "A common soldier, a child, a girl at the door of an inn, have changed the face of fortune, and almost of Nature." History is full of these momentous trifles – the accident which kills or preserves in life some figure of destiny; the weather on some critical battlefield, like the fog at Lutzen or the snow at Towton; the change of wind which brings two fleets to a decisive action; the severe winter of 1788 which produces the famine of 1789, and thereby perhaps the French Revolution; the birth or the death of a child; a sudden idea which results in some potent invention.

Men and Deeds: The Causal and the Casual in History

MILITARY GENIUS

V

Today we are very weary of war, and there is no one of us but hopes that in the future, by some happy conversion of heart and an adjustment of the mechanism of Government, the danger of it may be lessened and may ultimately disappear from the world. But our interest in war will not cease with its abolition. Even if that interest be only historical it must continue, for since the beginning of recorded time war has been the preoccupation of the leaders of mankind, and we mortals must have a perpetual curiosity about all great human effort. Again and again the course of things has been altered by the soldier, and if we set ourselves to make a catalogue of the greatest men of all ages, the odds are that even the most pacific among us will have several soldiers in the shortest list.

What is that which we call military genius? What is it that constitutes the great captain?... Even if the need for this form of genius should no longer exist, it is worth while to understand that with which we are dispensing. For one thing such genius has been immensely potent. It has changed the fate of peoples and the face of the world. For another, it is one of the rarest of human endowments. There have been fewer captains of the first rank than there have been poets, philosophers, or statesmen... It is not different in kind from other forms of genius. There has never been a very great soldier who was only a soldier. The foremost captains have been statesmen actually or potentially; they have been poets – without the gift of singing... It is the accident of environment and opportunity that gifts of that high order are applied to the conquest of armies or the shaping of states rather than to the devising of philosophies or the creation of masterpieces in art. The special interest of the soldier's achievement is that it is accomplished in a medium of exceptional stress and strain. The poet and the thinker work at ease with words and thoughts; the soldier's material is the intractable stuff of living humanity. The statesman, no doubt, has also for his material human beings, but he has leisure and the opportunity of retrieving mistakes. The soldier alone leads a life of perpetual crisis. He is fighting always against time, and a false step can rarely be retraced. From this it follows that in the great captain genius cannot be divorced from character. A fine artist may be a trivial fellow apart from his art, but in the profession of arms a major talent involves some, at any rate, of the major virtues.

Homilies and Recreations: The Great Captains

CHAPTER II

PORTRAITS

I. CLASSICAL
II. SCOTS AND ENGLISH
III. SOME THINKERS AND WRITERS
IV. MODERN VIGNETTES

The day of wars may be over and our military text-books may forever gather dust on the top shelves. But the interest of war cannot cease, for with all its cruelty and futility it has a power of raising men to their highest and exhibiting human nature at its greatest.

Homilies and Recreations: Two Ordeals of Democracy

I. CLASSICAL

JULIUS CAESAR

I

He never forgot that success in the field was only a means to an end, and that his purpose was not to defeat an army but to conquer and placate a nation.

Julius Caesar

II

Two main types may be discerned in the inner circle of human greatness. One is the cyclopean architect, the daimonic force who swings the world into a new orbit, whose work is as plain as the result of some convulsion of nature, but whose personality is hard to discover behind the colossal facade of his achievements, and at whose mental processes we can only guess. Such are the conquerors, the men of the sword, the Alexanders and Charlemagnes. The second is the man whose business is directly with souls, the thinker, the priest, and the prophet. His influence is to be looked for in no solid concrete creation, but must be traced through a thousand intricate channels, like the advent of spring. The minds of such we know fully, for the mind was their tool, and the mind of man was the object on which they wrought.

Caesar belongs to neither type. He performed the greatest constructive task ever achieved by human hands. He drew the habitable earth into an empire which lasted for five centuries, and he laid the foundations of a fabric of law and government which is still standing after two thousand years. He made the world possible for the Christian faith, so that there was reason in the mediaeval belief which saw in him a Bishop and a Father of the Church. He gave humanity order and peace, and thereby prepared the ground for many precious seeds. His genius as soldier and law-maker is amply proven. The greatest of poets believed him to have been "the noblest man that ever lived in the tide of times." But although we can come under the spell of his magnificence and appraise his character, we cannot probe to its inner springs. About the mind of this man, his inmost thoughts and dreams, there is still a mystery. We know the things that he did, but not why he did them.

He emerges from the clouds of mythology, lives his life in clear air, and then disappears in a divine mist. He was sprung from the ancient kings of Rome, and had the Goddess of Love herself as an ancestress. Before his death he was regarded by the Roman populace as a god, and later he was believed to have literally ascended into Heaven. To the Middle Ages he was a vast cosmic portent out of which men devised miracle-plays; fairy legend laid hold of him and made him, by Morgan la Fay, the father of Oberon the fairy king. But between these banks of vapour his life is as clear as a bright autumn day. The exact nature of his civil and military exploits is rarely in doubt. We have his own writings to guide us, and those of his marshals, and Cicero's many letters and speeches. We know much about his manners and tastes, and we have authentic busts. He is easier to picture than any other figure of classical antiquity.

Yet mystery remains. We have no contemporary who read his thoughts...

Julius Caesar

III

The campaigns in Gaul are Caesar's chief title to what has never been denied him, a place in the inner circle of the world's captains. He was in the first place a superb trainer of troops. He raised at least five new legions, and he so handled them that they soon ranked as veterans. Again, he was a great leader of men, having that rare gift of so diffusing his personality that every soldier felt himself under his watchful eye and a sharer of his friendship. Strategically he had an infallible eye for country, a geographical instinct as sure as Napoleon's. He had that power of simplification which belongs only to genius, and he never wasted his strength in divergent operations, but struck unerringly at the vital point. A desperate crisis only increased his coolness and the precision of his thought. He understood the minds of men, and played unerringly on the psychology of both his own soldiers and the enemy's; indeed he made the enemy do half his work for him; and he had a kind of boyish gusto which infected his troops with his own daring and speed. He had able marshals, like Labienus and Quintus Cicero and Publius Crassus, but he was always the controlling spirit. He was essentially humane – "mitis clemensque natura," Cicero wrote – but he was implacable when policy required it. Nor must it be forgotten that in his generalship, as in that of all great captains, there was a profound statesmanship.

Julius Caesar

IV

He gave the world a long breathing-space, and thereby ensured that the legacy of both Greece and Rome should be so inwoven with the fabric of men's minds that it could never perish. He taught no new way of life, no religion; he had no comfort for the weary and the sick at heart; he was a child of this world, content to work with the material he found and reduce it to order and decency. But he made it certain that the spiritual revelation for which mankind hungered would not be lost in the discords of a brutish anarchy. His standards were human, but the highest to which humanity can attain, and his work may well be regarded as the greatest recorded effort of the human genius.

The man who achieved it – and herein lies Caesar's unique fascination – was no leaden superman, no heavy-handed egotist, but one with all the charms and graces. The burden of the globe on his shoulders did not impede his lightness of step. War and administration never made him a narrow specialist. His culture was as wide as that of any man of his day; he loved art and poetry and music and philosophy, and would turn gladly to them in the midst of his most critical labours. He was the best talker in Rome and the most gracious of companions. There was no mysticism or superstition in his clear mind, but he was not without certain endearing sentimentalities. He was tolerant of other men's prejudices and respected their private sanctities. Combined in him in the highest degree were the realism of the man of action, the sensitiveness of the artist, and the imagination of the creative dreamer – a union not, I think, to be paralleled elsewhere.

But the spell of his intellect was matched by the spiritual radiance which emanated from him to light and warm his world. He could be harsh with the terrible politic cruelty of a society based upon slavery, but no one could doubt the depth of his affections and the general benignity of his character. He had no petty vanity; the *Commentaries* is the most unegotistic book ever written. This man, whose courage in every circumstance of life was like a clear flame, had a womanish gentleness and the most delicate courtesy. He never failed a friend, though his friends often failed him. He was relentless enough in the cause of policy, but he could not cherish a grudge and he was incapable of hate; his dislike of Cato was rather the repugnance of a profound intellect to a muddy and shallow one. In Cicero's words, he forgot nothing except injuries. When Catullus abused him he asked him to dinner, and when an enemy fell into his power he dismissed him with compliments. The meanness and the savagery which are born of fear were utterly alien to his soul. The most penetrating and comprehensive of human minds and the bravest of mortal hearts were joined in him with what is best described in a phrase of Mark Antony's which Dio Cassius reports, an "inbred goodness."

Julius Caesar

V

Moreover, Caesar was one who did not trouble to reveal himself to the world except by deeds. He went his smiling way among men, hiding his thoughts behind a gentle and impenetrable courtesy. The bust in the British Museum, the noblest presentment of the human countenance known to me, tells us much, but not all. The broad, full brow and the sinewy neck we take for granted, but what of the strange contradiction of the jaws, and the fine, almost feminine, moulding of the lips and chin? Caesar is the only great man of action, save Nelson, who has in his face something of a woman's delicacy. The features conceal more than they reveal. As in the hour of death at the base of Pompey's statue, he has muffled his face. It may be permitted to attempt once again to draw aside the folds of the cloak.

Julius Caesar

AUGUSTUS CAESAR

VI

The true achievement of Augustus is that he saved the world from disintegration.

Augustus

VII

He was a fatalist, like most great men of action.

Augustus

VIII

...that noble fatalism which is a source of weakness in fools but of inspiration in the great...

Homilies and Recreations: Two Ordeals of Democracy

IX

We are engaged in the study of a creative mind. Of the character apart from the mind there is not a great deal to note. It can be said truly of Augustus that the mind was the man. His moral qualities were in full accord with his intellectual powers; they were such as were needed for the fulfilment of his task; in his work he completely realized himself, and there were no unsatisfied longings left over, no gift or quality which missed its mark. His public life was also his private life, and he had no secret world hid from his fellows. All his days were passed in the glare of publicity, and to his contemporaries, as to later generations, he was fully intelligible; a man like themselves, only built on a grander scale, a figure as obvious as the Zeus of Olympia, revered, saluted, but not discussed, for there were no mysteries about it. The gossip-writers a century later found much to admire in him, but little of personal interest to record. The picture they give is on the whole a pleasant one, but it is colourless; to them he was something statuesque, grandiose, marmoreal, with few of the ragged ends of life.

He was a man with a mission, which he pursued with as austere a devotion as any saint or prophet, but there was very little mysticism in it.

Augustus

X

He was a builder whose concern was with things, not fancies. He could appreciate a far-reaching plan, but towers and adminicles must wait for the deep foundations. He had his preferences like other people, but he brought them always to the test of plain reality. Julius had been a dreamer; Augustus admired, examined and discarded many of his dreams. There were dreamers in plenty in Greece and the East; his sharp practical logic saved the world both from oriental extravagance and the sterile mysticism of the philosophers. He had none of the dangerous fanaticism which is to be found in men so diverse as Machiavelli and Calvin, an exaggerated view of the sanctity of the state; he would give the state the sanctity which belonged to it and no more. He was free from egalitarian whimsies, a malady from which the ancient world did not greatly suffer; he did not believe in that degeneration of democratic theory which imagines that there is a peculiar inspiration in the opinions of the ignorant and a singular nobility in the character of the penniless. But he had equally no belief in a crude authoritarianism; he would have assented to Aristotle's definition of the purpose of the state – that it originated for the sake of life and was continued for the sake of the good life. He sought not only to give every class a modest comfort, but to assign it a function in the community.

Augustus

XI

This doctrine of function was no new thing, for it derived from the Greek philosophers, and at the time was accepted by most thinking men; but after Augustus it had to wait for many centuries until it was revived as a principle of democracy. We must be careful in using this last term, for it has acquired a flavour today which would have been incomprehensible to the ancient world. Of the familiar democratic technique certain parts, like the representative idea, were in the circumstances impracticable. But one democratic essential – government by discussion – Augustus would fain have established. He sought to make the Senate, constantly refreshed from below and therefore in a sense representative, a true consultative assembly, whose decisions the Princeps must accept or refute by argument. He would have applauded, too, the definition of Pericles: "Our constitution is named a democracy because it is in the hands not of the few but of the many. Our laws secure equal justice for all in their private disputes, and our public opinion welcomes and honours the best in every branch of achievement, not for any class reason, but on grounds of excellence alone." The Republic had been a close oligarchy; the empire brought a large new recruitment to the public service and endeavoured to give to the humblest a modicum of civic interests.

Augustus

XII

Augustus had notable advantages. He had to deal with the stubborn reactionary, but he was little troubled by the foolish progressive. The voice of the revolutionary was stilled. Rome had had too much of him and craved above all things for order and decorum. Nor did he suffer from the minor intellectual, the man whose talent is for a cheap disintegration. Rome did not want the atomizer; her one desire was to escape from chaos. Moreover, the sophist was everywhere at a discount when men were seeking a positive faith. Callicles and Thrasymachus were rare types even in the academies; Plato three centuries before had put them out of business and they had not recovered. Lastly, Augustus was free from intellectual pride. He was not dogmatic, but content to feel his way modestly, and when he blundered to retrace his steps. And he did not overrate himself or his achievements. Like Ecclesiastes, he could rejoice in his labour, and yet admit that much of it was vanity and its reward vexation of spirit. He had his task which must be done without thought of the price. The mainspring of his life was the Stoic precept: "We also must be soldiers, and in a campaign where there is no intermission and no discharge."

The career of Augustus may be likened to a high plateau approached by a long, steep and perilous ascent. For fifteen years his feet were on the crags, and for forty-three he surveyed the world from the tableland. In the first stage his problem was how to win supreme power, and in the second how best to use it. His character remained the same throughout his life, in the sense that the qualities which enabled him to outstrip his rivals were those which made it possible to remould the world – iron self-command, infinite patience, and an infallible judgment of facts and men. Few have ever entered upon a more apparently hopeless task than Augustus when, in his nineteenth year, he left Apollonia, and few have ever won a more triumphant success. For years he led a life of unremitting physical toil and mental anxiety combined with miserable health – no small test of fortitude. Close-lipped, tenacious, cautious and yet intrepid, he is amazing, but he is not attractive. The earlier Augustus is the Industrious Apprentice raised to the highest power, the Eldest Son of the fairy tales, whom nothing will keep from his heritage. He lived in constant peril, but his prudent days had none of the glamour of adventure. He took desperate risks, but only after meticulous calculation. He is the least romantic of great men.

When Actium was fought and won he revealed the same qualities, but they were given a new direction and tempered by something of which hitherto there had been few traces. The common *arriviste* is apt to find himself lost at his journey's end. He does not know how to use what he has gained. The very gifts which made him formidable on the road keep him puzzled and uncertain at the goal. Here – on the side of character – lies the marvel of Augustus's career. A cold, self-contained youth was exchanged for a genial maturity; he who had held himself apart became the friend of all the world; what had appeared to be a devouring personal ambition was transmuted into an anxious benevolence, a selfless care for the vast oecumene of which he was the head. To "pietas" and "gravitas" were added "civilitas" and "clementia" and "providentia," and between them they made up a complete "auctoritas." These latter qualities he had always possessed, but they had been necessarily frostbound during the bleak years of struggle and frustration. The miracle was that they did not die, but, when at last the sun shone, could break into blossom and fruit.

His character, as I have said, was adequate to his powers of mind, a thing unfissured, four-square, simple, wholly intelligible. He had most of the major virtues which Aristotle enumerates, but especially he had *phronesis*, that practical wisdom which is the proper attribute of the ruler. Here we are faced by something far from simple. We have seen its results in the system of government which he created; it will be well to look into it more closely, for it is in this respect that he excelled other men.

Augustus

XIII

The work of Augustus was for centuries too much the accepted background of their life for men to question or assess it; it was taken for granted like the equinoxes and the seasons. In the Middle Ages, under the name of Octavian, he became a cloudy figure of necromancy. But now, at the second millenary of his birth, scholarship has enlarged our knowledge of him, and the problems he faced have a livelier interest for us, since they are not unlike our own. History does not repeat itself except with variations, and it is idle to look for exact parallels, but we can trace a resemblance between the conditions of his time and those of today. Once again the crust of civilization has worn thin, and beneath can be heard the muttering of primeval fires. Once again many accepted principles of government have been overthrown, and the world has become a laboratory where immature and feverish minds experiment with unknown forces. Once again problems cannot be comfortably limited, for science has brought the nations into an uneasy bondage to each other. In the actual business of administration there is no question of today which Augustus had not to face and answer.

If his "magna imago" could return to earth, he would be puzzled at some of our experiments in empire, and might well complain that the imperfections of his work were taken as its virtues, and that so many truths had gone silently out of mind. He had prided himself on having given the world peace, and he would be amazed by the loud praise of war as a natural and wholesome concomitant of a nation's life. Wars he had fought from an anxious desire to safeguard his people, as the shepherd builds the defences of his sheep-fold; but he hated the thing, because he knew well the deadly "disordering," which the Greek historian noted as the consequence of the most triumphant campaign. He would marvel, too, at the current talk of racial purity, the exaltation of one breed of men as the chosen favourites of the gods. That would seem to him a defiance not only of the new Christian creed, but of the Stoicism which he had sincerely professed. True, he had been sparing in his grants of Roman citizenship, but that had been for a temporary purpose, since the heart of the principate must be first made strong if the blood was to circulate freely to the members. From the Elysian Fields he had watched the development of his empire and had come to see the wisdom of Julius' liberalism, for had that empire not drawn much of its strength from the non-Italian stocks, in philosophers, poets, emperors and soldiers?

But chiefly, I think, he would be perplexed by the modern passion for regimentation and the assumed contradiction between law and liberty. To bring order out of anarchy he had been forced to emphasize the first, but he had laboured also to preserve the second. His aim had been to keep the masculine vigour of the republican character, and to cherish likewise all worthy local and provincial autonomies, for he recognized that the empire depended upon men, and that men to be of any account as citizens must have a decent measure of freedom. He would sadly admit that the machine which he had created had been too strong for Roman liberties, and that in its grip the Roman character had lost its salt and iron. Being too much governed, men had forgotten how to govern themselves. But in the centuries since his death he had observed that the world had discovered certain methods of which he had not dreamed, and that it was possible for greater numbers than he had ever ruled to live a life which was both orderly and free. With the disappearance of slavery and the spread of education the constituents of society had changed, and self-government need not be mob-government. Here lay a path to the solution of what had been his gravest problem, and he would be amazed that men should so light-heartedly reject it. And when this expert in mechanism observed the craving of great peoples to enslave themselves and to exult hysterically in their bonds, bewilderment would harden to disdain in his masterful eyes.

Augustus

SOME SOLDIERS, WOMEN, POETS, AND A TYRANT

VERCINGETORIX

I

Vercingetorix in defeat rose to heroic stature. He offered his life for his countrymen, for, as he said, he had been fighting for Gaul and not for himself; splendidly accoutred he appeared before Caesar, stripped off his arms and laid them silently at his feet. The victor for reasons of policy showed mercy to the broken Aedui and Averni, but he had none for Vercingetorix. He was sent to Rome as a prisoner, six years later he adorned his conqueror's triumph, and then he was put to death in a dungeon of the Capitol. No Roman, not even Caesar, knew the meaning of chivalry. Of Vercingetorix we may say that he was the first, and not the least, of that succession of Celtic paladins to whom the freedom of their people has been a burning faith. He was the greatest soldier – greater than Pompey – that Caesar ever faced in the field, and no lost cause could boast a nobler or more tragical hero.

Julius Caesar

BRUTUS

II

With Brutus perished the republican cause, for he alone of its leaders had the moral authority which can dignify stagnation and reaction. It is a strange accident which has given him so great a name in history, for the man himself was inconsiderable. Of the two chief enemies of Julius, Cassius was the more vigorous and resolute in action, but he was a type common in history, the ambitious *condottiere* who can readily adapt a principle to self-interest. Brutus was a rarer species, who both impressed and puzzled his contemporaries. Julius out of friendship for his mother Servilia was his constant patron, and seems to have regarded him with a half-amused respect as an interesting relic; it was his policy, too, as it was Napoleon's, to be polite to the old nobility. The famous comment on him, "Quicquid vult valde vult," is as much a criticism of his limited outlook as of his intensity of purpose. Cicero wrangled with him and flattered him, but does not seem to have greatly liked him. Brutus had a solemn condescending manner, a hard face, a pedantic style in speech and writing, and a stiff ungracious character. He was capable of extreme harshness, as he showed in his treatment of the Asian cities before Philippi, and he was to the last degree avaricious. There was little principle about him when his investments were in question, and he extorted forty-eight per cent from one wretched Cypriote community. His philosophy of life was not profound, and he died abjuring his creed. He was an egotist and a formalist, yet he won an extraordinary prestige, for to his contemporaries he seemed the living embodiment of certain ancient virtues which had gone out of the world. To adopt Sydney Smith's phrase about Francis Homer, he had the Roman equivalent of the Ten Commandments written on his countenance and about him an air of inaccessible respectability. History has by one of its freaks perpetuated this repute, and he remains the "noblest Roman" when in truth he was a commonplace example of artistocratic virtues and vices. Cicero was in a far truer sense the last republican.

Augustus

CLEOPATRA

III

Cleopatra has long ago passed beyond the libels with which her reputation was blackened by a terrified Rome – even the maledictions of great poets, whose hate confers an unwelcome immortality. Charmion's tribute, "a lass unparalleled," is the world's verdict. She stands with Helen of Troy as one of the two women whose influence over the hearts of men has become a legend and a symbol. But the common picture of her as a martyr of love, a mortal Aphrodite, does scant justice to her powers of mind. To Egypt she was a wise and capable ruler, and in Egypt for long her memory was cherished. A Coptic bishop of the seventh century could speak of her as the most illustrious of her sex, "great in herself and in her achievements." She was a notable woman of business, she inaugurated and directed industries, and she organized the supplies for Antony's army and fleet. If she wrote a book on cosmetics, she is also credited with works on coinage and weights and measures. She was a friend of philosophers, like Philostratus the Platonist and Nicolaus the Peripatetic. She had a courage so clear and fine that no man or woman ever made her afraid. In the downfall of Antony's fortunes she did not despair, but struggled on to the end, and welcomed death only when all was over. With much earthy dross in her, she was yet pre-eminently a creature of "fire and air."

It is easy to dismiss the false Cleopatra, but the true one can only be conjectured, for the material for a reasoned verdict is lost. Could we know what Julius thought of her we should be in a better case, for it is likely that Julius inspired much of her policy, and was the only man who ever captured her mind as well as her heart. Her main purpose is clear. She was the heir of Alexander, and, as we have seen, sought to rebuild the monarchy of Egypt with the help of Rome. But there was more in her than mere dynastic ambition, for she had "immortal longings." She was the prophetess of an ancient culture which she believed to be doomed without her aid. From Julius she may have learned the ideal of an empire which should be a true fellowship of humanity, and in which all the old cultural bequests would be harmonized. Her months in Rome had convinced her of the hardness and narrowness of the Roman temper, and her association with Antony and his friends did not abate her dislike of its grossness. She was in revolt against the Roman philistinism which would crush under its chariot wheels a multitude of ancient and beautiful things, and constrict into a mercantile uniformity the infinite variousness of the world she loved. The virtues of the Italian temper were hidden from her, and she saw only its vulgarity. She stood for Hellenism and for something else – something which only Julius had understood – strange and wonderful things descended from primeval monarchies in the Asian and African spaces, secret lore for which Latin had no idiom:

Imperishable fire under the boughs
Of chrysoberyl and beryl and chrysolite,
And chrysoprase and ruby and sardonyx.

If such was her creed, history can pass judgment on her failure. Hers was a bastard Hellenism, and her conception of world empire was a whimsy. The grave beauty of the great age of Greece had gone from the world, and the gem-like flame of its spirit had been replaced by the fires of baser altars. The Hellenistic had ousted the Hellenic. The simplicity and *ascēsis* of an elder Greece were to be sought in Italy rather than in Egypt, with its garish, superheated court, its pedantic universities and its servile peoples. Alexandria had little to teach Rome. The enduring bequest of the

East was to spring half a century later, not from the effete successors of the old monarchies, but from the bare Palestinian hills. As for the dream of the habitable earth peaceful under a universal empire, the dream of Alexander and Julius and Cleopatra, the motive power to realize it must come from the West, where men could still be both disciplined and free. Behind the cold front of Octavian lay the vision, the will, and the power.

Augustus

JULIA

IV

A woman, born into such a society, could, if she were happily wedded, find satisfaction in husband and children; but if she missed that, the only other avenues were ambition and adultery. She could set her heart on power or on pleasure. Julia seems to have had something of the fineness and *esprit* of her father's race, marred by the caprice of her mother Scribonia. Her portraits show that she had beauty, but her dark hair was early streaked with grey, which gave her much concern. Her childhood in the house on the Palatine cannot have been gay. Livia, her stepmother, was a woman of the old school, with strict ideas about the upbringing of youth, and Augustus, while anxious to play a father's part, was too busy to see much of his daughter. A girl was not likely to find much charm in the grave and preoccupied Agrippa, or in a dry lawyer like Ateius Capito, or in the airs and attitudes of Maecenas. Julia, as a child, seems to have been on easy terms with her father, and to have been allowed to chaff him and to answer him pertly. She was carefully shielded from young men, and was inordinately proud of her rank, having little else to think about.

At fourteen she was married to her cousin Marcellus, which might have been well enough had Marcellus lived; but at sixteen she was left a widow, and was promptly espoused to the elderly

Agrippa. She bore him five children, Gaius, Lucius, the younger Julia, Agrippina, and a posthumous son, Agrippa. She seems to have been reasonably happy with him. She accompanied him on his Eastern travels, was nearly drowned in the Scamander, and was hailed as a goddess in various Asian cities – a bad thing for a woman with her overweening pride of birth. But it was the old story of crabbed age and youth. She had much time on her hands when Agrippa was abroad on duty, and she amused herself with books, but principally with dress, and won a name for extravagance. She began, too, to see too much of young men, especially of one of the Gracchi. Augustus scolded her but failed to keep an eye on her, though Livia was a vigilant duenna.

Agrippa died, and Julia was again on the market. Presently at the age of twenty-eight she was married to Tiberius, who was three years older. Her new husband, whose heart was with the wife whom he had been compelled to divorce, was ill-fitted to be the mate of a brilliant and audacious woman. At first she seems to have done her best, for she accompanied him on his Dalmatian campaign, and there bore him a son who died. But after that the breach widened. Julia in Rome lived wholly among the younger set, and stories began to circulate of her doings. She was seen with drunken revellers in the streets, and was a frequent guest at dubious male parties. Tiberius was well aware of the scandals and suffered them in silence, but the position, for a proud man, was intolerable, and was one of the reasons for his retreat to Rhodes.

Then suddenly Augustus learned from Livia what was happening, since all Rome rang with the story. He was wounded to the quick in his pride and self-respect. At the very time when he was attempting to purify Roman morals his own child was revealed as the leader of that light-witted raffishness which he detested. He must have been aware, too, that he was not free from blame, and in the extremity of his anger we may detect the prick of conscience. He referred the business to the Senate and asked for the legal penalty. Her two chief lovers were a son of Mark Antony and Fulvia, and the young Gracchus; the former committed suicide and the latter was banished. Julia herself was exiled to the island of Pandataria, off the Campanian coast.

Such was the fate of this bright and brittle creature who, under happier circumstances, might have been great, for she had an excellent mind, and, as her popularity with the Roman mob showed, the magic of personality. Neither her father nor her husband ever saw her again.

Augustus

CICERO

V

Among the first to die was Cicero. He had little estate, only debts, but Antony could not forgive the lash of the Philippics. Plutarch has told the tale of that winter afternoon in the wood by the sea-shore when the old man stretched out his frail neck to the centurion's sword, and of that later day in Rome when the head was fixed by Antony's order above the Rostra, and "the Romans shuddered, for they seemed to see there not the face of Cicero but the image of Antony's soul." He met his death in the high Roman fashion – the only misfortune of his life, says Livy, which he faced like a man. The verdict is scarcely fair; juster is the comment of the same historian that he was so great a figure that it would require a Cicero to praise him adequately. In the wild years when the Roman Republic fell, the thinker and the scholar does not fill the eye in the same way as the forthright man of action, and Cicero is dim in the vast shadow of Julius. His weaknesses are clear for a child to read, his innocent vanity, his lack of realism, his sentimentality about dead things, his morbid sensitiveness, his imperfect judgment of character, his frequent fits of timidity. The big head, the thin neck, the mobile mouth of the orator could not dominate men like the eagle face of Julius. He failed and perished because he was Cicero. The man of letters in a crisis, who looks round a question, cannot have the single-hearted force of him who sees the instant need. Yet it is to be remembered that he could conquer his natural timorousness and act on occasion with supreme audacity, a far greater achievement than the swashbuckling valour of an Antony. And let it be remembered, too, that it was Cicero's creed which ultimately triumphed. His dream came true. His humanism and his humanity made him the prophet of a gentler world. The man to whom St Augustine owed the first step in his conversion, who was to St Ambrose a model and to St Jerome "rex oratorum," the scholar whose work was the mainspring of the Renaissance, has had an abiding influence on the world. While others enlarged the limits of the Roman empire, he "advanced the boundaries of the Latin genius."

Augustus

VIRGIL

VI

Virgil had been the complete Roman, a lover of wild nature and the North, but also a devotee of cities, for after his youth he left Mantua behind him and lived wholly in Rome and Naples. All Italy, all the empire, was his home. With a sound instinct Augustus forbade the poet's executors to fulfil his wishes and burn the manuscript, thereby preserving for the world an inestimable treasure. To the Romans Virgil was the preacher of a nobler creed of morals and the prophet of a larger destiny, for he gave expression to all that was best in the stock and made the imperial ideal, a thing of vision and high poetry. But not less he was the interpreter of humanity in every age, its sufferings and consolations, and therefore the poet not only of the Rome which has gone, but of a spiritual Rome, an Eternal City which can never perish since it is built of man's hopes and dreams.

Augustus

HORACE

VII

He was in his fifty-seventh year, and had just finished his *Ars Poetica*. He was a plump little man with hair prematurely grizzled, and he always had been something of a valetudinarian. Towards Maecenas he felt a warm gratitude, and for that strange *poseur* he may also have had a temperate liking, but between him and Augustus there was a strong affection. Horace was a court poet, but no courtier; he was not afraid to laugh gently at Augustus' paternalism and his belief in making people virtuous by statute, and he cherished and gave constant expression to a kind of literary republicanism. There was never a more independent poet-laureate. The two men, indeed, had much in common, for both looked at life with a cool realism which was not allowed to become cynical; both loved the old ways of the land; both detested snobbery, luxury and ill-bred display. There was a hard core in the mind of each and a pleasing, astringent dryness. To the poet, whom he would have made his private secretary, Augustus wrote in the undress style which a man keeps for his intimates. "Consider yourself a privileged guest in my house...you will always be sure of a welcome... What a warm feeling I have for you, you can learn from Septimius among others, for the other day I was talking about you in his presence. You need not suppose because you are so grand as to reject my overtures that I mean to get on the same high horse and pay you back." Yet Horace's urbane and critical soul was fired by Augustus' aims, and he turned the dull things of policy into a poetic vision. In his odes, with their thunder of place-names, he makes vivid the territorial immensity of the empire. He paints with exquisite art the charm of the deep country and the lure of the simple life. He pays to the makers of empire a tribute which has ever since echoed in men's ears. This poet, whose works, like Virgil's, soon displaced in Roman schools the aridities of Livius Andronicus, made it his task to interpret the Augustan ideal to that educated middle class which was the true strength of Rome.

Augustus

HEROD

VIII

Looking round the world at this time one is struck by the absence of commanding figures. Augustus had a lonely pre-eminence. There was no man in any part of the empire likely to challenge his authority, or in the lands beyond the frontier, though such an one was coming to maturity in the German forests. Nor, with a single exception, was there any protected prince who rose above mediocrity. The exception was Herod of Judaea, and his territory and his people were of all the client-kingdoms the most interesting to the Roman mind. Palestine, like Armenia, had high strategical importance in the defence of the eastern frontier against Parthia. The Jews, now scattered throughout the globe, were a perpetual conundrum to Rome, and Herod himself, in his extraordinary career, captured the Roman imagination. He had that touch of genius which makes a man incalculable.

There had been a Jewish colony in Rome since the days of the Gracchi, and now there were perhaps as many of the race there in proportion to the population as there are in America today. Rome had been generous to them, and had granted them exemption from any service inconsistent with their creed. Julius had given them privileges, and Augustus and Agrippa had been notably respectful to their faith. They had considerable underground influence, for their banking business played a large part in imperial finance. Of their religion the Romans had a very confused idea. Obviously their rites were very different from the common heady mysteries of the East. A few of the educated classes recognized the grandeur of their monotheism, and some were even converts, but to the ordinary man their creed was unintelligible. There were many stories about the great temple in Jerusalem, where some said the object of worship was a silver ass, and others a mysterious spirit that dwelt in an old box. In Rome they lived for the most part in the suburb beyond the Tiber, and, while tolerated and even respected, they were not loved.

The ruler of the homeland of this odd people was Herod, a convert, who had been born in Idumea. The epithet of "Great" is not misapplied in his case, for he was a man of infinite audacity and resource. He had consistently taken the wrong side in the civil wars, and had always emerged the friend of the victor. He had been for Cassius against Antony, and for Antony against Octavian, and in each case had won power by his treasons. Having obtained by crime the wretched little domain of Judaea, he made of it a considerable kingdom. He professed Judaism but he was no true Jew, and he repeatedly outraged the sanctities of that faith. His aim was to combine Judaism and Hellenism, and to have behind him the strong arm of Rome. Augustus appreciated and supported his purpose, for he wanted someone to control the turbulent populace of Jerusalem and to be a barrier against Parthia.

Herod attempted to ride two horses and failed with both. He did succeed in making Judaea the most important of the client-kingdoms, but he won the undying hatred of all orthodox Jews, especially the aristocracy, and he failed to hellenize his land beyond the surface. On the one side he sacrificed to Jupiter Capitolinus; he turned Samaria into Sebaste, and created the great port of Caesarea, both in honour of Augustus; he made of the High Priesthood a family benefice; filled his court with Greek-trained Jews, like Nicolaus of Damascus; established theatres and games on the Roman model even in Jerusalem; made his subjects swear by the name of the Princeps, and sacrificed daily in his honour. About 18 BC he paid a state visit to Rome. At the same time he professed himself a devout Jew, pled the cause of the Jews in Asia Minor before the Princeps, and began on a magnificent scale the rebuilding of the Temple at Jerusalem. About 8 BC he fell out of favour with Augustus, who said bitterly that he would rather be Herod's pig than his son. After that till he died in 4 BC, a sense of failure sharpened his passion for cruelty. He broke every law of Jewry, put his sons to death, massacred the Pharisees, and descended to the grave in an orgy of blood. It is probable that he had become mad. The way was prepared for the end of the client-kingdom, the transformation of Judaea into an ordinary Roman province, and that exacerbation of Jewish feeling which ended in the destruction of Jerusalem.

In 7 BC Quirinius, the governor of Syria, who had just completed a successful campaign against the brigands of the Taurus, decreed a census of this distracted little land, that census which, for taxation purposes, was held every fifteen years. All Jews had to attend at the centre of their tribe. A certain Joseph – a carpenter from Nazareth in the pleasant country of Galilee – was compelled to journey south in the winter weather to Bethlehem in the Judaean uplands, the city of David, for he was of the tribe of David. With him went Mary, his betrothed. There on December 25, in a hovel where the stars shone through the thatch, a son was born. The name given to the child was Jesus.

Augustus

II. SCOTS AND ENGLISH

SOME LORDS, COMMONERS, KINGS, A PRIEST, AND A QUEEN

CROMWELL
CHARLES I
CHARLES II
STRAFFORD
HAMPDEN
LAUD
MONTROSE
ARCHIBALD, DUKE OF ARGYLL
ELIZABETH OF BOHEMIA

The hero in history is a terrible nuisance to the lover of dapper generalities.

Men and Deeds: The Causal and the Casual in History

CROMWELL

I

He who studies Cromwell must be prepared for many conundrums.

Cromwell

II

He had no egotism, and would readily take advice and allow himself to be persuaded. He would even permit opponents to enlarge on his faults and point out his spiritual defects, than which there can be no greater proof of humility.

Cromwell

III

A great man lays upon posterity the duty of understanding him. The task is not easy even with those well-defined, four-square personalities, who belong to a recognizable type, whose purpose was single and whose career was the product of obvious causes; for we have still in our interpretation to recover an atmosphere which is not our own. It is harder when the man in question falls under no accepted category, and in each feature demands a new analysis. It is hardest of all with one who sets classification at defiance, and seems to unite in himself every contrary, who dominates his generation like some portent of nature, a mystery to his contemporaries and an enigma to his successors. In such a case his interpreter must search not only among the arcana of his age, its hidden forces and imponderable elements, but among the profundities of the human spirit.

Oliver Cromwell has long passed beyond the mists of calumny. He is no longer Hyde's "brave bad man"; still less is he the hypocrite, the vulgar usurper, the bandit of genius, of Hume and Hallam. By common consent he stands in the first rank of greatness, but there is little agreement on the specific character of that greatness. He is admired by disciples of the most divergent faiths. Some see in him the apostle of liberty, the patron of all free communions, forgetting his attempts to found an established church and his staunch belief in a national discipline. Constitutionalists claim him as one of the pioneers of the parliamentary system, though he had little patience with government by debate, and played havoc with many parliaments. He has been hailed as a soldier-saint, in spite of notable blots on his scutcheon. He has been called a religious genius, but on his religion it is not easy to be dogmatic; like Bunyan's Much-afraid, when he went through the River none could understand what he said. Modern devotees of force have seen in him the super-man who marches steadfastly to his goal amid the crash of ancient fabrics, but they have forgotten his torturing hours of indecision. He has been described as tramping with his heavy boots relentlessly through his age, but his steps were mainly slow and hesitating, and he often stumbled.

Paradox is in the fibre of his character and career. Like Pompey, he was *suarum legum auctor ac subversor*; a devotee of law, he was forced to be often lawless; a civilian to the core, he had to maintain himself by the sword; with a passion to construct, his task was chiefly to destroy; the most scrupulous of men, he had to ride roughshod over his own scruples and those of others; the tenderest, he had continually to harden his heart; the most English of our greater figures, he spent his life in opposition to the majority of Englishmen; a realist, he was condemned to build that which could not last. Even at his death the dream-fabric was dissolving, so that Cowley, after watching the splendid funeral, could write: "I know not how, the whole was so managed that, methought, it somewhat expressed the life of him for whom it was made – much noise, much tumult, much expense, much magnificence, much vainglory, briefly a great show, and yet, after all this, but an ill sight." "The joyfullest funeral I ever saw," wrote Evelyn, "for there were none that cried but dogs."

Cromwell

VI

His theology was simple, like all theologies of a crisis. He accepted the Calvinist's unbending fatalism, which instead of making its votaries apathetic moved them to a girded energy. But his unspeculative mind was careless about niceties of dogma; probably he would have come off badly in any doctrinal examination; and he never assented to the view that intellectual error was a sin to be implacably punished in this world and the next. The foundation was a personal experience, a revelation which he might have described in Luther's words: "I do not know it and I do not understand it, but, sounding from above and ringing in my ears, I hear what is beyond the thought of man." This revelation demanded the assent of the mind, but, above all, the submission of the will. God manifested Himself as creator, reconciler and redeemer, and while the horror of sin was intensified its burden was removed. Against the darkness of sin shone the light of grace, and it is upon grace that he dwells most often, grace the only link between the worlds of God and of man. The state of salvation into which the soul entered was not a continuation of the old life on a higher plane, but a wholly different life. The kingdom of God was an *ingressio*, the advent of a new thing. The soul was washed and transformed through the mystery of the atonement, and thereafter breathed a different air. The legalism – that hardy English growth

– which so narrowed puritan theology, meant nothing to Oliver. He talks often of "covenants," but he means promises, not bargains. No fear of future punishment was the reason of his conversion, but a passion for purity and a horror of evil. Like Dante's Farinata degli Uberti he "entertained great scorn of Hell."

The majesty and transcendence of God is the rock of his faith, a majesty so awful that without grace man must be shrivelled like a leaf in its burning light. Oliver is what Novalis called Spinoza, a *Gott-betrunkener Mann.* He is stupefied by the wonders of the Almighty, and is lost in an abasement of worship. It is a mood which is strange to the bustling religiosity of later times and the Mr Brisks and Mr Talkatives of our casual creeds, but it is a mood which must always appear in a time of crisis. The single purpose of those who share it is to bring the will into subjection to the divine will; to attain, in the words of Clerk Maxwell, "an abandonment of wilfulness without extinction of will, but rather by means of a great development of will, whereby, instead of being consciously free and really in subjection to unknown laws, it becomes consciously acting by law and really free from the interference of unrecognized laws."

In front of this background of eternal Omnipotence stood the figure of Christ, the revelation of the love and the fatherhood of God, the God-man, the world's redeemer. In his contemplation of Christ awe is mingled with a personal devotion such as is revealed in Pascal's fragment, the *Mystère de Jésus.* Through Christ his relation to God became that of a son, and sometimes he writes of the mysteries of faith as he writes to his children, with a familiar human affection:

> Love argueth in this wise: What a Christ have I, what a Father in and through Him! What a name hath my Father; merciful, gracious, long-suffering, abundant in goodness and truth; forgiving iniquity, transgression and sin! What a nature hath my Father! He is Love – free in it, unchangeable,

> infinite. What a Covenant between Him and Christ, for all the seed, for everyone, wherein He undertakes all, and the poor soul nothing.

Had he had the poet's gift he might have written something akin to Henry Vaughan's celestial nursery rhymes.

Cromwell

V

To the end of his life he remained the countryman, and his happiest hours were spent in the long weekends at Hampton Court, where he had constructed fish-ponds and inclosed a warren. That was the sole relaxation permitted him, for the times were too critical to go far from London. The only game he played was bowls, but in field sports he had a most catholic taste. Hawking had been an amusement of his earlier days and he never lost his zest for it. Old, out-at-elbows, cavalier falconers won his favour, and he did his best to entice away Whitelocke's servant who had good skill in hawks. But hawking demanded a freedom of movement and a leisure which he did not possess, and as Protector he had few opportunities for it beyond an occasional day on Hounslow Heath. So also with hunting, another pastime of his youth, Marvell speaks of

> *his delight*
> *In horses fierce, wild deer, or armour bright.*

His love of the dun deer was famous, and Queen Christina of Sweden collected as a present for him a small herd of reindeer, which was unfortunately destroyed by wolves before it could be despatched to England. As Protector he had to confine his indulgence in the chase to the park at Hampton Court, where after dinner he would sometimes course a buck, and amaze the foreign ambassadors by his bold jumping.

Horses were his abiding passion. He suppressed bear-baiting and cock-fighting because of their cruelty, but his prohibition of horse-racing was only local and temporary, and due solely to its political danger as an excuse for royalist meetings. The old cavalry leader was the best judge of a horse in England. There is no evidence that he raced himself, but his stud was his delight, and he laboured to improve the breed. We hear of his well-matched coach-teams – reddish-grey and snow-white – better, said rumour, than any king of England had ever possessed. The Godolphin Barb and the Darley Arabian had their predecessors in his stables, and every English agent on the Mediterranean shores held a roving commission from the Protector. He bought barbs in Tripoli and arabs in Aleppo, for he had had enough of the heavy Flanders brand and knew that what the English stock wanted was the fineness of the East. At one crisis of his life, when a deputation from parliament visited him on the matter of the crown, he kept it waiting for two hours while he inspected a barb in the garden. This constant touch with the natural world was one of his rare founts of refreshment. It was a link with the old simple country life for which he always hankered, and it kept him in tune with his fellow-men. A spirit, which otherwise might have lost itself in aerial flights, had this wholesome tether to English soil.

Cromwell

VI

His working rule was that of Marchamont Needham; government was “an art or artifice found out by man’s wisdom and occasioned by necessity,” and not a deduction from “principles of natural right and freedom.” He had as deep a contempt for the compact and riveted logic of the republican and the leveller as for the fantasies of the Fifth Monarchy men. His mind was wholly unspeculative, and he never felt the compulsion which others have felt to weave his views into an harmonious system of thought.

It was impossible for him, being the man he was, to leave any permanent construction behind him, any more than he could leave a code of principles. He was the creature of emergencies, and he died while he was still feeling his way. England, let it be remembered, blundered and sidled into modern parliamentaryism. Oliver more than any other of her historic rulers had the hard bourgeois sense of reality, and he decided that Pym's notions simply would not work. In that he was right. The spirit of the Restoration was largely negative; certain old things disappeared for ever, but it took several generations, and many false starts, to frame a system which combined expert administration with a measure of popular control. Something in the nature of a permanent civil service had first to be created.

But if Oliver left nothing that endured, no more did the Vanes and Ludlows who opposed him. It may be argued that democracy, in the sense of government by the whole people, is not a system for a fallible world; in England at all events it was not achieved, and it was not seriously desired. The land had had too much of being governed, and the ordinary man wished as little as possible of the attentions of the State. In normal times whiggism, *laissez faire*, is the temper of England. In Macaulay's words, she looks for success not to "the intermeddling of an omniscient and omnipotent State, but to the prudence and energy of the people." So long as in the last resort she has the right of interference she will be apathetic about most of the business of government. The two centuries after Oliver's death saw a marvellous advance in her fortunes. The nation marched forward to undreamed-of wealth, to a humaner and freer social life, to triumphant heights in letters and science and thought. But this was due to the untrammelled vigour of the individual, and very little to any corporate or State-directed effort. There were governing classes but no government. The merit of successive administrations was that they left the people alone, or at the most removed obstacles. The system is best described as oligarchy or aristocracy – with a popular sanction. Burke, its prophet, goes no further in democratic principle than to admit that the whole people, in any matter which deeply stirs them, is wiser than any group or individual, and that a free constitution requires that they may have some power of making their wishes felt; and his doctrine of the true character of the representative is aeons removed from the kind of theory which Oliver combated. During the past century Burke's creed has been relinquished and the mechanism of politics has steadily become more plebiscitary, but it is still far from the democratic ideal of a whole people organically enlisted in the work of governing themselves. It remains in substance a fluid oligarchy, which has the task, daily becoming more difficult, of pacifying its uninstructed masters.

Oliver stands out in history as the great improviser, desperately trying expedient after expedient, and finding every tool cracking in his hand. He dies, the experiments cease, and there is a fatigued return to the old ways. But it is possible to discover in that cloudy mind an ideal of the State which he was not fated to realize, but which he did not cease to cherish. Dryden had a glimmering of this when he wrote in his memorial verses,

Poor mechanic arts in public move,
Whilst the deep secrets beyond practice go.

Like Caesar, another man of a crisis, we must judge him, not only by his actual work but by his ultimate purpose, the substance of things hoped for.

His profoundest conviction, which on occasion could make him tender even towards the zealots of the Fifth Monarchy, was that government should be in the hands of the good and wise, of those whom he thought of as the people of God. For the fundamental tenet of plebiscitary democracy, the virtue of a majority of counted heads, he had only contempt. The justification of such a method on the ground of practical convenience – its only serious justification – would have seemed to him a sin against the divine purpose. The mechanism of the ballot-box was no more to him than a child's toy. He believed in government by the general will, but he did not define that as the will of all. The essence of common democracy is quantity, and he desired quality. The mind was the man, he told parliament; with an impure mind man was no better than a beast, and a beast could not rule: the State must be controlled by the seeing eyes and the single hearts.

But to this conviction he added another, which made him a democrat of an extreme type in his ultimate ideals. His religion taught him the transcendent value of every immortal soul, even though dwelling in the humblest body. He dreamed of an aristocracy of quality where the best would govern, but all would be the best. The State he thought of as, in Kant's words, "a kingdom of ends, where all are sovereign because all are subjects." His zeal for education and for the faithful preaching of the Word is the practical proof of a belief which appears in broken gleams everywhere in his speeches and letters. He was no leveller to seek a monotonous, unfeatured community. He believed in diversity of station – noble, squire, yeoman, merchant and peasant – as congenial to human nature and as giving stability to society, but he would have made each class a partner in the duties and a sharer in the rights of the English polity. His toleration was based on the same principle, that variety of emphasis in faith tended to strengthen the spiritual life of a nation. Tolerance ultimately triumphed through the cynics and sceptics who taught that such differences were trivial, and therefore negligible; Oliver with a brave optimism stood for them because of their value.

Cromwell

VII

As Oliver rode south in April to the meeting of the Short Parliament – perhaps making a circuit to pick up his cousin Hampden in the Chilterns – he must have been conscious that he had reached the turning-point of his career. He had no impulse to plan out his life by the rules of worldly ambition, but he had strange premonitions, and his instinct must have told him that he was done with the tithes of Ely as with the cow-pastures of St Ives. He was now forty-one years of age, which was then regarded as far on in middle life. He was a different man from the ruddy young squire who took his bride to Huntingdon – even from him who, eleven years before, had had his first taste of parliament. There were lines on his brow, streaks of grey in his hair, and his features were leaner and harsher, for his spirit had been through deep waters. An uncouth but an unforgettable face...

Oliver had not found himself – that he was never to do in this world – but after much striving he had learned a rule of life. He had a profound and passionate, if undogmatic, religious faith. In politics, except in as much as they touched upon his religion, he was less decided; indeed so far he had been curiously unpartisan. His only speech in Parliament had been a plea not for coercion but for fair dealing to all sides, and in his local quarrels he had actually been on the side of the king, and had opposed the Russells and Montagues and other puritan grandees. He had somewhat of a cross-bench mind, not easily brigaded with sect or party. His supreme convictions were the worth of what Lincoln called the "plain people," and the responsibility of a man to his fellows as well as to his God.

In the eleven years of country life he had come slowly to maturity. They had not been years of idyllic retreat, as Andrew Marvell sang, in private gardens:

where
He lived reservèd and austere,
As if his highest plot
To plant the bergamot.

They had been years of active social life, when he had come to know the hearts of the Fenland people and something of the heart of England. They had been years of strenuous self-examination and much lonely pondering – dejection too, till the doings in Scotland gave him hope. He had watched the course of events at home and abroad with anxious eyes, fretted at Laud's doings, trembled over Wentworth's success, gloried in Hampden's defiance, shuddered at Tilly's sack of Magdeburg, exulted in the victories of the King of Sweden and sorrowed for his death. He had no experience of war, but when in a year or two he took the field he showed himself already a master of its first principles, and it is reasonable to believe that a close study of works like the *Swedish Intelligencer* had opened to him the mind of Gustavus.

But the formative power of those years lay most, perhaps, in the magical environment of the fens, with their infinite spaces of water and sky. Out of them for immemorial time grew one of the stubbornest of English stocks... Like the desert, it is a land inhospitable to man, where humanity must toil hard to keep its feet and each vantage has to be grimly won from nature. Like the desert, too, it holds life close to its elements, leading to monotheism in religion and a certain stark virility in conduct and manners, for nature there has no delicate cosmetics with which to flatter the soul. Out of such places have come mystics and prophets, iron autocrats and iron levellers – all of them simple men.

Cromwell

VIII

...if his faith after his death went out of public view, indeed almost out of the memories of men, it did not therefore perish, for it was born of an age when the nation was emptied from vessel to vessel, and it was certain of a rebirth should time bring some new great loosening of the foundations. In a sense the seventeenth century plumbed depths of human experience which later centuries have neglected... The mind of the world changes, and it can be argued that the quality of a work of art alters with the change in the mood of the mind which appreciates it. This is even truer of political creeds. They may have been justly discarded for generations when circumstances made them meaningless, but the day comes when they cease to seem futile or irrelevant and have again a compelling power. Today the world has suffered that ***discordia demens*** which England knew three hundred years ago, and nations are prepared for the sheer sake of existence to sacrifice the easy freedom of more comfortable times. A corporate discipline, of which quality is the watchword, seems to many the only way of salvation. Minds surfeited with a sleek liberalism are turning to a sterner code, and across the centuries Oliver speaks to us strangely in the accents of today.

But his bequest to the world was not institutions, for his could not last, or a political faith, for his was more instinct and divination than coherent thought. It was the man himself, in his good and ill, his frailty and his strength, typical in almost every quality of his own English people, but with these qualities so magnified as to become epic and universal. He belongs to the small circle of great kings, though he never sat on a throne; like Milton's Adam:

in himself was all his state
More solemn than the tedious pomp that waits
On princes.

His figure still radiates an immortal energy. "Their distinction," Burke has written of him and his kind, "was not so much like men usurping power as asserting their natural place in society. Their rising was to illuminate and beautify the world. Their conquest over their competitors was by outshining them. The hand that like a destroying angel smote the country communicated to it the force and energy under which it suffered." Though he wrought in a narrower field and influenced far less profoundly the destinies of mankind, and though in sheer intellect he was manifestly their inferior, he had the same power as Caesar and Napoleon, the gift of forcing facts to serve him, of compelling multitudes of men into devotion or acquiescence.

But it is on that point alone that he is kin to those cyclopean architects and roadmakers, the world's conquerors. Almost without exception they were spirits of an extreme ambition, egotism and pride, holding aloof from the kindly race of men. Oliver remained humble, homely, with a ready sympathy and goodwill. For, while he was winning battles and dissolving parliaments and carrying the burdens of a people, he was living an inner life so intense that, compared with it, the outer world was the phantasmagoria of a dream. There is no parallel in history to this iron man of action whose consuming purpose was at all times the making of his soul.

Cromwell

CHARLES I

IX

...That singular character is one of the paradoxes, but not one of the enigmas, of history, for its weakness and strength are abundantly plain. His mild but immovable fanaticism, his lack of any quick sense of realities, his love of wooden intrigues, his defect in candour, his inability to read human nature, his incapacity to decide swiftly and act boldly, – they are as patent as his piety, his fortitude, and his fidelity to what he held to be right. But he had in the highest degree the charm of his race, and could cast a glamour over the most diverse minds. It was those who knew him best who were most under his spell, so that Clarendon could describe him as "the worthiest gentleman, the best master, the best friend, the best husband, the best father, and the best Christian," and Sir Philip Warwick could write: "When I think of dying, it is one of my comforts that, when I part from the dunghill of this world, I shall meet King Charles."

Montrose

X

His gentleness and charm might attach his friends to him, but his public conduct had been in the highest degree fantastic, disingenuous and uncertain. He had no gift of resolute purpose or single-hearted action; the prominent velvet eyes under the heavy lids were the eyes of an emotional intriguer. They were the eyes, too, of a fanatic, who would find in the last resort some curious knuckle of principle on which he would hear no argument. "He loved not the sight of a soldier, nor of any valiant man," it had been written of his father, and Charles had no single gift of the man-at-arms except personal bravery. The old monarchy could only survive if its representative had those qualities of plain dealing and sturdy resolution which were dear to Englishmen; and it was the irony of fate that this king should be part woman, part priest, and part the bewildered delicate boy who had never quite grown up. A freakish spirit had been unloosed, as a shrewd observer noted: "such an unhappy genius ruled these times (for historians have observed a genius of times as well as of climates or men) that no endeavour proved successful, nor did any actions produce the right though probable effects."

Cromwell

CHARLES II

XI

Let us take the man first on his professional side, as a politician. Politically he was a foreigner. He knew more of Spain and France than of England...

Some Eighteenth-Century By-ways: Charles II

XII

He was too idle to be very ambitious, and however clearly he might see the facts, his nature led him in the path of least resistance. But his indolence, which might have left him in the power of strong men, was counteracted by his self-indulgence, which put him in the hands of worthless women. He starved the Navy to adorn his mistresses. Since he needed money, he sought for it in the likeliest quarter, France, and so by compelling England to take the wrong side in the great international quarrel of Europe, prepared the way for the expulsion of his house. He let himself grow weary of Clarendon, as Nero grew weary of Seneca, and the man to whom he owed his throne left the palace in disgrace, pursued by Lady Castlemaine's mocking laughter. He was guilty of two crimes of unparalleled political baseness, – the war with the Dutch in 1672 and his attitude towards the Popish Terror. The only manly act we can set against them was his refusal to be bullied into barring his brother from the succession. And with it all he came to have an extraordinary insight into the real position of parties, as he had always had a remarkable understanding of individual hearts. He saw through the rather shoddy patriotism of the Whigs as he had discounted the Anglican fervour of Clarendon, and by that act of genius, the dissolution of the Oxford Parliament, he checkmated all parties, appealed to the people, and won. He died thoroughly successful, for though he had taken countless false steps and prepared the way for the Revolution, he had got all he asked, and had James been as wise a player William might never have landed. True statesmanship demands patriotism and foresight, but if Charles was far from this, he was yet an incomparable politician and a great intelligence.

Of the rest of his character the trait which has captured men's fancy is his good-humour. Much of it, to be sure, was mere robust health and a careless mind, but something was due to his great knowledge of men. He could adapt his conversation to every circle, and be a "gracious youth" to Robert Baillie, a boon companion to the Mays and Chiffinches, a vulgarian with Lauderdale and Nell Gwynn, a scholar with Rupert and Burnet, and a fellow sportsman with the Newmarket set. He could jest, and jest wittily, at anything, from his own appearance to Bishop Ken's sermons. Part was cynicism, into which his early insouciance had developed; part was simple absence of vanity. Frivolity is perhaps the best word, the frivolity not of the Stuarts, that dark melancholy race, but of the Bourbons, whom the Grande Mademoiselle had called "gens fort appliqués aux bagatelles et peu solides." He would spend an evening with his women hunting a moth while the Dutch were at Chatham, and Captain Douglas, of the *Royal Oak*, had sent his men ashore and was burning along with his ship rather than desert his post. Business to him was a "foolish, idle, impertinent thing."...

But more remarkable than this frivolity of Charles was his ingrained selfishness and self-deception; for sincere though he was with himself in minor affairs, in things which touched his honour he had a great gift of moral blindness. His whole treatment of the Popish Plot agitation, and his conduct about the death of Lord Stafford, are illustrations. He was not without the easy generosity of the selfish man; he was naturally kind, when he had not to trouble himself too much; but his charity was never more than a casual impulse. He was free from superstition, like all sceptics; he was moderate and tolerant; and, say his apologists, he could see through and despise his companions. Such virtues are all traits of the half-hearted and selfish man, without religion or ideals.

In one thing, to be sure, he was single-hearted – his amusements. He was an excellent athlete, a great walker, sailor, huntsman, a superb horseman, and so devoted to angling that he went out in all weathers, to the despair of his doctors. He was not a drunkard, but he drank often to excess, and shortened the days of the Court dandies, who had not his constitution. It was the fashion of the time...

Some Eighteenth-Century By-ways: Charles II

XIII

But his relations with women were so far in advance even of that loose age that Pepys, "the prurient bourgeois," blushes to think of them. Every type, well-born lady and child of the London streets, English and foreign, pretty and comparatively ugly, was the same to his capacious heart. Of his treatment of his unhappy wife it is best to say nothing...

Some Eighteenth-Century By-ways: Charles II

XIV

In the whole history of his affections we can discover only two bright spots, – his constant friendship for the great Ormond, and his love for his child-sister, the short-lived and adorable Henrietta of Orleans. On the whole, he was perhaps the most worthless fellow who ever sat on the English throne, worthless because he had great talents and great chances, and, in a sense, great qualities. He had courage which he never exercised, shrewdness which he misused, health and charm which he frittered away.

Some Eighteenth-century By-ways: Charles II

XV

It is not easy to judge Charles with either patience or fairness... In the compost of graces and infirmities which made up his character, a fine sense of honour had no part, since for that some spiritual discipline is required. He was an engaging creature of impulse, with a tolerant humour which could laugh at himself as well as at others, with the courage which comes from a good constitution and a high vitality, and which could face misfortunes with equanimity – both his own and his friends'.

Montrose

STRAFFORD

XVI

Few characters have been so travestied by legend, for he was far from being the melodramatic devotee of blood and iron of the old history books. He was a simple man, with strong affections, and he wrote the most endearing letters to his children. He would have been happy as a plain country gentleman, busy about his gardens and stables and kennels, for he had a great love of nature and wild sport. In Ireland, whenever he could escape from his duties, he was off to fish for trout, or to hawk – he complains of the absence of partridges around Dublin which compelled him to fly his falcons only at blackbirds – or to oversee the erection of his little shooting-lodge.

His first task was, as president of the Council of the North, to see that the king's law was enforced beyond Trent, to protect every man in his belongings, and to raise money for the Crown – that is to say for the services of the State. As a privy councillor he was a member of what was the equivalent of the cabinet. He had to administer the poor law, supervise the draining of the Yorkshire fens, keep the militia up to strength, and wrestle with obstructive nobles and stupid gentry. His methods often lacked tact, for he did not suffer fools gladly, and his fiery honesty made him intolerant of rogues. He could be hasty and harsh, but he put the north into some kind of order, and his many enemies in those parts could substantiate no single charge against him at his trial.

Then came his appointment in 1632 as Lord Deputy of Ireland, in succession to the incompetent elder Falkland. If England was disturbed, Ireland was ancient chaos; the land was poverty-stricken, and the "great" Earl of Cork was making a fortune out of money-lending; the coasts were harried by pirates, the plantation system was breaking down, and the rule of the lord-justices in Dublin was a farce. A more seemingly hopeless task never confronted a man with a passion for order. It is on his eight years of Irish government that his chief title to fame must rest, and it may fairly be said that no British pro-consul ever undertook a severer labour or in a short time produced more miraculous results. He raised the status of the alien Protestant Church and the character of the divines. He did not attempt to press the Laudian policy of conformity, and he disbelieved in penal measures; "it is most certain," he wrote to Laud, "that the to-be-wished Reformation must first work from ourselves," so he made war on simony and corruption, and told refractory bishops that he would have their rochets pulled over their ears. He refused to bear hardly on the Catholics, postponing any attempt at their conversion till he had provided a Church worth being converted to, while Pym across the water, was declaring that he "would have all Papists used like madmen." In Ulster he tried mild measures to bring the high-fliers to reason, though he detested "the vanity and lightness of their fantastic doctrine," and it was only in the interest of public peace that he was compelled in the end to make the life of men like Robert Blair so uncomfortable that they retired to Scotland. His method with the ministers had much of the initial patience and ultimate firmness of Cromwell's. He believed that for the sake of peace Ireland should be economically dependent upon England, but he did not interpret this maxim harshly, and in many respects his economic views were ahead of his time. He succeeded to a revenue which fell short of the expenditure, and to a very heavy debt, and he left the country solvent, largely by checking peculation. He had to struggle against the vested interests of monopolists and land-grabbers and corrupt officials, who had great purchase in England both at court and in parliament, and, like most servants of the Stuarts, he had to fight with his flank turned and his rear threatened. He was determined that Ireland should not be the milch cow of "that nation of people, or rather vermin, which are ever to be found in the courts of great princes."

He toiled with resolution, energy and invincible courage, and his successes far outbalanced his failures. He ended with a surplus instead of a deficit, and a large reserve fund. He put the plantations in order, and, though he had no military experience, provided an efficient defence force, much of which he trained himself; he cleansed the foul stables of officialdom, set the church on a sound basis of temporalities, and vastly improved its quality; he so enlarged the export trade that it was nearly double the value of the imports; above all, he put into the land a new spirit of ease and hopefulness. Ireland, as he told the king, was now "a growing people in their first Spring." He did all this by a prodigal expenditure of mind and body. He had never been strong, and all his life was plagued with gout and the stone. Ireland made him an old man in his early forties. "I grow extremely old and full of grey hairs since I came into this kingdom," he wrote, "and should wax exceeding melancholy, were it not for two little girls that come now and then to play by me. Remember, I tell you, I am of no long life." He was always oppressed by the thought that his time on earth would be too short for the work he had to do. But he consoled himself with the reflection that "he lives more that virtuously and generously spends one month, than some other that may chance to dream out some years and bury himself alive all the while."

There was no doubt felt in England of the success of Wentworth's work, for every post and every traveller out of Ireland told the tale of it. He had few illusions about how his old parliamentary comrades would now look on him. "I am not ignorant," he wrote to Laud in 1634, "that my stirring herein will be strangely reported and censured on that side, and how I shall be able to sustain myself against your Prynnes, Pims and Bens, with the rest of that generation of odd names and natures, the Lord knows." By his former colleagues he was regarded with mingled admiration, hatred and fear, but principally fear. They felt towards him as an extreme Marxist might feel towards an enlightened, humane and successful capitalist. He was making autocracy efficient and therefore respectable, breaking cheerfully all their pet laws to the profit of the lieges, and thereby buttressing that very fabric which they sought to demolish.

Cromwell

HAMPDEN

XVII

...His (Pym's) chief lieutenant was John Hampden, one of the richest men in England, to whom the ship money case had given a nation-wide fame. Hampden was a poor speaker, but, like Falkland, he cast a spell over his contemporaries. Clarendon calls him a "very wise man, and of great parts, and possessed with the absolute spirit of popularity, that is the most absolute faculties to govern the people, of any man I ever knew." His power lay in two things, his singlemindedness, for he knew precisely what he wanted, and his subtlety and tact, for like many of the single-hearted he was an adroit diplomatist. He was eminently persuasive, for he was never dogmatic, and so gently insinuated his views into other men's minds that they believed them to be their own unaided creation. He was that rare combination, an idealist with an acute judgment of ways and means, perhaps at the moment the wisest head in England...

Cromwell

LAUD

XVIII

The character of Laud has waited long for a fair assessment, for till the other day Macaulay's coarse abuse was apparently the verdict of history. But this little man, with his horseshoe brows and prim mouth and sharp restless eyes, is too subtle a figure for an easy verdict. It is clear that he had great natural gifts of head and heart, and that there was honesty in his dreams and much valuable matter in his work. He had a spacious conception of the church as the guardian of sane progress not in England only but throughout the globe, a missionary church, the spiritual counterpart of a great terrestrial empire. Only through such a church, he believed, could the perilous encroachments of Rome be stayed. He was tolerant in matters of dogma. The disciple of Lancelot Andrewes and the friend and counsellor of George Herbert and Nicholas Ferrar had a sincere personal religion. He had always an honourable tenderness towards poverty. He had a passion for sound learning, and as chancellor he set Oxford upon a new and better road.

Even on the more dubious side of his career, his work in the Star Chamber and the High Commission, there is something to be set to his credit. These courts, on the testimony of Sir Matthew Hale, filled a gap in the legal system, and could reach offenders who laughed at the ordinary tribunals. Laud knew neither fear nor favour, and his normal administration was not harsh, for he put no man to death, and the fines imposed were beyond all comparison less than those imposed by parliament. He had to administer a cruel law – of which he did not recognize the cruelty, for there was a cold donnish insensitiveness about him – and we are shocked at the barbarous punishments inflicted upon Prynne and Leighton, Bastwick and John Lilburne; but it may be questioned if they really shocked the moral sense of the community though they gave superb material to his enemies. These men had been guilty of libels which in earlier times would have been construed as treasonable and for which they would have suffered death, and it is better to lose your ears than to lose your head.

Laud's tragedy, and that of his country, was that he was an able and honest man set in a place where his ability and honesty were the undoing of himself and his master. "A busy logical faculty, operating entirely on chimerical element of obsolete delusions, a vehement shrill voiced character, confident in its own rectitude as the narrowest character may the soonest be. A man not without affections, though bred as a College Monk, with little room to develop them; of shrill, tremulous, partly feminine nature, capable of spasms, of much hysterical obstinacy, as female natures are." So Carlyle, and his verdict does not greatly differ from that of James I: "he hath a restless spirit, and cannot see when things are well, but loves to bring matters to a pitch of reformation floating in his own brain." Laud forgot Bacon's profound sentence: "it were good that men in their innovations would follow the example of Time itself, which, indeed, innovateth greatly, but quietly, and by degrees scarce to be perceived." He applied the brain of a college pedant to the spacious life of England.

We cannot deny vigour to a mind to which Wentworth turned for advice, but it was vigour without perspective. He had Wentworth's love of order, but he insisted on it in the one sphere which was not ripe for it, and, unlike Wentworth, he could not distinguish between essentials and things "purely and simply indifferent." Laud was at utter variance with the great mass of the English people. He put the emphasis on uniformity of worship when the serious minds of his age were absorbed in spiritual struggles which had nothing to do with ceremonial. He preached the doctrine of one great, unified, comprehensive church, when the popular tendency was towards minute schisms. He was a devotee of ritual, and most of the usages he would have made compulsory seemed to the plain man to be what Oliver called "poisonous popish ceremonies." His church courts were so active and meddlesome that the ordinary man's life was made a burden. If Wentworth's doings filled the parliamentarians with fears because he seemed to be making a success of autocracy, Laud's were a blessing to them because they made the Church, and the king the Church's protector, hated and despised. The small, untiring, resolute, courageous archbishop is a tragic figure, for he had no inconsiderable faith to preach but not the gifts to make it acceptable. He was a devoted priest and a great ecclesiastic, but what the world sought was a prophet.

Cromwell

MONTROSE

XIX

His qualities in the retrospect seem to be drawn to a fine edge of burning light. But, as we wonder and revere, there comes a voice from behind the flame, and awe is changed to wistfulness; for it is a voice of comradeship and joy and youth which "sweetly torments us with invitations to his own inaccessible homes."

Montrose

XX

Few careers have such romantic unity. In one aspect he is the complete paladin, full of courtesy and grace, a Volcker of Alsace with his sword-fiddlebow, whose every stroke is a note of music. He wins fights against odds, and scribbles immortal songs in his leisure, and dies in the end like some antique hero, with the lights burning low in the skies and the stage darkened. In another he is the thinker, who read, as no one else did, the riddle of his times, and preached a doctrine of government which had to wait for nearly two hundred years till it found an audience. In that fierce seventeenth century, when men died for half truths or less, when the great forces of the State were apt to be selfish competitors for material gain, and the idealists were driven into the wilds or overseas – in that gross and turbid age he lit the lamp of pure duty and pure reason. There were those who followed duty, but it was too often blindly. There were those who loved reason, but they either retired from the struggle or, like Falkland, fought with the air of martyrs rather than of soldiers. Montrose was armed and mailed Reason, Philosophy with its sword unsheathed. He is a far rarer type than the quietist who has fascinated historians, or than the grim Ironside, "the most formidable of combinations, the practical mystic." He had all the grave lucidity of a Falkland, but he had none of his sad despair, for he went out joyfully to do battle for his faith. He was as stubborn and passionate in his cause as any Ironside, but he was no fanatic; he was not even any kind of mystic. He saw life clearly and calmly, and his spiritual force did not come, as it often comes, from a hectic imagination or a fevered brain. The springs of his being were a pellucid reasonableness of soul, joined to a power of absorption in duty which is commonly found only in the ranks of fanaticism.

It is a figure which must always haunt those who travel the rough roads of Scottish history. We see him in the brave clothes which still dazzle us in his portraits, the long, north-country face, the broad brow, the inscrutable grey eyes. He is thinking, wondering, brooding on the needs of his land, while others are preying on them. Then he reaches his conclusions, and, with something between the certainty of the thinker and the enthusiasm of the boy, he sets out on his desperate errand. We see him in battle, a flush on his cheeks, a youthful ardour in his eye, but his mouth set like iron. We see him among his friends, conquering all hearts with his wit and grace. We see him in triumph and in failure, careless of self, his course set unfalteringly towards his dreams, carrying, in Keats' words, "an awful warmth about his heart like a load of immortality." He is always very human, very much the man, for Alasdair and his kerns would never have followed the ordinary dreamer. And then, when the last blow has been struck, he has neither fears nor reproaches. Clearly and reasonably he states his defence, and when it is flouted and he is condemned to a shameful death, he takes it meekly, knowing something of the fallibility of mankind. The Edinburgh mob is awed into a hush by his appearance; his enemies declared that it was his fine clothes and noble looks; more truly we may read it as that inward vision which is the beatitude of the pure in heart.

Montrose

XXI

On the political side Montrose was a modern man, as modern as Burke and Canning, and speaking a language far more intelligible to our ears than that of the Butes and Dundases of a later Scotland. The seventeenth century produced two curiously premature characters in the great Marquis and Sir George Mackenzie; but Mackenzie, lawyer-like, made a sharp distinction between theory and practice, and while his theory was modern his practice was of the Dark Ages; whereas Montrose knew no cleavage between thoughts and deeds. Most great men have been in advance of their day. Some have had the insight to see several stages ahead and have tried to expedite the wheel of change; some have thrown out ideas which were to fructify afterwards in a form of which they did not dream. Montrose was before his time, not from paradox or from hurry, but because, almost alone in his age, he looked clearly at the conditions of all government, and, having formed his conclusions, was not deterred by prudence or self-interest from acting upon them. As we have seen, he was notably free from contemporary prejudices. He had none of the current belief in Divine Right; he had no excessive reverence for a king as such, and very little for a nobility; he would not have shrunk from the views of Cromwell's Ironsides as to the historical origin of the peerage, which so scandalized the decorous soul of Richard Baxter. He was willing to accept any form of government, provided it fulfilled the requirements which are indispensable in all governments; and these he defined with an acumen and a precision which cannot be challenged.

Statesmanship demands two gifts – the conception of wise ends and the perception of adequate means. The first Montrose possessed in the highest degree, the second scarcely at all. He was a most fallible politician, and he was without skill in the game of parliamentary intrigue. He did not read the temper of the people with the accuracy of Argyll, or the possibilities of the moment with the profound sagacity of Cromwell. He was an optimist about his dreams; he saw the Lowland peasantry looking for a deliverer, when they regarded him as a destroyer; he did not understand the depths of the antipathy of Saxon to Celt, or how fatally the use of Alasdair's men prejudiced his cause; he looked for loyalty in quarters which knew only self-interest, and courage among those who had it not. Practical statesmanship works essentially by compromises, accepting the second or third best as an instalment, and by slow degrees leading the people to acquiesce in an ideal which they have come to regard as their own creation. It must judge shrewdly the situation of the moment, and know precisely what elements therein are capable of providing the first stage in the great advance. It must have infinite patience, and infinite confidence in the slow processes of time.

Such a gift Montrose did not possess – indeed it may be questioned whether the problem before his age permitted of such evolutionary methods. There was no material to his hand in the shape of a nation at least partially instructed or a group of likeminded colleagues. But he was a statesman, if it be the part of statesmanship to see far ahead and to stand for the hope of the future. He stood for the Scottish democracy against those who would have crushed it and those who betrayed it with a kiss. In views and temperament it is not easy to find his parallel. He had Marlborough's contemptuous superiority to parties, but he lacked his passionless Olympian calm. With his kinsman Claverhouse – *Montrosio novus exoritur de pulvere phoenix* – he had little in common except the power of leadership. There is some resemblance to Ireton in political creed, in his scorn of abstractions, and his belief in the need of a strong central government, monarchical, parliamentary, or both; he shared the same view with Strafford, but, unlike him, he did not come to regard monarchical and parliamentary authority as mutually exclusive. He never relinquished his doctrine of a just balance, and if in his last years he was compelled to put the emphasis on the royal power, it was for the same reason as Sir Thomas More was forced into opposition to Henry VIII – because the balance had been unduly depressed.

The truest kinship is perhaps with the troubled humanity of Cromwell. The Lord Protector fought for "the poor godly people"; Montrose for the plain folk without any qualification. Both were tolerant, both were idealists, striving for something which their age could not give them. Montrose had one obstacle in his way above all others, and that was Scotland. Her jealous nationalism was not ripe, even had the century been ripe, for his far-sighted good sense. She was still hugging to her breast her own fantastic creations, her covenants, her barren survivals, her peculiar royalism, still prepared to sacrifice peace and fortune to her pride. If Cromwell shipwrecked upon the genial materialism of England, Montrose split upon the rock of the sterile conservatism of his own land. Scotland was not ready for civic ideals or luminous reason. She had not found the self-confidence which was to give her a far truer and deeper national pride. She had still to tread for long years the path of coarse and earthy compromises, lit by flashes of crazy quixotry, till through suffering and poverty she came at last to find her own soul. Montrose was in advance of his age, he was in advance of England at her best, but he was utterly and eternally beyond the ken of seventeenth-century Scotland. Yet of the two great idealists he has had the happier destiny. Cromwell, brilliantly successful for the moment, built nothing which lasted. Except for his doctrine of toleration, he left no heritage of political thought which the world has used. The ideals of Montrose, on the other hand, are in the warp and woof of the constitutional fabric of today.

Montrose

ARCHIBALD, DUKE OF ARGYLL

XXII

To one who studies such portraits as exist of the chief figures in the Scotland of that epoch, there must come a sense of disappointment. Few convey the impression of power which is found among the Puritans and Cavaliers of England. There is Hamilton, self-conscious, arrogant, and puzzled; Lanark, his brother, dark, sullen, and stupid; Huntly, a peacock head surmounting a splendid body; Rothes, heavy-chinned, goggle-eyed, Pickwickian; Glencairn, weak and rustical; old Leven, the eternal bourgeois; the Border earls, but one remove from the Border prickers; Wariston, obstinate and crack-brained; James Guthrie, lean and fanatical. But there are three exceptions. One is the haunting face of Montrose, whose calm eyes do not change from the Jameson portrait of his boyhood to the great Honthorst of his prime. The second is the face of Alexander Henderson, yellow from the fevers of the Leuchars marshes, lined with thought, and burning with a steady fire. The third is that of Archibald, eighth Earl of Argyll. We see him at nineteen, in his marriage clothes, his reddish hair falling over his collar, his grey-blue eyes with ever so slight a cast in them; we see him in his twenty-fourth year, with the air and accoutrements of a soldier; in the Castle Campbell portrait, unfortunately burned in the Inverary castle fire of 1877, he is in armour, but the face has a scholar's pallor and a curious melancholy; in the familiar Newbattle picture, painted in his late forties, he is in sober black with the skull-cap of a divine on his head, the features are drawn with ill-health and care, the mouth is compressed and secret, the nose is pendulous, and the cast in the eyes has become almost a deformity. But at whatever period we take it, it is a face of power, with intellect in the broad brow, and resolution in the tight lips and heavy chin...

The head of the great house of Campbell was now some thirty-four or thirty-five years of age, eight years the senior of Montrose. He had the widest possessions of any Highland chief except Huntly, and at his back by far the most powerful clan, for he lived close to the Lowlands, and could put 5,000 men into the field. His father, to whom the sobriquet of Gilleasbuig Gruamach – "Gillespie the Sullen" – properly belonged, was an odd character and led an odd life. He was defeated at Glenrinnes in 1594 by the Gordons, but later added to his possessions by subduing the Macdonalds of Islay and Kintyre. But his fortune was not commensurate with his lands, he fell deeply into debt, married a Catholic second wife, joined the Church of Rome, and had to flee the country. He was permitted to return, and lived some ten years in England before his death. His first wife was a daughter of the house of Morton, so his son had in his veins the unaccountable Douglas blood. Like the father, the son had an unhappy childhood, for he lost his mother in his infancy, and during his youth was perpetually at variance with his wandering sire. He had to fight hard during his minority for his rights, and the experience must have made him wary and distrustful, and taught him diplomacy and dissimulation. Charles is said to have assisted him against his vindictive parent, and Clarendon reports some dubious gossip about the old man warning the king against his son...

What is clear is that in his youth he was deeply in debt, and found his great estates less of a boon than an incumbrance. He determined to husband and increase his fortune; and there is record of a curious venture to annex an imaginary island beyond the Hebrides... With high politics he did not meddle... Up to 1638 we may regard him as principally occupied with family troubles and the care of his estates, a little suspect by Presbytery as the son of a Catholic and the brother-in-law of Huntly, well regarded by the king in spite of his father's warnings, and with no special predilection towards the Kirk. He was one of the few nobles who, in the summer of 1638, took the king's alternative covenant at the request of Hamilton.

In this mood he attended the Glasgow Assembly. There it would appear that he underwent a profound spiritual experience, and in the theological sense was "converted."... It was this change of heart, and not the discovery that the Covenant was the side of the majority, that determined Argyll's course. He was an acute judge of popular opinion, but it was something more than policy that took him over to the Covenant side. For from that day this man, who in the past had been wholly concerned with his worldly possessions, and had held himself conspicuously aloof from the Kirk, became a religious enthusiast, a fanatic; and no mortal, however consummate an actor, could simulate such enthusiasm as Argyll revealed during the remainder of his troubled life.

In assessing his character we have therefore to start from the fact that in religious matters he was most deeply in earnest... To this add his Campbell and Douglas ancestry. He had the chief's love of power, and it is possible that, as in Hamilton's case, visions of a crown may have haunted one who boasted that he was the "eighth man from Robert Bruce." Such dreams were common among the higher Scots nobility. His bitter youth had left him suspicious and aloof, without warmth, with few friends and fewer intimates. He could not charm easily; he must win his way by patience, assiduity, and talent; but he learned in time a grace of manner to which even the hostile Clarendon bears witness. He was, so far as can be judged, without any interest in humane letters; his mind was mediaeval in its cast, holding firm by law and scholastic divinity. Hence it is vain to look to him for any profound ideal of statecraft. He was essentially a politician, a shrewd judge of character and opinion, able to use both the raw material of fanaticism in the ministers and of gross self-interest in the nobles to further his ends, because he shared the one and wholly understood the other. There was no quicker brain in Britain to probe the possibilities of a situation. Mr Gardiner thinks him as much superior to Montrose as a statesman as he was inferior in the art of war; and Clarendon, after remarking that Montrose despised him, "as he was too apt to contemn those he did not love," adds that Argyll "wanted nothing but honesty and courage to be a very extraordinary man, having all other good talents in a great degree."

Honesty and courage are difficult matters upon which to dogmatize. Argyll was a poor soldier, because he lacked the power of grasping a tactical or strategical problem – a gift as specialized as that for poetry or the higher mathematics – and because he had not the kind of personality which can impress itself upon large bodies of men under arms. But it is idle to deny courage, even of the rude physical kind, to a man who time and again risked his neck, who was prepared to meet an enemy in a duel, and who went without a tremor to the scaffold. As for honesty, there is little enough of the high and delicate kind at any time in the political game, and if we define it as scrupulous loyalty to cause and colleagues, it was a fruit which scarcely grew in seventeenth-century Scotland. In that mad kaleidoscope Argyll had as much of the rare commodity as most of his contemporaries. His troubles came primarily from a divided soul – a clear, practical intellect pulling against an obscurantist creed, the Highland chief at variance with the Presbyterian statesman, a brain, mediaeval for all its powers, fumbling with the half understood problems of a new world. With such a one subtlety will appear as irresolution, perplexity as cowardice, and a too quick mind will seem to argue a dishonest heart.

Such a man will be a power among fanatics and self-seekers, for he can read the souls of both. But there will be one chink in his armour. He will not comprehend so readily other motives, and, in failing to understand, he will miscalculate and undervalue. Single-heartedness will not come within the scope of his capacious understanding.

Montrose

ELIZABETH OF BOHEMIA

XXIII

Elizabeth of the Palatine, for some brief winter months Queen of Bohemia, had the strange compelling power of her grandmother, Mary of Scots, over the hearts of men. As a girl she had been the idol of her country, for she had the fire and brilliance and endearing simplicity of her brother Henry. Her wedding to the Prince Palatine had set all England junketing for weeks. Then came the disastrous episode of the Bohemian throne, the beginning of the Thirty Years' War, the loss of both Bohemia and the Palatine, her husband's death, and the squalor of a court in exile, dependent upon foreign bounty. But misfortune, no more than age, could dim her charm. When Montrose first met her she was in her early fifties, as we see her in the portraits by Honthorst and Mierveldt – a woman who had left youth behind her, one who had known the whole range of mortal joys and sorrows, with a mouth a little narrowed by pain and disappointment, but with great brown eyes still full of the hunger of life. Few crossed her path but were beguiled, and either became her devotees and the sharers in her broken fortunes, or to their dying day cherished the memory of her as if in a shrine. Zachary Boyd, in far-off Glasgow, came under a spell which is patent even in his halting verses. Donne sent her his sermons and his prayers. To the staid Sir Henry Wotton she was "the eclipse and glory of her kind," and he wrote in anguish, "Shall I die without seeing again my royal mistress?"

"*You meaner beauties of the night,*
That poorly satisfy our eyes
More by your number than your light,
You common people of the skies,
What are you when the moon shall rise?"

Was ever woman praised more nobly? But the glamour fell on others than the poets. "I see it is not good to be my friend," she once wrote, and indeed a following so loyal could not but suffer in a cause so calamitous. But for Elizabeth's sake men forgot worldly wisdom, and were back in the high days of chivalry. There were the young gentlemen of the Middle Temple, who kissed a sword and swore a solemn oath to live and die in her service. There was Sir Ralph Hopton, who, fresh from Oxford, accompanied her in the flight from Prague; and Conway, and Lord Carlisle, and Sir Dudley Carleton, and Lord Cromwell, and Sir Thomas Roe, and Christian of Brunswick. Soldiers, courtiers, ambassadors, bravos, each subscribed himself, like Christian, "your most humblest, most constant, most faithful, most affectionate, and most obedient slave, who loves you and will love you, infinitely and incessantly to death." And there was Lord Craven, who laid his great fortune at her feet, and lived only to serve her.

What was there in Elizabeth to draw forth this wealth of love? Reckless, extravagant, exacting, perhaps a little heartless, there was about her a kind of stellar greatness, a spirit that could not be soiled or subdued by fate. Like Constance, she had "instructed her sorrows to be proud," but it was a laughing pride which endeared as well as awed. "Though I have cause enough to be sad," she wrote to Sir Thomas Roe, "yet I am still of my wild humour to be as merry as I can in spite of fortune." She was a better friend than a mother, for her daughter Sophia declared that her monkeys and her dogs came before her children. The buffets of the world had a little calloused her. But her flawless courage remained, her winning humour, her subtlety, her abounding zest for life.

Montrose

III. SOME THINKERS AND WRITERS

CALVIN
RABELAIS
MOMMSEN
SIR WALTER SCOTT

...genius, the rare quality which was needed to heal the world's ills.

A Prince of the Captivity

"It's the strength of the human spirit that matters."

A Prince of the Captivity

CALVIN

I

Calvin was perhaps the most potent intellectual force in the world between St Thomas Aquinas and Voltaire. Though he rejected in his system whatever the Bible did not warrant, and not, like Luther, only what the Bible expressly forbade, he was in many ways nearer to Catholicism than the German reformer. Like most great men, he was greater than the thing he created. He was a profounder statesman than his followers, and far less of a formalist. He could be so inconsistent as to be accused of heresy: he saw the dangers into which his church might drift, and declared that he had no desire to introduce "the tyranny that one should be bound, under pain of being held a heretic, to repeat words dictated by someone else"; a man to whom Plato was of all philosophers *religiosissimus et maxime sobrius*, had more affinities with humanism than is commonly believed. But a lawgiver must be dogmatic, and the founder of a church must narrow his sympathies. He faced the eternal antinomies of thought – the reign of law and the freedom of the human spirit – and provided not a solution but a practical compromise. He begins with the conceptions of an omnipotent God of infinite purity and wisdom, of man cradled in iniquity, and of salvation only through God's grace. The sinner is foreordained – since God orders all things – alike to sin and to destruction. It is the omnipotence of God that he stresses, rather than the fatherhood, for he faces the problem from another angle than Luther: the triviality of the created and the majesty of the creator; the eternal damnation of man unless lifted out of the pit by God's election.

These doctrines and this angle of vision were not new...they were the orthodox creed of the Fathers of the Church... On such a view man's reason and man's moral sense must alike be discarded as temptations of the devil.

This was the creed of Augustine, stated by him more passionately and harshly than by any Reformer; from him Calvin largely derived his dogmas, but he took the doctrine and discarded Augustine's church. Its central principle, the inexorableness of law, the impossibility of free will, has been held by many secular thinkers from Spinoza to Mill, who would have rejected its theological implications. It was the creed of William the Silent and Coligny and Cromwell, of Donne and Milton and Bunyan – men in whom both conscience and intellect were quick. Only by a noble inconsistency and a tacit forgetfulness could it be a worthy rule of life, and this was in fact what happened. Calvin was greater than Calvinism, and the Calvinist was a humaner and wiser man than his creed. But with all its perversities it put salt and iron into human life. It taught man his frailty and his greatness, and brought him into direct communion with Omnipotence. It preached uncompromisingly the necessity of a choice between two paths; in Bunyan's words the mountain gate "has room for body and soul, but not for body and soul and sin." It taught a deep consciousness of guilt and a profound sense of the greatness of God, so that they who feared Him were little troubled by earthly fears. Historically its importance lay in its absoluteness, for a religion which becomes a "perhaps" will not stand in the day of battle.

Montrose

RABELAIS

II

He sums up the energy of the Renaissance in a way peculiarly his own, and with this in mind we can find a meaning in his ribaldry...

He represents...a theory of life in itself noble and rational, and yet we cannot regret that he has found his opponents. Humanism is a fine creed, but it is insufficient, for it has its limits as much as the old monastic shibboleths. The most illuminating comparison of Rabelais is with Erasmus. Both represented culture, humour, the fine sentiments of life, a high and generous morality, and a real seriousness. Compared with this shining creed, the other side, Puritanism, Calvinism, whatever we care to call it, looks at first sight a drab and melancholy dogma. But it was the latter which the world needed, and still needs, and it could afford to keep the former as a plaything for its leisure. Admirable as humour is, it is of minor importance in morals. The man who has a clear eye and an excellent heart and a great zest for the pleasures of life will in the long-run go down before the man who sees all things in a grim alternative, sin and death on the one hand, and life everlasting on the other. The active life is not enough, if one merely lives for the activity, and it was towards this materialism that all the humanists tended. So, while their work has eternal value as a corrective, it is as the corrective and not as the staple. But in literature it is triumphant, for while Puritanism was overturning thrones and moulding the character of nations, the true Pantagruelist, with his mellow wisdom and infinite humour, was weaving his fancies about Theleme and that far-off land of good fellows, where it is possible to be both virtuous and merry.

Some Eighteenth-Century By-ways: Rabelais

THEODOR MOMMSEN

III

At his death Theodor Mommsen occupied a unique position in contemporary Europe. By common consent he was the foremost scholar, both by virtue of the extent and variety of his attainments and the extraordinary literary value of one or two of his works. He was also the accepted *savant* of the German people, the tutelary intellectual genius of his country. For many years it had been his business to expound German ideals, and to give voice to racial ambitions. His verdict on any question, whether of the day or of all time, was accepted by the large proportion of his countrymen... An enthusiastic Liberal from the first, and a strenuous opponent of Bismarck, he remained to the end a keen critic of policies and politicians. Whatever our verdict on his work, all must feel that a great figure has departed from the world.

Being a man before he was a scholar, he carried into scholarship a profound sense of the importance of the man of action. Like Freeman, he always insisted upon the unity of history, and refused to change his attitude towards the protagonists merely because they had been two thousand years in their graves. He was as keenly interested, and, let it be said, as violent a partisan, in the quarrels of Sullans and Marians as he was in the debates of the Reichstag. For him there was no distinction in nature between 1805 and 90 BC. Hence we never find in him the severely-balanced judgments and the scrupulous impartiality of calmer historians. He wrote his history with certain fixed presuppositions in his mind, but happily they are so very clear on every page that the student can detect them and allow for them. In the first place he was a democrat, rejoicing in the strength of the people, and when he found a man capable of leading the masses, ready to fall down and worship him... The ineffective philanthropist gets from him nothing but contempt. It is the strong man, the Caesar or Napoleon, who can discern the power of the "bodyguard from the pavement," and use it to shatter effete institutions, that commands his admiration. That Teutonic characteristic, which is found in different degrees in such very opposite people as Bismarck and Nietzsche, is very strong in this historian's mind. He believes in and preaches the gospel of strength, and the strong unjust man seems to him more worth having than a century of the ineffectual good. Hence his democracy is a fighting force, and only one step removed from a tyranny.

... For the cast-off rags of feudalism and clericalism he had nothing but contempt, but in discarding one set of bonds he imposed another. He was at all times a thorough-going Individualist. He detested slavery, and the war between North and South America seemed to him a holy crusade. But his conception of freedom, like that of most Individualists, was narrow and abstract; and he was prepared to submit to other bonds. He was nominally opposed to the doctrine of Imperialism, but in practice he was an enthusiast for the domination of his own Teutonic race. His nationalism was strong enough to make him a violent critic of the policy of other people's, as in his ill-judged comments on the Boer War, but it was a nationalism quite inconsistent with itself. The old democratic cult of the "strong man" is always somewhere in the back of his mind. The people are the only source of power and of political wisdom, so ran his creed; but they must be led, and their leader should tolerate no malcontents. He was so like Bismarck that we need not wonder that he quarrelled with him. The truth is that no Conservatism is so unshakable as a certain kind of Liberalism which professes a small number of Liberal dogmas, but is by temperament bureaucratic and absolutist. To Mommsen the Hague Convention was merely a misprint in history, Socialism a dangerous heresy, and popular liberties an uncertain growth which should be blessed but also jealously curtailed. His honesty and political courage were remarkable, and were so recognized by his countrymen that towards the end of his life he was granted a kind of indulgence for free speech, and held a position of whimsical independence. But the net result of his teaching seems to us to have been the riveting of militarist and bureacratic shackles upon his compatriots, and the encouragement of every grandiose racial ambition. Like the Republican Whigs of the eighteenth century, he showed how reaction can masquerade in the cap of liberty.

Some Eighteenth-Century By-ways: Theodore Mommsen

SIR WALTER SCOTT

IV

The strong wine of genius too often cracks and flaws the containing vessel. The mind revolts against the body, the subconscious against the conscious, and there is an expense of spirit in a waste of fears and frustrations. But just as there was no strife or sedition in Scott's intellectual powers, so there were no fissures in his character.

Sir Walter Scott

V

Out of the immense and varied mass of his work a picture of the worker emerges which is substantially the truth... The man and his achievements were of a piece, and there was no schism between fact and dream.

Sir Walter Scott

VI

Such an one makes a light and a warmth around him.

Sir Walter Scott

VII

It is curious how rarely he has been made the subject of serious criticism. His encomiasts have been eloquent and sincere like Ruskin, his detractors have been boisterous and bitter like George Borrow, but he has been praised and blamed in a spirit of rhetoric rather than of science.

Homilies and Recreations: Essay on Sir Walter Scott

VIII

It is not difficult to make a picture of one whose nature is all crude lights and shadows and sharp angles, for a character with anything of the fantastic or perverse in it lends itself to easy representation. But it is hard to draw on a little canvas the man whose nature is large and central and human, without cranks or oddities. The very simplicity and wholesomeness of such souls defy an easy summary, for they are as spacious in their effect and as generous in their essence as daylight or summer. In these days of emotional insecurity we are apt to confuse the normal with the mediocre, and to assume that largeness is also shallowness. We are a little afraid of the high road and find more attraction in the crooked by-ways. Such a mood is not conducive to a fair judgment of Scott, or even to an understanding of him at all. For he is the normal man raised to the highest power, eschewing both fantastic vices and freakish virtues.

He stood at the heart of life, and his interests embraced everything that interested his fellows. That is the keystone of his character and mind – they were central and universal. He was impatient of nothing that God had made; and he did not merely tolerate, for he was eager to understand. His interest was as acute in the way a merchant managed his counting-house and a banker his credits as in the *provenance* of a ballad or some romantic genealogy. No lover of the past had ever his feet more firmly planted in the present. He was pre-eminently a social being, recognizing his duty to others and the close interconnexion of humanity. The problem of his character is, therefore, the way in which imaginative genius and practical sagacity ran in harness, how the spiritual detachment of the dreamer was combined with this lively sense of community.

Sir Walter Scott

IX

Few men have ever approached the task of fiction more superbly endowed than this lawyer-squire of forty-three. He was widely read in several literatures, and so deeply learned in many histories that he could look upon a past age almost with the eye of a contemporary. His life had brought him into touch with most aspects of men's work; he knew something of law, something of business, something of politics, something of agriculture; he had mixed with many societies, from the brethren of the Covenant Close to the politicians of Whitehall, from the lairds of the Forest to the lords and ladies of St James's. Every man he met he treated like a kinsman, and there was no cranny of human experience which did not attract his lively interest. Moreover he knew most of them from the inside, for by virtue of his ready sympathy and quick imagination he could penetrate their secrets. He valued his dignity so highly, he used to say, that he never stood upon it. He could understand the dark places of the human spirit, but especially he understood its normal sphere and the ordinary conduct of life. It could not be said of him, as it was said of Timon of Athens, that he never knew the middle of humanity but only the extremities. He had that kindly affection for the commonplace which belongs to a large enjoying temperament…

Sir Walter Scott

X

The instinct to express himself in words was at the root of his being… He felt himself a member of a great fraternity and cherished a masonic loyalty towards his colleagues. But he had no heroics about it and claimed for it no privileges.

Sir Walter Scott

XI

He considered that the man who retired from the bustle of the world to spin his fancies was something of a deserter from the combatant ranks of humanity. He had so many fighting strains in his ancestry that he hungered always for action, for a completer life than could be lived only in the mind... It was this instinct which was responsible for his commerical and political ventures and – largely – for the *folies des grandeurs* of Abbotsford, but it also gave him his insight into the heart and the prepossessions of the ordinary man. He never lost himself in the stuffy parlours of self-conscious art.

Sir Walter Scott

XII

...He saw that an art is degraded if its practitioners demand privileges in matters of conduct beyond other men. He himself had no vanity or peevishness. He thought that most of his contemporaries wrote better than he did, and that the simplest soldier who carried a gun for his country was a sounder fellow than he was. He refused to indulge in false heroics about his craft or to think that the possession of great gifts released him from the humblest human obligation. He could not see that rules of morality which held in the case of the soldier, the merchant, and the country labourer should be slackened for the artist, or that an imaginative temperament and a creative mind gave a plenary indulgence to transgress. He ranked himself with the plain man, and because he ranked himself with him he understood him.

Homilies and Recreations: Essay on Sir Walter Scott

XIII

Scott had not the metaphysical turn of his countrymen, and he had no instinct to preach, but the whole of his life and work was based on a reasoned philosophy of conduct. Its corner-stones were humility and discipline. The life of man was difficult, but not desperate, and to live it worthily you must forget yourself and love others. The failures were the egotists who were wrapped up in self, the doctrinaires who were in chains to a dogma, the Pharisees who despised their brethren. In him the "common sense" of the eighteenth century was coloured and lit by Christian charity. Happiness could only be attained by the unselfregarding.

Sir Walter Scott

XIV

To this philosophy he added a stalwart trust in the Christian doctrines, a trust which was simple, unqualified and unquestioning.

Sir Walter Scott

XV

He was not disposed to set much value on new theories of society and morals, for he put all theory in the second class of importance. If he was told that such and such a thing was in accordance with the spirit of the age, he replied that the spirit of the age might be a lying spirit with no claim to infallibility.

Sir Walter Scott

XVI

He believed in persons rather than in policies.

Sir Walter Scott

XVII

The very characteristics which cramped him as a poet were shining assets for the novelist, since he did not dramatize himself and see the world in terms of his own moods, but looked out upon it shrewdly, calmly and steadfastly. He was no raw boy, compelled to spin imaginative stuff out of his inner consciousness, but mature in mind and character, one who had himself struggled and suffered, and rubbed against the sharp corners of life. Yet, in his devouring relish for the human pageant, he had still the ardour of a boy.

Above all he knew his native land, the prose and the poetry of it, as no Scotsman had ever known it before. He thrilled to its ancient heroics, and every nook was peopled for him with familiar ghosts. He understood the tragedy of its stark poverty, and the comedy of its new-won prosperity. It was all a book in which he had read deep; the cities with their provosts and bailies, the lawyers of the Parliament House and the High Street closes, the doctors in the colleges, the brisk merchants who were building a new Scotland, the porters and caddies and the riff-raff in the gutter; the burgh towns – was he not the presiding judge of one? – with their snuffy burgesses and poaching vagabonds; the countryside in all its ways – lairds and tacksmen, ale-wives and tinkers, ministers and dominies, the bandsters and shearers in harvest-time, the drovers on the green roads, the shepherds in the far shielings. He had the impulse and the material which go to the making of great epics...

Sir Walter Scott

XVIII

Always in his bustling world Scott is aware of the shadow of mortality. It is a gay world, but at the last it is a solemn world, and few can so cunningly darken the stage and make the figures seem no longer men and women, but puppets moving under the hand of the Eternal.

Sir Walter Scott

He was perfectly conscious of the half-world of the soul and glances at it now and then to indicate its presence, but he held that there were better things to do than to wallow in its bogs. The truth is, the pathological is too easy...

Homilies and Recreations: Essay on Sir Walter Scott

XIX

...He has a very clear philosophy, of which the basis is the eternity and the wisdom of the divine ordering of things. His aim is that of Greek tragedy, to secure a valiant acquiescence in the course of fate and in the dispensations of human life. To him Zeus always governs; Prometheus may be a fine fellow, but Zeus is still king of gods and men. He believed that in the world as it was created there was a soul of goodness, and that, in spite of evil, the "inward frame of things" was wiser than its critics. Throughout history there have been rebels against this doctrine.

Sir Walter Scott

XX

...it is the quiet anchorage of good sense from which we are able to watch with a balanced mind the storm without. I am inclined to think that no great art is without it, and that the absence of it prevents certain writers such as Dostoievsky from being in the highest class. Scott never loses his head;...he never forgets the "main march of the human affections"; and the artistic value is as undeniable as the moral value. The fantastic, the supernatural, the quixotic are heightened in their effect by being shown against this quiet background; moreover, they are made credible by being thus linked to our ordinary world... Compare Scott with Victor Hugo and you will understand the difference which the lack of this quality makes. In the great Frenchman there is no slackening of the rein, no lowering of the top-note, till the steed faints from exhaustion and the strident voice ceases to impress our dulled ears.

Homilies and Recreations: Essay on Sir Walter Scott

XXI

Scott's purpose is the classic reconciliation. Like Meredith's Lucifer in starlight, he is always aware of the "army of unalterable law." To him peace and fortitude are to be found in a manly and reverent submission. *In la sua volontade é nostra pace.*

But his reconciling power lies not only in submission to law but in his joyous recognition of its soul of goodness. If he makes the world more solemn, he also makes it more sunlit. That is the moral consequence of comedy, and of comedy in the widest sense Scott is an especial master. He has Shakespeare's gift of charging our life with new and happier values. His people do not, like Tourgeniev's, fight a losing battle; they are triumphant, they must be triumphant, for there is that in them which is in tune with the inner nature of things.

Sir Walter Scott

XXII

He has the Greek quality of *sophrosyne*, which means literally the possession of "saving thoughts." He can penetrate to the greatness of the humble, the divine spark in the clod. No other writer has done quite the same thing for the poor. Many have expounded their pathos and their humours, and some few have made them lovable and significant, but Scott alone has lifted them to the sublime. Through their mouths he proclaims his evangel.

Sir Walter Scott

XXIII

Scott has what Stevenson found in Dostoievsky, a "lovely goodness." He lacks the flaming intensity of the Russian; his even balance of sould saves him from the spiritual melodrama – to which the latter often descends. But like him he loves mankind without reservation, is incapable of hate, and finds nothing created altogether common or unclean. This Border laird, so happy in his worldly avocations that some would discard him as superficial, stands at the end securely among the prophets, for he gathers all things, however lowly and crooked and broken, within the love of God.

Sir Walter Scott

XXIV

The novels enlarge our vision, light up dark corners, break down foolish barriers, and make life a happier and more spacious thing. If they do not preach any single philosophy, they, in Shelley's words, "repeal large codes of fraud and woe." They restore faith in humanity by revealing its forgotten graces and depths.

Is there nothing here for comfort and edification? Is there no more than the utterance of the intelligent country gentleman? One instance of this enlargement I will give you, and then I have done. No professed prophet of democracy ever achieved so much for the plain man as this Tory Border laird. Others might make the peasant a pathetic figure, or a humorous, or a lovable, but Scott made him sublime, without departing one hair's-breadth from the strictest faithfulness in portraying him. It is not a queen or a great lady who lays down the profoundest laws of conduct; it is Jeanie Deans.

Homilies and Recreations: Essay on Sir Walter Scott

XXV

...I submit further that Scott was a very great artist in words, playing with them as a musician plays with notes of music, and weaving harmonies as subtle and moving as you will find in the whole range of English prose. On a certain level his gifts are admitted by all. He was a master of easy, swift, interesting narrative; he was a master of dialogue, especially that of humble folk; he invented a mode of speech for the figures of past ages, which is at once romantic and natural. But on the highest levels, where alone he is to be judged, he is more wonderful still. When the drama quickens and the stage darkens he attains to a style as perfect and unforgettable as Shakespeare's, and it is most subtly compounded.

Homilies and Recreations: Essay on Sir Walter Scott

IV. MODERN VIGNETTES

WILHELM II
WOODROW WILSON
GEORGES CLEMENCEAU
FERDINAND FOCH
T E LAWRENCE

All of us, however modest our station, are called now and then to be leaders. We must make decisions which affect not only ourselves, but a greater or lesser number of our fellow mortals. We must face situations in public or in private life where we have to choose between two roads, one hard and one easy, one, it may be, right and the other wrong. We have to take risks, to gamble in life, and we have to persuade other people to follow us in our decision and to trust us. The matter may be of small moment, or it may be of the first importance, but the nature of the decision is the same. We have to act as leaders, and therefore we have to act alone…

Men and Deeds: Essay on Montrose and Leadership

WILHELM II

I

"The generality of princes," Gibbon wrote, "if they were stripped of their purple and cast naked into the world, would immediately sink to the lowest rank of society, without a hope of emerging from their obscurity." This harsh saying was not true of William II: in whatever class he had been born he would have been a figure of note. It was his misfortune that destiny had placed him in a position where his faults were too readily hailed as virtues and his virtues were encouraged to degenerate into vices. He came to the throne at a difficult moment, an eager, curious youth, with a weak nervous system and a restless energy, profoundly impressed by the greatness of his place and full of incoherent and undisciplined ambitions. Such a temperament is fatal to a constitutional monarchy, but it may suit moderately well with autocracy, and an autocrat William was from the start. Bismarck read him shrewdly. "I pity the young man," he said in May 1890. "He is like a young hound; he barks at everything, he touches everything, and he ends by causing complete disorder in the room in which he is, no matter how large it may be." That same year the Emperor "dropped the pilot" and became his own adviser, for his youth and the crabbed age of the great Chancellor could not live together.

The new autocrat was a type of monarch to dazzle the populace in his own and other lands. He had great charm of manner and knew how to condescend gracefully to all classes of men. In his multitudinous uniforms he made a fine spectacular figure, and this dignity increased the effect of his frequent condescensions. He had much facile kindness of heart, and on occasion he had even a sense of humour. His abounding and half-neurotic vitality made him amenable to new ideas, his ready emotionalism made him translate these ideas into popular rhetoric, and the self-confidence which grew with every year of his reign convinced him of the profundity of each of his fleeting views. He took all knowledge for his province, and suffered the fate of such adventures, for his excursions in scholarship, art, theology, and metaphysics produced amusement rather than edification. His mind was incapable of real originality or sustained and serious thought; it was the mind of the journalist or the actor, and therefore susceptible to every wave of feeling, to every fragment of an idea, that might pass through the brain of the people which he ruled. He became the barometer of German opinion; he did not direct it, but he registered and was directed by it. This susceptibility made him a lover of theatrical parts, most of which he played moderately well. They were wrong who accused him of insincerity. He was sincere enough while the mood lasted; the trouble was that it was only a mood and did not last long. The conception of William II as an iron-hearted Borgia preparing ruthlessly for conquest was as far from the truth as that picture of him as a mild angel of peace which was at one time foisted upon the world.

If we look deeper into his mind we shall find a strange compost of tastes and aptitudes. He had an acute, if perverted, sense of history, and his soul was hag-ridden by his forerunners. From the contemplation of the legends of the German races and the empire of Otto and Barbarossa he acquired a kind of mystic mediaevalism. He was the heir of the old Caesars, and he would revive the Holy Roman Empire with a Lutheran creed. As early as 1890 he told the world: "I look upon the people and the nation handed on to me as a responsibility conferred upon me by God, and I believe, as it is written in the Bible, that it is my duty to increase this heritage, for which one day I shall be called upon to give an account. Those who try to interfere with my task I shall crush." The doctrine of Divine Right had had a new birth, and its exponent filled in turn all the parts which his reading of history dictated – the heir of Siegfried, the successor of Charlemagne, the Crusader who prayed at the Holy Sepulchre, the prophet who wore Luther's mantle, the wielder of the sword of Frederick the Great. The Imperial mind was like the Siegesallee in the Berlin Thiergarten – filled with flamboyant effigies of the illustrious dead. But there was another side to him, for he was also the man of his age, a leader in commercial propaganda, very sensible of the power of money, and zealous to make his country wealthy as well as great. He cultivated the society of the new-rich, and the aristocracy which he created was largely a plutocracy. He laboured to prove that he was not only the vicegerent of God and the successor of Barbarossa, but the first of the world's bagmen. *Mars commis-voyageur* – the cruel French phrase is the best epitome of the role he had chosen.

With all his faults he was a ruler admirably suited to the Germany of his day. His passion for the top-note, his garish personality, his splendid vitality, his amazing speeches, were in tune with the grandiose temper of his people. He was popular as a man must always be who puts into words what a nation desires to think. He was reverenced by masses of men because his pretensions seemed to swell their own greatness. His vulgarity did not offend, because it was the vulgarity of modern Germany. Moreover, his untiring energy was commercially invaluable, for an autocrat in a hurry is the most efficient of hustlers. Had he been only a figure-head, his quick, shallow intelligence would have been no danger to the world, for its inconstancy would have provided a corrective to its extravagance. Unhappily he was also the chief executive power in his land, and had the ordering of German policy. Unable to read the hearts of other peoples, he had to conduct negotiations with them, and *bêtises*, which would have been harmless enough as the pranks of a negligible royalty, became dangerous when they appeared in the fragile world of diplomacy. He loved the pageantry of war, but had no knowledge of its practical meaning, and rattled his sabre as a rhetorical gesture. As a statesman he was without aptitude or judgment, and yet with him lay the last word in his country's statecraft. Into his capricious hands the Fates had put the issues of life and death... On the 7th September, 1914, the German Emperor had viewed the fight at Nancy from a hill near Moncel. We shall see him again, in his grey cloak and spiked helmet, watching the menace of the Russians from a Polish castle, or looking at the desperate charge of his volunteers among the wet fields of Flanders. He flits restlessly between east and west, everywhere making brave speeches, everywhere announcing a speedy and final triumph. A melancholy figure he cuts, as he stands on the fringe of the battle-smoke at Nancy, looking west to Burgundy and that promised land which he could not enter. An object for pity, perhaps, rather than commination, for he is the dreamer whose dreams do not come true, and who in his folly has imagined that his caprices are the ordinations of destiny.

A History of the Great War, Vol. I

WOODROW WILSON

II

The struggle closed with three men directing the councils of the Allies, and standing forth as the representatives of their peoples; and in each case the leader was not wholly typical of the nation he led. M. Clemenceau had much of the essential Gallic genius, but his inspired audacity was perhaps less characteristic of the France of 1918 than was the patient caution of Pétain. Mr Wilson guided his country without being in temperament a representative American, and Mr Lloyd George irritated and puzzled millions who accepted his inspiration. In these three men the Allies found their ultimate leaders, who controlled the spirit as well as the form of the final stages. Two of them were in the first order as War Ministers, blending courage and tenacity with imaginative fervour and a sure instinct for essential needs. The third had no special faculty for the task, and he owed his power to the chance which made him the official head of a great people, as a monarch must play a foremost part in his country's wars from the accident of his sitting upon the throne. The same chance made him for a season the apparent arbiter of the world's destinies, and the position placed an undue strain upon a stiff and somewhat arrogant temperament and a powerful but intolerant mind. He withdrew into an austere seclusion, refusing to share his responsibility except with lesser men, and as a consequence he was to prove impotent in the final councils of peace. Here we are not concerned with the flood of criticism which followed his fall; but as the leader of America during twenty months of campaigning, and as the prophet of certain vital truths which he alone was in the position to formulate, he has an indefeasible claim to the gratitude of mankind...

On his conception of the duty of a President he behaved with complete correctness, and he rightly interpreted the wishes of the vast majority of the American people. It was not an easy path to tread for a man of his antecedents, for it involved the deliberate shutting of the eyes to many matters which in his past life had interested him most deeply. But he moved on the tight-rope of legality with perfect balance. Whatever defects his critics might find in him of sympathy and the larger intelligence, it could not be denied that his conduct was resolute, and, in a sense, courageous.

Facts, however, were destined to make his resolution look like weakness. If a man is determined not to fight, and his enemy knows this, it is unlikely that he will escape without finding himself in strangely undignified positions. Mr Wilson's mind was essentially of the juridical type. He was admirable in formal argument, and had he been pleading before an international court his case would have been good, and the judges would no doubt have found for him. But he was still unable to envisage that rough-and-tumble world where decisions are won not by words but deeds. He still believed that he could secure victory by making debating points against his adversary. This remoteness from facts was shown in the three disastrous years during which, in Mr Roosevelt's phrase, he "waged peace" against Mexico. It was most conspicuously shown in the situation created by the sinking of the *Lusitania* and by the later outrages. The President stated his case with dignity and force; he was flouted, and he did nothing. Germany, like a street urchin, regarded her mentor with her finger to her nose. Fair words alternated with foul deeds, and though eventually he won an admission of liability from the German Government on the *Lusitania* point and a promise of compensation, it was the most barren of victories, for the outrages continued. The words of the President's severest critic were not without warrant. The Germans "had learned to believe that, no matter how shocked the American Government might be, its resolution would expend itself in words. They had learned to believe that it was safe to kill Americans – and the world believed with them. Measured and restrained expression, backed to the full by serious purpose, is strong and respected. Extreme and belligerent expression, unsupported by resolution, is weak and without effect. No man should draw a pistol who dares not shoot. The Government that shakes its fist first and its finger afterwards falls into contempt." [1]

A History of the Great War, Vols II and IV

[1] "*Dogberry.* This is your charge: – you shall comprehend all vagrom men; you are to bid any man stand, in the prince's name.

"*Second Watchman.* How if 'a will not stand?

"*Dogberry.* Why, then, take no note of him, but let him go; and presently call the rest of the watch together, and thank God you are rid of a knave."

Much Ado about Nothing, Act III, Sc. 3

GEORGES CLEMENCEAU

III

On the 16th November (1917) M. Clemenceau took office. The military situation since Caporetto had become grave, and he called upon the good sense of republican France to show a steady front to the enemy. His countrymen responded with a support which no French Ministry since the outbreak of war had enjoyed, and the world was presented with the exhilarating spectacle of a man who despised party intrigue, rejected all counsels of worldly prudence, appealed, like Chatham, to the nation behind the placemen – and won.

Georges Clemenceau was at this time seventy-six years of age, and since his early youth had played a notable part in public affairs. He was the French spirit incarnate – a master of the *beau geste,* a maker and destroyer of governments, a man with an inexhaustible zest for life, brilliant, warm-hearted, catholic in his interests, and endowed with unhesitating courage. He was such a figure as at the back of his heart every Frenchman loves, and he could count upon this national inclination, as he could count upon the confidence of the men in the trenches. The peculiar strength of his position was that he was utterly single-hearted, suffering from no doubts as to the perfect justice of his cause and the complete villainy of his adversaries. His creed was nineteenth-century radicalism – nationalist, anti-clerical, rational – with no mysticism or loose fringes. Hence every hesitation, moral or intellectual, every subtlety that might distract the national mind or weaken the national front, he met with relentless and contemptuous opposition. In a world of wavering counsels his courage, his ardour, even his narrowness were the qualities most needed – especially in France, whose heart was being made sick by hope deferred. His business was to guide and encourage his country in the fiery trials he saw approaching, and not less to cleanse public life from the foul stuff which clogged the nation's effort. Ever since the spring France had been gravely perturbed by treacherous elements in her midst – German agents who seduced her baser press and her venal politicians, sinister figures that strove to bring the pacificism of the extreme socialists into line with *défaitisme* in other lands, and so play the game of Berlin. Against such treason M. Clemenceau declared truceless war.

A History of the Great War, Vol. IV

FERDINAND FOCH

IV

By whatever standards we judge him, Ferdinand Foch must take rank among the dozen greatest of the world's captains. Long before the outbreak of war he had made himself a master of his art, and a happy fate gave him the chance of putting into practice in the field the wisdom he had acquired at leisure. He had studied closely the work of Napoleon, and had brought his mind into tune with that supreme intellect so that he absorbed its methods like a collaborator rather than a pupil. Discarding the pedantic cobwebs which a too laborious German Staff had woven round the Napoleonic campaigns, he mastered those principles which to the great Emperor were like flashes of white light to illuminate his path. Few soldiers have been more learned in their profession, and few have worn their learning more lightly. His broad, sane intelligence was without prejudice or prepossession. He turned a clear eye to instant needs, and read the facts of each case with a brave candour. But he did not forget that the maxims of strategy are eternal things, and he brought his profound knowledge of the past to elucidate the present. No aspect was neglected; he knew how to inspire men by the *beau geste* as well as how to labour at the minutiae of preparation. He was both artist and man of science; he worked at a problem by the light of reason and knowledge, but when these failed he was content to trust that instinct which is an extra sense in great commanders. His character was a happy compound of patience and ardour; he could follow Fabian tactics when these were called for; and he could risk everything on the sudden stroke. He was not infallible, any more than Caesar, or Napoleon, but he could rise from his mistakes to a higher wisdom. In a word, he had a genius for war, that rarest of human talents. In the splendid company of the historic French captains he will stand among the foremost – behind, but not far behind, the greatest of all.

A History of the Great War, Vol. IV

T E LAWRENCE

V

I do not profess to have understood T E Lawrence fully, still less to be able to portray him; there is no brush fine enough to catch the subtleties of his mind, no aerial viewpoint high enough to bring into one picture the manifold of his character.

Before the War I had heard of him from D G Hogarth, and so many of my friends, like Alan Dawnay, George Lloyd and Aubrey Herbert, served with him in the East that he became a familiar name to me; but I do not think that I met him before the summer of 1920. Then we found that we had much in common besides Hogarth's friendship – and admiration for the work of C E Doughty, including his epics; similar tastes in literature; the same philosophy of empire.[1]

Until his death I saw him perhaps half a dozen times a year while he was in England. He had gathered round him a pleasant coterie, most of whom I knew. But we never worked together, though we once projected a joint-editing of the Gadarene poets – there were others from Gadara besides Meleager. He would turn up without warning at Elsfield at any time of the day or night on his motor-cycle Boanerges, and depart as swiftly and mysteriously as he came.

Yet in a sense I knew him better than many people whom I met daily. If you were once admitted to his intimacy you became one of his family, and he of yours; he used you and expected to be used by you; he gave of himself with the liberality of a good child. There was always much of the child in him. He spoke and wrote to children as a coeval. He had a delightful impishness. Even when he was miserable and suffering, he could rejoice in a comic situation, and he found many in the ranks of the RAF and the Tank Corps. What better comedy than for a fine scholar to be examined as to his literacy by the ordinary education officer? And the game of hide-and-seek which he played with the newspapers amused him as much as it annoyed him.

When I first knew him he was in the trough of depression owing to what he thought to be the failure of his work for the Arabs, which involved for him a breach of honour. Mr. Churchill's policy eventually comforted him, but it could not heal the wound. Physically he looked slight, but, as boxers say, he stripped well, and he was as strong as many people twice his size, while he had a bodily toughness and endurance far beyond anything I have ever met. In 1920 his whole being was in grave disequilibrium. You cannot in any case be nine times wounded, four times in an air crash, have many bouts of fever and dysentery, and finally at the age of twenty-nine take Damascus at the head of an Arab army, without living pretty near the edge of your strength. But he had been endowed also with a highly keyed nervous system which gave him an infinite capacity for both pleasure and pain, but never gave him ease. There was a fissure in his nature – eternal war between what might be called the Desert and the Sown – on the one side art and books and friends and leisure and a modest cosiness; on the other action, leadership, the austerity of space.

His character has been a quarry for the analysts and I would not add to their number. It is simplest to say that he was a mixture of contradictories which never were – perhaps could never have been

– harmonized. His qualities lacked integration. He had moods of vanity and moods of abasement; immense self-confidence and immense diffidence. He had a fastidious taste which was often faulty. The gentlest and most lovable of beings with his chivalry and considerateness, he could also be ruthless. I can imagine him, though the possessor of an austere conscience, crashing through all the minor moralities to win his end. That is to say, he was a great man of action with some "sedition in his powers."

For the better part of three years he was a leader of men and a maker of nations. Military students have done ample justice to his gifts as a soldier. Perhaps his contribution to the art of war has been a little overstated, but beyond question he foreshadowed a new strategy and tactics – audacity in surprise, the destruction of material rather than of men, blows at the enemy's nerve centre and therefore at his will to resist. And he could put his doctrine into effect with speed and precision. If he had come out of the War with a sound nervous system and his vitality unimpaired, he might have led the nation to a new way of life. For he had a magnetic power which made people follow him blindly, and I have seen that in his eye which could have made, or quelled, a revolution. He had also an astonishing gift for detail. He knew more about the history and the technique of war than any general I have ever met. He understood down to the last decimal every weapon he employed and every tool he used. He was a master both of the vision and of the fact.

What deflected him from his natural career of action? For deflected he was; he made deliberately *lo gran rifuoto*; he cut himself off from the sphere in which he was born to excel. It is idle to speculate on what would have happened if he had ended the War with perfect balance and undamaged nerves; if he had he would not have been Lawrence. There was a fissure in him from the start; the dream and the business did not march together; his will was not always the servant of his intelligence; he was an agonist, a self-tormentor, who ran to meet suffering half-way. This was due, I think, partly to a twist of puritanism, partly to the fact that, as he often confessed, pain stimulated his mind; but it was abnormal and unwholesome. He was a great analyst of himself, but he never probed the secret of this crack in the firing. Sometimes he put it down to his war experiences, sometimes to his post-War disillusionment, when he was inclined to talk the familiar nonsense about youth having been betrayed by age. But I think it was always there, and it tended to gape under stress. When there was no call to action he was torn by his divided thoughts. "The War was good," he once wrote, "by drawing over our depths that hot surface wish to do or win something."

He was disillusioned, too, about mundane glory, disillusioned too early. "I wasn't a King or Prime Minister, but I made 'em and played with 'em, and after that there was not much more in that direction for me to do." The man of action in him gave him an appetite for fame, even for publicity, and the other side of him made him despise himself for the craving. His conscience forbade him to take any reward for his War services, but there were times when he thought it a morbid conscience. So, pulled hither and thither by noble and contradictory impulses, he had moods when he hated life. "Oh, Lord, I am so tired! I want so much to lie down, to sleep and die. Die is best because there is no réveillé. I want to forget my sins and the world's weariness."

He craved, like a mediaeval monk, for discipline and seclusion. To use a phrase of his own, he was done with trying to blow up trains and bridges, and was thinking of the Well at the World's End. He wanted padlocks, as Hogarth said, and that was why he enlisted in the RAF as a mechanic. It was a true instinct, for, unless after 1922 he had found mechanical work under discipline, the fissure might have become a gulf. I remember that at that time I came across some words written by the Sir Walter Raleigh of our day about the Elizabethan Raleigh, who was a collateral kinsman of Lawrence. "The irony of human affairs possesses his contemplation... The business of man on this earth seems trivial and insignificant against the vast desert of eternity."

He had found refuge from the life of action in another kind of activity, for he had always an itch to write. He was contemplating the *Seven Pillars* as early as September 1917, and he had no sooner entered the Air Force than he planned a book on his experiences. "Writing has been my inmost self all my life," he wrote in his last years, "and I can never put my full strength into anything else." This interest brought him after the War into literary and artistic circles. In one way this was very good for him, since it gave him a host of new interests and much welcome companionship, but I fear that it also increased his tendency to introspection. What was an intellectual pastime to those cultivated ingenious friends of his might to him be deadly serious. But one thing it did – it made him write.

To me he seems to be a great writer who never quite wrote a great book. All his writing was a sort of purgation, a clearing from his mind of perilous stuff, and consequently the artistic purpose was often diverted by personal needs. The *Seven Pillars* is ostensibly the story of a campaign and it contains brilliant pieces of story-telling; but, as he said of it himself, it is "intensely sophisticated." It is a shapeless book and it lacks the compulsion of the best narrative, for he is always wandering off down the corridors of his own mind. The style has its great moments, but it has also its lapses into adjectival rhetoric. The *Mint* is a *tour de force*, an astonishing achievement in exact photography; no rhetoric here, but everything hard, cold, metallic and cruel. His power of depicting squalor is uncanny, though there is nothing in the *Mint*, I think, which equals a later passage describing a troopship on its way to India[2] that fairly takes the breath away by its sheet brutality. In the *Mint* he weaves words and phrases from the gutter – *les gros mots* – into a most artful pattern. But I cannot think the book a success. It lacks relief and half-tones; also shape. In his own phrase it is a "case-book; not a work of art, but a document."

I never cared for his version of the *Odyssey*, for I did not share his view that that poem was Wardour Street. Lawrence had had the ideal experience for an Homeric scholar. "For years we were digging up a city of roughly the Odysseus period. I have handled the weapons, armour, utensils of those times, explored their houses, planned their cities. I have hunted wild boars and watched wild lions, sailed the Aegean (and sailed ships), bent bows, lived with pastoral peoples, woven textiles, built boats and killed many men." But he was not simple-souled enough to translate Homer, so he invented a Pre-Raphaelite Homer whom he could translate. I believe that the *Letters* will rank as high as any of his books, because they show nearly all the facets of his character; and he never wrote better prose than his description of the bleak sea-coast of Buchan.[3]

His fame will endure, and as time goes on the world may understand him better; as he wrote of Thomas Hardy, "a generation will pass before the sky will be perfectly clear of clouds for his shining." I last saw him at the end of March, 1935, when on a push-bike he turned up at Elsfield one Sunday morning and spent a long day with me. He was on his way from Bridlington to his Dorsetshire cottage. He looked brilliantly well, with a weather-beaten skin, a clear eye, and a forearm like a blacksmith's. His nerves, too, seemed to be completely at ease. He had no plans and described himself as like a leaf fallen from a tree in autumn, but he was looking forward avidly to leisure. He spoke of public affairs and his friends with perfect wisdom and charity. When he left I told my wife that at last I was happy about him and believed that he might become again the great man of action – might organize, perhaps, our imperfect national defences. She shook her head. "He is looking at the world as God must look at it," she said, "and a man cannot do that and live." ... A few weeks later he was dead.

I am not a very tractable person or much of a hero-worshipper, but I could have followed Lawrence over the edge of the world. I loved him for himself, and also because there seemed to be reborn in him all the lost friends of my youth. If genius be, in Emerson's phrase, a "stellar and undiminishable something," whose origin is a mystery and whose essence cannot be defined, then he was the only man of genius I have ever known.

1 "I think there's a great future for the British Empire as a voluntary association, and I'd like to have Treaty States on a big scale attached to it... We are so big a firm that we can offer unique conditions to small businesses to associate with us" (*Letters*, p. 578).

2 *Letters*, p. 50.

3 *Ibid.*

Memory Hold-the-Door

CHAPTER III

THE LAW AND SOME LAWYERS

THE LAW
LORD MANSFIELD
LORD ST LEONARDS
LORD LYNDHURST
LORD WESTBURY
A CHARACTER STUDY

The Law is a hard mistress, but she never denies a single-hearted votary.

Some Eighteenth-Century By-ways: The Victorian Chancellors

THE LAW

I

It is only by a vigorous mental effort that I can realize that I was once a lawyer. When a man has deserted the pastoral uplands of the Bar for the low levels of commerce, when he has ceased to be a manipulator of the legal mill and has become the crude material which is ground in it, when in his future relations with courts of justice he must content himself either with the insignificant position of the lay client, or the dullness of the jury box or the witness box, or the garish and comfortless notoriety of the dock, something is radically altered in his soul. He has lost his first innocence. He has embarked upon a career which may be more profitable and less laborious, but can never be as respectable as that which he has forsaken.

Homilies and Recreations: The Judicial Temperament

II

...I became an enthusiast for the law. In those days the Bar examinations were trivial, and I succeeded in being ploughed once in my finals through treating the thing too cavalierly. But I toiled prodigiously at my own kind of study. I read the Law Reports avidly. I discovered an antiquary's zeal in tracing the origins of legal doctrine. My favourite light reading was the lives of lawyers. I developed a special admiration for Mansfield, and, finding that the life of a great Chief Justice had never been written, I set myself to remedy the lack. To this day I possess three stout volumes in which I have analysed and classified every one of his decisions. I had no ambition at the time except legal success, and politics I thought of only as a step to that goal. It seemed to me that the position of a judge was the most honourable, dignified and independent of any – ease without idleness, an absorbing intellectual pursuit in which daily one became more of a master. My view was that of *Weir of Hermiston*: "to be wholly devoted to some intellectual exercise is to have succeeded in life; and perhaps only in law and the higher mathematics may this devotion be maintained, suffice to itself without reaction, and find continued rewards without excitement." Moreover, another side of me loved the appurtenances of it all – the Inns of Court with their stately dining-halls and their long histories, the ritual of the Bar and Bench, the habits of mind and the ways of speech of the profession, the sense that here was the hoar-ancient intimately linked to modern uses.

It was a pleasant apprenticeship, for I had not the nervous strain of a busy lawyer who has to struggle with obtuse juries and captious judges. I had the mental interest of determining the precise significance of words, using what sailors call cross-bearings, elucidating shades of meaning and nuances of atmosphere – the interest of a mathematical proof or a chess conundrum, or an elaborate piece of classical music. I had the historical interest of tracing doctrines back to their dim beginnings. I had the more human interest of watching the play of able minds and of seeing life vividly from a special angle. I am convinced that an education in the humanities should be supplemented and corrected by a training either in law or in some exact science. Besides, it admits one to a great and loyal brotherhood. Once a lawyer always a lawyer. Though I soon ceased to practise, for years I read the law reports first in the morning paper, and fragments of legal jargon still tend to intrude themselves in my literary style.

Memory Hold-the-Door

III

I have sometimes had an idea of compiling a legal anthology of those judgments which are good literature as well as good law. It would be a fascinating book, and it would put most professional stylists to shame... I am prepared to maintain that there is a surprising amount of fine literature in the Law Reports.

Homilies and Recreations: The Judicial Temperament

IV

There is something about a barrister's spells of overwork which makes them different in kind from those of other callings. His duties are specific as to time and place. He must be in court at a certain hour. He must be ready to put, or reply to, an argument when he is called upon; he can postpone or rearrange his work only within the narrowest limits. He is a cog in an inexorable machine and must revolve with the rest of it.

The Gap in the Curtain: Whitsuntide at Flambard

V

...that rare thing, the judicial temperament, which is something born in a man.

Homilies and Recreations: The Judicial Temperament

VI

...Alike in England, in Scotland and in America the Bench has a formative task which, when properly performed, is the highest of all judicial duties. The law, as I have said, should be regarded as an elastic tissue which clothes the growing body. That tissue, that garment, must fit exactly. If it is too tight it will split, and you will have revolution and lawlessness, as we have seen at various times in the history of this country when the law was allowed to become a strait waistcoat. If it is too loose, it will trip us up and impede our movements. Law, therefore, should not be too far behind, or too far ahead of the growth of society. It should coincide as nearly as possible with that growth. So it is the judge's duty to be in touch with contemporary life, to be awake to the emergence of new facts and forces, and to bring the new facts inside the circumference of law. Now and then statutes may be necessary, but the Common Law is a marvellously adaptive thing, and it is wonderful what can be done with it by one who understands it.

Homilies and Recreations: The Judicial Temperament

VII

It is a fact, I think, that the greatest judges have been usually men of a wide general culture. Such were Hardwicke, Mansfield, Wensleydale, Selborne, Bowen; such very notably in America was Story. There have been exceptions such as Sir Edward Coke, but they go to prove the rule.

Homilies and Recreations: The Judicial Temperament

VIII

We have judges witty and dull, learned and unlearned, high-minded and less high-minded, industrious and idle; we have on the whole a most respectable level of intellect and character. But the judicial temperament, the *vera differentia* of the judge, is so rare that I doubt if it appears as often as once in a decade.

Homilies and Recreations: The Judicial Temperament

IX

The greatest judge is one who might have been great in politics, in administration, in business, or in war. Which is simply to say that a great judge must be also a great man.

Homilies and Recreations: The Judicial Temperament

X

Since a judge is a human being, he must be permitted to have his share in the attributes of mortality. But he must be capable of putting them aside. He must have the power of separating a question from the "turbid mixture of contemporaneousness" with which it is clogged. It is a task which requires supreme intellectual honesty, a complete absence of the "lie in the soul," and it is the first duty of a judge. I think it has been the rule and not the exception in the history of the English and American Benches, and to that I believe is due the high popular esteem in which these Benches have so long been held.

Homilies and Recreations: The Judicial Temperament

XI

I do not deny that the pure and unadulterated fool has occasionally strayed on to the Bench.

Homilies and Recreations: The Judicial Temperament

LORD MANSFIELD

XII

...In many ways he is the most imposing figure in the history of the English bench. He had a profound effect upon the development of law; he held one or other of the great law offices for almost half a century; and he dominated his colleagues as no other Chief Justice has ever done. But it is possible to disregard this technical side, and still find a wonderful figure of a man, a statesman and a scholar... His was a nature born to success, and free from the little roughnesses which impede; a soul self-contained, clear-sighted, dispassionate, and patient. He was given a fair chance, for he had the best education which his time could afford, and he had a certain ready-made circle of friends. But, when all has been said, his achievement is remarkable. He was famous when little more than a youth; he conquered his profession while living as a friend of wits and poets and a gentleman of the town. And when he had reached his desire, then came those many years of serene and dignified work, where there is no sign of effort, the fine flower of an industrious youth.

He was the eleventh child of the fifth Lord Stormont, descended from the Murrays of Tullibardine, and connected with the houses of Buccleugh and Montrose. The family fortune was not great, and in the tumble-down castle of Scone, where he was born, the bringing-up of the fourteen children must have been Spartan...

He had no talent in a colossal degree; but he had all, or nearly all, in some proportion, and the whole was harmoniously compounded. His mind was clear and penetrating; all faculties were at his command for use, and none were blunted by years of routine. He attained to that perfect consciousness of power and ready facility which is the highest pleasure in life. For all his industry and his learning, there is never a hint of stress about him. After a long day in the courts, he turns to Horace or De Thou or the salons of St. James's with an unfailing alacrity of spirit. Nimble, keen, subtle, unwearied, if these be not characteristics of supreme genius, they at least denote a perfect talent. It is the perfection of the legal talent, a lawyer being rather an interpreter than a leader; mediocrity, if you like, but of the *aurea mediocritas* stamp.

...his character stands as something polished and complete, the "four-square man" that Simonides spoke of. But this perfection, if it has few flaws, has its limitations, as his enemies were ready to perceive. The chief charge is the expected one of a radical coldness of heart. Here, again, while admitting truth in the accusation, we must protest against the ordinary acceptation of the word. He could be very kind, and he could form the warmest friendships...we must confess that he was a little insensible to the warmth of common humanity...in his freedom from the prejudices of the crowd he fell short of the prejudice which is also wisdom. It is the old complaint against the entirely rational and clear-sighted man that, in his unbroken march, he misses the wayside virtues which fall to the blind and feeble.

Some Eighteenth-Century By-ways: Lord Mansfield

LORD ST LEONARDS

XIII

Of those whose reputation will ever be green in the law reports, but to whom the ordinary man will scarcely do justice, St Leonards is the chief. The qualities which make a great judge are not always those which make a man eminent at the Bar. An advocate is carried to fortune by the natural gift of the orator, by endowments of presence, manner, or voice, by a peculiar insight into human nature and a ready sympathy, or by some pre-eminent skill of intellectual fence. But the judge is concerned with none of those things: he may have them all, and be a signal failure. The meticulous interpretation of statutes, the orderly balancing of precedents and the deduction of principles, need none of the showy endowments of successful advocacy. Of the three Victorian Chancellors who will be remembered mainly as great judges, none won exceptional fame at the Bar. There is no such tradition of their prowess as attaches to Erskine, or Loughborough, or Scarlett, or, in a later day, to Charles Russell. Indeed St Leonards, the greatest of the three, seems, apart from vast learning and a clear mind, to have had scarcely any of the conventional qualities of the advocate. Like Lord Tenterden, he was the son of a barber, and went to neither of the universities. Amazingly precocious, and the author of standard law books while still in his early twenties, he came rapidly to the front through sheer competence. Once, after dining early, he got through thirty-five briefs before going to the House of Commons at eleven – which shows how complete was his mastery of his profession. He was respected by all parties, – by the Radicals for his efforts towards law reform, by the Tories for his unbending Toryism in all other matters, and by the Bar for his learning and his formidable temper. He was Lord Chancellor of Ireland before succeeding to the English office, and no doubt has ever been cast upon his value as a judge. He knew every case in the books, he went straight to the heart of the subject, and woe betide the counsel who tried to fob him off with irrelevancies. The reading of his decisions produces the impression of a powerful intellect working joyfully on the driest material. There has probably never been a greater judge, so far as the mere satisfactory decision of complex cases goes.

Some Eighteenth-Century By-ways: The Victorian Chancellors

LORD LYNDHURST

XIV

The son of Copley, the portrait-painter, he settled down, after a brilliant career at Cambridge, to make a living in the most uncertain of all professions. His rise was slow, and for years he shut himself off from the world. His chance came when he forswore the Whig principles of his youth and entered the House of Commons as the legal champion of the Tories. Thereafter his career was one long triumphal progress. He thrice occupied the Woolsack, and it is possible that, like Mansfield, he might have been Premier had he pleased. If he was not one of the greatest of English lawyers, he was certainly one of the greatest minds that ever applied itself to law. His intellectual vitality was such that no subject came under his cognisance which he did not master. He was earnest in the cause of law reform, however Tory might be his views in politics; but the truth is that he probably did not care enough about political problems to trouble to have opinions. He shaped his course from day to day, asking only one thing – the chance of exercising his superb powers of mind. "He played the game of life," wrote Bagehot, "for low and selfish objects, and yet, by the intellectual power with which he played it, he redeemed the game from its intrinsic degradation." He was a typical exponent of the "grand manner" – a great judge, who liked to look like a cavalry officer, and preferred smart to legal society. He was completely successful, and for long he and his wife were the most brilliant features in the fashionable world. In his attitude towards enemies and rivals in the Press and in Parliament he never lost the air of the *grand seigneur*. He disregarded abuse, and when fate put an opponent in his power, went out of his way to treat him magnanimously. To the end of a long life he retained a boyish gaiety, and bore his honours with the same lordly ease with which he had won them. His last words were: "Happy? Yes, supremely happy."

Some Eighteenth-Century By-ways: The Victorian Chancellors

LORD WESTBURY

XV

...Despising mankind, especially that portion of it which embraced his colleagues, he became the foremost scourge of fools in his generation. He was born with a gift of English style which might have made him a great man of letters. Exact, appropriate, and adequate sentences flowed easily from his lips. With this appalling clarity of thought and deftness of phrase he joined a gentle voice and a lisping, mincing accent, so that his sarcasm had the piquancy of gall in honey. His early years at the Bar were years of unremitting toil. He dined habitually in chambers off a mutton chop and a glass of water. Passionless lucidity was the mark of his advocacy, and no man was ever more fertile in resource, more wholly self-possessed, or more contemptuous of an adversary. He could so state his own case that any opposition seemed to involve the lunacy of the opponent. He entered Parliament as a Conservative, but he was as scornful of political principles as of other things, and calmly went over to the Liberals when their prospects seemed rosier. With his usual courage he faced alone an angry meeting of the Conservative Club while his name was being struck off the books. An Erastian in Church affairs, and of no persuasion at all in secular policy, a passion for law reform and better modes of legal education, and a deep love of Oxford, were almost his only interests beyond himself and his household. He was soon made Solicitor-General; and with Cockburn as Attorney smote Amalek hip and thigh. He bought a country estate, and became an assiduous if indifferent sportsman, occasionally peppering his friends and upbraiding someone else for the blunder. In 1861 he received the Great Seal in succession to Lord Campbell, and ascended the Woolsack followed by the admiring dislike of the whole Bar and most of the public. We know from the Letters of Queen Victoria that her Majesty shared to the full in the popular view.

As a judge he gave general satisfaction, for he had Lord Halsbury's knack of getting through verbiage to facts, and through subtleties to principles. Like Lord Young, he detested precedents, and wished that all the law reports could be burned. But his career as Chancellor is more remarkable on the political than on the legal side, for his Erastianism found full scope in his struggle with what he regarded as clerical usurpation. In his judgment in the "Essays and Reviews" case, he "dismissed hell with costs, and took away from orthodox members of the Church of England their last hope of everlasting damnation."... He treated the Episcopal Bench, to adopt a famous metaphor, as the

Almighty might treat refractory black-beetles... "I would remind your Lordships," he once said, "that the law in its infinite wisdom has already provided for the not improbable event of the imbecility of a bishop." Many of his jibes are merely rude, but we must remember that they were delivered in a dulcet voice, with a prim and measured accent, which greatly increased the effect. It is awesome to think that he once addressed a Young Men's Christian Association on the virtues of benevolence and charity, to which qualities he attributed the success of his career. Certainly he was a terrible old gentleman, and yet his bark was much worse than his bite. Hating sentiment and moral protestations, he leaned too far to the other extreme. But the virtues at which he publicly scoffed he was apt to practise in private, and many a man had to thank this rough-tongued cynic for advice and help. Whatever his faults, he was a splendid clean-cut figure, with something antiseptic and bracing in his air. One such man is no bad tonic for a generation. "From my youth up," he once said, "I have truckled to no man, sought no man's favour." His courage never failed him to the end. He died in harness, sitting as an arbitrator with a bag of ice on his spine, on the very eve of his death.

Some Eighteenth-Century By-ways: The Victorian Chancellors

A CHARACTER STUDY

XII

The Home Secretary was a joy to behold. He had the face of an elderly and pious bookmaker, and a voice in which lurked the indescribable Scotch quality of "unction." When he was talking you had only to shut your eyes to imagine yourself in some lowland kirk on a hot Sabbath morning. He had been a distinguished advocate before he left the law for politics, and had swayed juries of his countrymen at his will. The man was extraordinarily efficient on a platform. There were unplumbed depths of emotion in his eye, a juicy sentiment in his voice, an overpowering tenderness in his manner, which gave to politics the glamour of a revival meeting. He wallowed in obvious pathos, and his hearers, often unwillingly, wallowed with him. I have never listened to any orator at once so offensive and so horribly effective. There was no appeal too base for him, and none too august: by some subtle alchemy he blended the arts of the prophet and the fishwife. He had discovered a new kind of language. Instead of the "hungry millions" or "the toilers," or any of the numerous synonyms for our masters, he invented the phrase "Goad's people." "I shall never rest," so ran his great declaration, "till Goad's green fields and Goad's clear waters are free to Goad's people." I remember how on this occasion he pressed my hand with his famous cordiality, looked gravely and earnestly into my face, and then gazed sternly into vacancy. It was a fine picture of genius descending for a moment from its hill-top to show how close it was to poor humanity.

The Moon Endureth: A Lucid Interval

CHAPTER IV

AUTOBIOGRAPHICAL

...I cannot believe that the external incidents of my life are important enough to be worth chronicling in detail.

Memory Hold-the-Door

I

Looking back, my industry fills me with awe.

Memory Hold-the-Door

II

From my earliest youth I have been what the Greeks called a "nympholept," one who was under the spell of running waters. It was in terms of them that I read the countryside. My topography was a scheme of glens and valleys and watersheds. I would walk miles to see the debouchment of some burn with whose head-waters I was familiar, or track to its source some affluent whose lowland career I had followed. There was no tributary of the upper Tweed that I could not name, and, when I came to possess a bicycle, the same was true of the adjacent waters of Clyde and Annan, Ettrick and Yarrow. At any time in my childhood I could have drawn a map of my neighbourhood, which, so far as the streams went, would have been scrupulously exact.

Memory Hold-the-Door

III

My first impressions of Oxford were unhappy. The soft autumn air did not suit my health; the lectures which I attended seemed jejune and platitudinous, and the regime slack, after the strenuous life of Glasgow; I played no game well enough to acquire an absorbing interest in it. Above all, being a year older than my contemporaries I felt that I had been pitchforked into a kindergarten. The revels of alcoholic children offended me, and, having an unfortunate gift of plain speech, I did not make myself popular among those emancipated schoolboys. I must have been at that time an intolerable prig. Consequently the friends I made at first were chiefly hard-working students like myself, or older men in other colleges. Also I was very poor. For two years I could not afford to dine in hall. My Oxford bills for the first year were little over a £100, for my second year about £150. After that, what with scholarships, prizes and considerable emoluments from books and articles, I became rather rich for an under-graduate.

Memory Hold-the-Door

IV

...The real Scotland for me was discovered in my spring walking tours and my summer holidays. I had been a miserable headachy little boy, but at the age of five I had a serious carriage accident, when my skull was fractured, and I lay for the better part of a year in bed. I arose a new child, and throughout all my youth I was as hardy as a seal; indeed, apart from dysentery and a slight malaria in South Africa, I scarcely had an ailment until the War. I was lean and tough in body, accustomed to sleep out of doors in any weather, including December frosts, and, though never an athlete, capable of a good deal of physical endurance. Once I walked sixty-three miles on end in the Galloway Hills. It was my custom in the long vacations to bury myself in the moorlands, taking up my quarters in a shepherd's cottage. There I rose early, worked for five or six hours, and then went fishing until the summer midnight. I throve on a diet of oatmeal, mutton and strong tea...the works of Aristotle are for ever bound up for me with the smell of peat reek and certain stretches of granite and heather.

Memory Hold-the-Door

V

I learned a good deal in South Africa, and the chief lesson was that I had still much to learn about the material world and about human nature. I was given a glimpse into many fascinating tracts of experience which I longed to explore. I discovered that there was a fine practical wisdom which owed nothing to books and academies. My taste in letters was winnowed and purged, for the spirit of the veld is an austere thing. I learned to be at home in societies utterly alien to my own kind of upbringing.

Above all I ceased to be an individualist and became a citizen. I acquired a political faith...my notion of a career was radically changed. I thought no more of being a dignified judge with a taste for letters, or a figure in British politics. I wanted some administrative task, some share in the making of this splendid commonwealth. I hoped to spend most of my life out of Britain. I had no desire to be a pro-consul or any kind of grandee. I would have been content with any job however thankless, in any quarter, however remote, if I had a chance of making a corner of the desert blossom and the solitary place glad.

Memory Hold-the-Door

VI

I had friends in commerce and finance, in the army and navy and civil service, in most branches of science and scholarship, and especially in the law and politics. But as a writer it was my misfortune to be too little in the society of writers. This was partly due to my preoccupation with other interests. My upbringing never gave me the chance of the pleasant bohemianism associated with the writer's craft. As a publisher I came to know many authors, English and French, but it was only a nodding acquaintance. I must confess, too, I fear, that I rarely found a man of letters who interested me as much as members of other callings. A writer must inevitably keep the best of himself for his own secret creative world. I had no appetite for studio talk. I never knew the enthusiasm which is given by membership of a coterie designed to preach some new gospel in art. My taste was for things old and shabby and unpopular, and I regarded with scepticism whatever was acclaimed as the Spirit of the Age. I was born to be always out of fashion.

Memory Hold-the-Door

VII

It is now a good many years since I first became interested in books. But all my life I have also been interested, professionally interested, in other things, so that I have no title to speak on literature as a man of letters for whom the written word has been the working instrument of his career. The result of this imperfect absorption in the subject has been to make my views on many literary subjects highly unorthodox. I do not seem to have the right standard of values – at least I have not quite the same standard as the authoritative critics.

The Novel and the Fairy Tale

VIII

...In the 'nineties, when I first discovered the world of books, I had a most catholic taste in them. I was attracted by every new venture, I had few dislikes, my purpose was exploration rather than judgment, orthodoxy had no claims on me, and I identified appreciation with enjoyment. I was Montaigne's *ondoyant et divers* reader, undulating and diverse.

Then – some time in my early twenties the arteries of my taste seemed to narrow and harden. I became more fastidious, but with an eye less on eternal canons of excellence than on my own pleasure. I was now a critic, but on a purely subjective basis. Certain things satisfied me and certain things did not, and I was inclined to limit myself to the former. Since I knew what these were in the older literature and had no certainty of finding them in the new, I became conservative in my reading. As a publisher I had to keep a watchful eye on contemporary letters, but there my motive was commercial; for my pleasure I went to old fields. I speak, of course, of imaginative work. I was an assiduous student of the moderns in philosophy and history.

Not being a critic I was not called upon to formulate the reasons for my preferences, but I was conscious that I had standards of a sort. One was a belief in what the French call *ordonnance*, a supreme importance of an ordered discipline both in matter and in style. Another was a certain austerity – I disliked writing which was luscious and overripe. A third was a distrust of extreme facility. A work of art, I thought, should be carved in marble, not in soapstone. There were other half-conscious principles, and the whole batch constituted a strict, dry and rather priggish canon, which kept me from taking any real interest in the literature of my own day. One or two Romans (Virgil especially), Shakespeare and Wordsworth pretty well contented me among the poets, and in prose, apart from history and philosophy, I had recourse chiefly to the seventeenth-century writers. I had become what Dr Johnson called Gray, a "barren rascal."

Memory Hold-the-Door

IX

Generally speaking, I was of a conservative cast of mind, very sensible of the past, approving renovation but not innovation. Lord Falkland's classic confession of faith might have been mine – "when it is not necessary to change it is necessary not to change."

Memory Hold-the-Door

X

The road wound at a gentle slope, crossing little brown burns tumbling down from the heights. I met one solitary baker's van trundling sleepily along, and bought from the unkempt driver some biscuits and scones. If the occupations of life were left to ourselves instead of being created for us by meddling circumstances, I should certainly choose to drive such a van. There are some elements of greatness about the course, to dispense the staff of life to dwellers in outlying villages and to spend one's days in a placid, bountiful land. It is so infinitely to be preferred to the vexations of business and politics that it seems strange that the profession of van-driver is not desperately overcrowded.

The Scholar Gypsies

XI

I care little indeed for the odour of the finer kinds, but I dearly love the smell of bad tobacco. There is something about it at once so wild and homelike, recalling warm fires and desolate peat-bogs, fishermen and sailors and gypsy caravans, storms and summer days, keen-eyed, weather-beaten fellows, and all the things which give zest and savour to life. From your choicer kinds for the life of me I can get no associations beyond stifling thoroughfares and vacant young men.

The Scholar Gypsies

XII

"Romance is a word I am shy of using. It has been so staled and pawed by fools that the bloom is gone from it, and to most people it stands for a sugary world as flat as an eighteenth-century Arcadia. But, dry stick as I am, I hanker after my own notion of romance. I suppose it is the lawyer in me, but I define it as something in life which happens with an exquisite aptness and a splendid finality, as if Fate had suddenly turned artist – something which catches the breath because it is so wholly right. Also for me it must happen to youth. I do not complain of growing old, but I like to keep my faith that at one stage in our mortal existence nothing is impossible. It is part of my belief that the universe is on the whole friendly to man and that the ordering of the world is in the main benevolent... So I go about expecting things, waiting like an old pagan for the descent of the goddess."

Sir Edward Leithen in *The Dancing Floor*

XIII

I detest official work, but I love...plain dealing with facts.

From a letter

XIV

I am writing a book! I could not help it.

From a letter

XV

I find, as I grow older, that I write more and more to please myself and my old friends, and think of nothing else.

From a letter

CHAPTER V

LANDSCAPES

WOOD, SEA AND HILL
AN AFRICAN STREAM
THE AFRICAN VELD
CANADIAN LANDSCAPES
URBAN GARDEN
A HOUSE IN THE TROPICS
A PLACE TO LIVE
A PLACE TO DIE

WOOD, SEA AND HILL

I

Wood, sea and hill were the intimacies of my childhood and they have never lost their spell for me.

Memory Hold-the-Door

II

...All my life I have cherished certain pictures of landscape, of which I have caught glimpses in my travels, as broken hints of a beauty of which I hoped some day to find the archetype. One is a mountain stream running through a flat stretch of heather from a confusion of blue mountains. Another is a green meadow, cut off like a garden from neighbouring wildernesses, secret and yet offering a wide horizon, a place at once a sanctuary and a watchtower. This type I have found in the Scottish Borders, in the Cotswolds, once in New Hampshire, and plentifully in the Piedmont country of Virginia.

The Dancing Floor

III

I have two landscapes in my mind which have always ravished my fancy. One is a morning scene. It is spring – say mid-April; a small fresh wind is blowing; my viewpoint is somewhere among the foothills where a mountain land breaks down to the plains. Below me is a glen with green fields and a smoke of hearthfires and running water, and a far-off echo of human bustle, including the clack of a mill wheel. The glen runs out into the blue dimness of a great champaign, with the spires of cities in it, and on the far rim a silver belt of sea. A white road winds down the valley and into the plain, and I know that it will take me past a hundred blessed nooks into an April world of adventure and youth.

The other scene belongs to the afternoon, not the languorous afternoon of the poets, but a season which is only the mellowing of the freshness of morning. It is a wide tract of pasture, backed by little wooded hills, mostly oaks and beeches, but with clumps of tall Scots firs. Behind, fading into the sunset, are round-shouldered blue mountains. In the pasture there are shapely little coverts, as in the park of a great mansion. Through it winds a little river, very clear and very quiet, with long smooth streams and pools edged with fine gravel. The banks are open so that there is nothing to impede the angler. There are cattle at graze, and a faithful company of birds and bees. It is a place long-settled and cared for, with a flavour of a demesne, a place in close contact with human life.

Memory Hold-the-Door

IV

There are hours which live for ever in the memory – hours of intense physical exhilaration, the pure wine of health and youth, when the mind has no thoughts save for the loveliness of earth, and the winds of morning stir the blood to a heavenly fervour. No man who has experienced such seasons can be other than an optimist. Dull nights in cities, heartless labours with pen and ink, in the squalid worries of business and ambition, all are forgotten, and in the retrospect it is those hours which stand up like shining hill-tops – the type of the pure world before our sad mortality had laid its spell upon it. It is not pleasure – the word is too debased in human parlance; nor happiness, for that is for calm delights. Call it joy, that "enthusiasm" which is now the perquisite of creeds and factions, but which of old belonged to the fauns and nymphs who followed Pan's piping in the woody hollows of Thessaly.

The African Colony

V

Two pictures I have always carried to cheer me in dismal places. One is of a baking noon on the high veld, the sky a merciless blue, the brown earth shimmering in a heat haze. I am looking into a wide hollow where a red road like a scar descends and disappears over the next ridge. In the bottom there is a white farm with a clump of gum trees, a blue dam, and blue water furrows threading a patch of bright green alfalfa. An outspanned fire is sending up spirals of milky blue smoke. A hawk is hovering far above, but there are no sounds except the drone of insects, and very far off the jar of an ungreased axle. The air is hot but not very heavy, pungent and aromatic. I have never had such a sense of brooding primeval peace, as from that sun-drenched bowl brimming with essential light.

The other picture is the Wood Bush in the North Transvaal which lies between Pietersburg and the eastern flats. You climb to it through bare foothills where the only vegetation is the wait-a-bit thorn, and then suddenly you cross a ridge and enter a garden. The woods of big timbered trees are as shapely as the copses in a park laid out by a landscape-gardener. The land between them is rich meadow with, instead of buttercups and daisies, the white arum lily and the tall blue agapanthus. In each cup is a stream of clear grey-blue water, swirling in pools and rapids like a Highland salmon river. These unite to form the Bruderstroom which, after hurling itself over the plateau's edge, becomes a feeder of the Olifants. Here is a true lodge in the wilderness, with on the one side the stony Pietersburg uplands, and on the other the malarial bushveld. The contrast makes a profound impression, since the

Wood Bush itself is the extreme of richness and beauty. The winds blow as clean as in mid-ocean, soil and vegetation are as wholesome as an English down. I have entered the place from different sides – by the precipitous road up the Bruderstroom, by the Pietersburg highway, from the north along the scarp, and once from the bushveld by a tributary glen where my Afrikaner pony had to do some rock-climbing; and on each occasion I seemed to be crossing the borders of a *temenos*, a place enchanted and consecrate. I resolved to go back in my old age, build a dwelling and leave my bones there.

Memory Hold-the-Door

VI

...Dew was in the air and an overpowering sweetness of fern and pine and mosses, and through the aisles of the high trees came a shimmer of palest gold, and in the open spaces the moon rode in the dusky blue heavens – not the mild moon of April but a fiery conquering goddess, driving her chariot among trampled stars.

It was clear to him that he would not find Paradise except by happy chance, since he was utterly out of his bearings. But he was content to be lost, for the whole place was Paradise. Never before had he felt so strong a natural magic. This woodland, which he had once shunned, had become a holy place, lit with heavenly lights and hallowed by some primordial peace. He had forgotten about the girl, forgotten his scruples. In that hour he had acquired a mood at once serene and gay: he had the light heartedness of a boy and the ease of a wise philosopher; his body seemed as light as air, and, though he had already walked some twenty miles, he felt as if he had just risen from his bed. But there was no exuberance in him, and he had not the impulse to sing which usually attended his seasons of high spirits... The silence struck upon him as something at once miraculous and just. There was not a sound in the Wood – not the lightest whisper of wind, though there had been a breeze on the hilltops at sundown – not the cry of a single bird – not a rustle in the undergrowth. The place was dumb – not dead, but sleeping.

Suddenly he came into a broad glade over which the moonshine flowed like a tide. It was all of soft mossy green, without pebble or bush to break its carpet, and in the centre stood a thing like an altar.

At first he thought it was only a boulder dropped from the hill. But as he neared it he saw that it was human handiwork. Masons centuries ago had wrought on it, for it was roughly squared, and firmly founded on a pediment. Weather had battered it, and one corner of the top had been broken by some old storm, but it still stood four-square to the seasons. One side was very clear in the moon, and on it David thought he could detect a half-obliterated legend. He knelt down, and though the lower part was obscured beyond hope, the upper letters stood out plain. IOM – he read: "Jovi Optimo Maximo." This uncouth thing had once been an altar.

Witch Wood

VII

A stretch of green turf, shaded on all sides by high beeches, sloped down to the stream side. The sun made a shining pathway down the middle, but the edges were in blackest shadow. At the foot a lone gnarled alder hung over the water, sending its long arms far over the river nigh to the farther side. Here Tweed was still and sunless, showing a level of placid black water, flecked in places with stray shafts of light.

John Burnet of Barns

VIII

All the world was bright; an early lark sang high in the heaven; merles and thrushes were making fine music among the low trees by the river. The haze was lifting off the great Manor Water hills;

the Red Syke...looked very distant in the morning light; and far beyond all Dollar Law and the high hills about Manorhead were flushed with sunlight on their broad foreheads. A great gladness rose in me when I looked at the hills, for they were the hills of my own country; I knew every glen and corrie, every water and little burn. Before me the Lyne Water hills were green as grass with no patch of heather, and to the left, the mighty form of Scrape, half clothed in forest, lay quiet and sunlit. I know of no fairer sight on earth; and this I say, after having travelled in other countries, and seen something of their wonders; for to my mind there is a grace, a wild loveliness in Tweedside, like a flower garden on the edge of a moorland, which is wholly its own.

John Burnet of Barns

IX

We turn homeward over the long shoulders of hill, keeping to the track in the failing light. If the place is sober by day, it is transformed in the evening. For an hour the land sinks out of account, and the sky is the sole feature. No words can tell the tale of a veld sunset. Not the sun dipping behind the peaks of Jura, or flaming in the mouth of a Norwegian fiord, or sinking, a great ball of fire, in mid-Atlantic, has the amazing pageantry of these upland evenings. A flood of crimson descends on the world, rolling in tides from the flagrant west, and kindling bush and scaur and hill-top, till the land glows and pulsates in a riot of colour. And then slowly the splendour ebbs, lingering only to the west in a shoreless, magical sea. A delicate pearl-grey overspreads the sky, and the onlooker thinks that the spectacle is ended. It has but begun; for there succeed flushes of ineffable colour, purple, rose-pink, tints of no mortal name – each melting imperceptibly into the other, and revealing again the twilight world which the earlier pageant had obscured. Every feature in the landscape stands out with a tender, amethystine clearness. The mountain-ridge is cut like a jewel against the sky; the track is a ribbon of pure beaten gold. And then the light fades, the air becomes a soft mulberry haze, the first star pricks out in the blue, and night is come.

The African Colony

X

A high fragrance of heath and bog-myrtle was in the wind, and the mouth grew cool as after long draughts of spring water. Mists were crowding in the valleys, each bald mountain-top shone like a jewel, and far aloft in the heavens were the white streamers of morn. Moorhens were plashing at the loch's edge, and one tall heron rose from his early meal. The world was astir with life: sounds of the *plonk-plonk* of rising trout and the endless twitter of woodland birds mingled with the far-away barking of dogs and the lowing of the full-uddered cows in the distant meadows.

The Half-hearted

XI

The sheepfolds of Etterick lie in a little fold of glen some two miles from the dwelling, where the heathy tableland, known all over the glen as "The Muirs," relieves the monotony of precipitous hills. On this day it was alert with life. The little paddock was crammed with sheep, and more stood huddling in the pens. Within was the liveliest scene, for there a dozen herds sat on clipping-stools each with a struggling ewe between his knees, and the ground beneath him strewn with creamy folds of fleece. From a thing like a gallows in a corner huge bags were suspended which were slowly filling. A cauldron of pitch bubbled over a fire, and the smoke rose blue in the hot hill air. Every minute a bashful animal was led to be branded with a great E on the left shoulder, and then with awkward stumbling let loose to join her naked fellow-sufferers. Dogs slept in the sun and wagged their tails in the rear of the paddock. Small children sat on gates and lent willing feet to drive the flocks. In a corner below a little shed was the clippers' meal of ale and pies, with two glasses of whisky each, laid by under a white cloth. Meantime from all sides rose the continual crying of the sheep, the intermittent bark of dogs, and the loud broad converse of the men.

The Half-hearted

XII

It was a perfect midsummer morning, with that faint haze in the distance which means a hot noon. The park under my window lay drenched and silvered with dew. The hawthorns seemed to be bowed over the grasses under their weight of blossom. The birds were chattering in the ivy, and two larks were singing. Just under me, beyond the ha-ha, a foal was standing on tottering legs beside its mother, lifting its delicate nozzle to sniff the air. The Arm, where the sun caught it, was a silver crescent, and there was a little slow drift of amethyst smoke from the head keeper's cottage in a clump of firs. The scene was embodied, deep, primordial peace, and though, as I have said, my ordinary perception had become a little dulled, the glory of the June morning smote me like a blow.

The Gap in the Curtain

AN AFRICAN STREAM

XIII

...I have known and loved many streams, but the little Malmani has a high place in my affections. The crystal water flowed out of great reed-beds into a shallow vale, where it wound in pools and cataracts to a broad ford below a ruined mill. Thence it passed again into reed-beds fringed with willows and departed from our ken. There was a bamboo covert opposite full of small singing-birds; the cries of snipe and plover rose from the reed-beds, and the fall of water, rarest of South African sounds, tinkled like steel in the cold morning air. We shot nothing, for we saw nothing; the glory of the scene was all that mortal eye could hold at once.

The African Colony

THE AFRICAN VELD

XIV

With the end of the wood we come out upon the veld. What is this mysterious thing, this veld, so full of memories for the English race, so omnipresent, so baffling? Like the words "prairie," "moor," and "down," it is easy to make a rough mental picture of. It will doubtless become in time, when South Africa gets herself a literature, a conventional counter in description. Today every London shop-boy knows what this wilderness of coarse green or brown grasses is like; he can picture the dry streams, the jagged kopjes, the glare of summer, and the bitter winter cold. It has entered into patriotic jingles, and has given a *mise-en-scène* to crude melodrama. And yet no natural feature was ever so hard to fully realize. One cannot think of a monotonous vastness, like the prairie, for it is everywhere broken up and varied. It is too great for an easy appreciation, as of an English landscape, too subtle and diverse for rhetorical generalities – a thing essentially mysterious and individual. In consequence it has a charm which the common efforts of mother-earth after grandiloquence can never possess. There is something homely and kindly and soothing in it, something essentially humane and fitted to the needs of human life. Climb to the top of the nearest ridge, and after a broad green valley there will be another ridge just the same: cross the mountains fifty miles off, and the country will repeat itself as before. But this sameness in outline is combined with an infinite variety in detail, so that we readily take back our first complaint of monotony, and wonder at the intricate novelty of each vista...

At the summit of the ridge there is a breeze and a far prospect. The road still runs on up hill and down dale, through the distant mountains, and on to the great pastoral uplands of Rustenburg and the far north-west. On either side the same waving grass, now grey and now green as the wind breathes over it. Below is a glen with a gleam of water, and some yards of tender lawn on either bank. Farmhouses line the sides, each with its dam, its few acres of untidy crop land, and its bower of trees. Beyond rise line upon line of green ridges, with a glimpse of woods and dwellings set far apart, till in the far distance the bold spurs of the Magaliesberg stand out against the sky. A thin trail of smoke from some veld-fire hangs between us and the mountains, tempering the intense clearness of an African prospect. There is something extraordinarily delicate and remote about the vista; it might be a mirage, did not the map bear witness to its reality. It is not unlike a child's conception of the landscape of Bunyan, a road running straight through a mystical green country, with the hilltops of the Delectable Mountains to cheer the pilgrim...

No landscape is so masterful as the veld. Broken up into valleys, reclaimed in parts by man, showing fifty varieties of scene, it yet preserves one essential character. For, homely as it is, it is likewise untamable. There are no fierce encroachments about it. A deserted garden does not return to the veld for many years, if ever. It is not, like the jungle, the natural enemy of man, waiting for a chance to enter and obliterate his handiwork, and repelled only by sleepless watching. Rather it is the quiet spectator of human efforts, ready to meet them half-way, and yet from its vastness always the dominant feature in any landscape. Its normal air is sad, grey, and Quakerish, never flamboyant under the brightest sun, and yet both strenuous and restful. The few red monstrosities man has built on its edge serve only to set off this essential dignity. For one thing, it is not created according to the scale of man. It will give him a home, but he will never alter its aspect. Let him plough and reap it for a thousand years, and he may beautify and fructify but never change it. The face of England has altered materially in two centuries, because England is on a human scale – a parterre land, without intrinsic wildness. But cultivation on the veld will always be superimposed: it will remain, like Egypt, ageless and immutable – one of the primeval types of the created world.

But, though dominant, it is also adaptable. It can, for the moment, assume against its unchangeable background a chameleon-like variety. Sky and weather combine to make it imitative at times. Now, under a pale Italian sky, it is the Campagna – hot, airless, profoundly melancholy. Again, when the mist drives over it, and wet scarps of hill stand out among clouds, it is Dartmoor or Liddesdale; or on a radiant evening, when the mountains are one bank of hazy purple, it has borrowed from Skye and the far West Highlands. On a clear steely morning it has the air of its namesake, the Norwegian fields, – in one way the closest of its parallels. But each phase passes, the tantalizing memory goes, and we are back again upon the aboriginal veld, so individual that we wonder whence arose the illusion.

The African Colony

CANADIAN LANDSCAPE

XV

They came on it suddenly... The scraggy forest of jackpines, which seemed to stretch to the very edge of the snows, suddenly gave place to empty air, and Leithen found himself staring breathlessly not up, but down – down into a chasm nearly a mile wide and two thousand feet deep. From his feet the ground fell away in screes to a horizontal rib of black rock, below which, in a blue mist very far down, were the links of a river. Beyond it were meadows and woods, and the woods were not of scrub-pine, but of tall timber – from one or two trees in scattered clumps he judged them to be a hundred feet high. Beyond them again the opposite wall rose sheer to fantastic aiguilles of dark rock. He was looking at some mighty volcanic rift which made a moat to the impregnable castle of the snows...

He lay full in the pale sun and the air was mild and mellow. As his eyes thirstily drank in the detail he saw that there was little colour in the scene. Nearly all was subfusc, monochrome, and yet so exquisite was the modelling that there was nothing bleak in it; the impression rather was of a chaste, docile luxuriance. The valley bottom, so far as he could see it, seemed to be as orderly as a garden. The Sick Heart was like a Highland salmon river, looping itself among pools and streams with wide beaches of pebbles, beaches not black like the enclosing cliffs, but shining white. Along its course and between the woods, were meadows of wild hay, now a pale russet against the ripple of the stream and the evergreen of the trees... Something from his past awoke in Leithen. He was far up in the Arctic North; winter had begun, and even in this false summer the undercurrent of cold was stinging his fingers through his mitts. But it was not loneliness or savagery that was the keynote of this valley. Pastoral breathed from it; it was comforting and habitable. He could picture it in its summer pride, a symphony of mild airs and singing waters. Stripped and blanched as it was, it had a preposterous suggestion of green meadows and Herrick and sheep.

Sick Heart River

URBAN GARDEN

XVI

The wall which encircles the domain is of bricks, old, dim, and dirty. But somehow a mellow russet has evolved from the soot and the dingy mosses which clothe it, so that when the sun is on it they shine as rich as an autumn wood. The ivy which half-clothes it is aged and scanty of leaf, with ragged grey stems and straggling offshoots. But here a blackbird will sometimes build, and after the shower this sordid foliage will glisten with innumerable jewels. Two valiant elms guard the corners, and midway a herd of little ashes and lindens form a thin grove, beneath which the earth lies long damp, and a few pale valley-lilies raise their heads in spring. What else is there? A privet hedge, which, unclipped, bears a wilderness of blossom, a lawn with wide borders of flowers, a minute shrubbery, two great beds by the house wall flanked by two birch trees, and little more. It is a place "shorn and parcell'd," with just enough magnitude to give point to its littleness.

The flowers, too, are confined in variety, for not all can live well in such surroundings. Roses, curiously enough, grow and thrive, and old hardy veterans, wallflowers, pinks, lilies, gillyflowers pick up a bare living. Just now there is a great show of rakish turk's caps and many-hued carnations, and on the wall the white Prince Charlie roses flaunt with the honeysuckle. But the place is not noteworthy for flowers, for, apart from its adventitious interest, its charms lie mainly in the well-kept grass and the cool wide-spreading shade of the trees. Moreover, it is a spot for a distant prospect rather than a too intimate acquaintance. If you pluck the flowers you will find them speckled with soot, the leaves are darker than nature meant them to be, and the rich tints on the wall do not depend solely on age and weather. But if one be not over-critical, but rather content to make the best of things, he may gain from the place a feeling of deep solitude and ease.

If the town is memorized in countless ways in the garden, the country, too, is not forgotten. Many kinds of birds come hither. I have seen jackdaws and magpies of a spring morning, blue tits in the boughs of the elm, a fly-catcher among the ivy, and linnets, thrushes, and starlings as thick as flies on the lawn. There is a rookery somewhere in the wide distance, whence come crows to strut and possess the land. One April morning, looking from the window, I saw a rabbit on the grass, a wanderer from Heaven knows what distant warren. The cuckoo comes every year, and its dominating note booms amid the pipes of lesser birds and the half-echoes of the faint street-cries. Indeed, there are many hints of the sun and the green woodlands, which come to perplex the man who has set himself to arduous work, and who, when he opens his window, hears the alluring voice of the piper and longs to follow.

This urban garden is not without its association and fragments of past history. By the side over the young trees there rises an old square house, ivy-clad, with crow-step gables, and all the outward marks of antiquity. This was once the manor house of the place, when the suburb was still a smiling village among cornfields. The two big elms which lend dignity to the other trees were part of the green avenue which led to it. There dwelt Woodrow, the historian of the Scottish Church, a man full of absurdity and kindliness, whose books are a charming farrago of gossip and grave reflection. One can fancy him walking here, composing his letters to Cotton Mather, and asking if the wild men and beasts of which his correspondent complained could be worse than the ravening Prelatists and lukewarm professors in his own unhappy country of Scotland. Over this place, too, was fought a great battle, which brought to the ill-fated Queen of Scots the loss at once of her kingdom and her liberty. Not half a mile off, fragments of steel are still found to testify to the struggle, and in this very garden was once dug up a little cannon-ball of the kind used at the time, with the crust of three hundred years upon it. There is indeed a sort of faded gentility about all things here, a flavour of old wars and devilry, old godliness and peace.

And just as certain weather brings out certain tints in old buildings, so the afternoon calls these fleeting memories into existence. The colours are deeper, the smoke is not seen, the blossom and the greenery are at their finest. And over all is that subtle, ill-defined feeling of cessation in the midst of labour, of quiet among turbid memories, of romance in the very citadel of the unromantic.

The Scholar Gypsies

A HOUSE IN THE TROPICS

XVII

From a wayside station on the railway between Mombasa and Port Florence a well-made highway runs along the edge of the plateau through forests of giant cypress and juniper. To the east lies the great Rift valley, with the silver of its lakes gleaming eerily through the mountain haze. After a dozen miles the woodland ceases and the road emerges on a land of far-stretching downs, broken up into shallow glens where streams of clear water ripple through coverts of bracken and lilies. Native villages with beehive huts appear, and the smoke from their wood fires scents the thin upland air. Now the road turns west, and the indefinable something creeps into the atmosphere which tells the traveller that he is approaching the rim of the world. Suddenly he comes upon a gate, with a thatched lodge, which might be in Scotland. Entering, he finds himself in a park dotted with shapely copses and full of the same endless singing streams. Orchards, vineyards, olive-groves, and tobacco fields appear, and then the drive sweeps into a garden, with a lake in the centre and a blaze of flower-beds. The air blows free to westward, and he knows that he is almost on the edge, when another turn reveals the house against the skyline; It is long and low, something in the Cape Dutch style, with wide verandahs and cool stone pillars. The sun-shutters and the beams are of cedar, the roof is of warm red tiles, and the walls are washed with a delicate pure white. Standing, as I have seen it, against a flaming sunset, with the glow of lamplight from the windows, it is as true a fairy palace as ever haunted a poet's dream. Beyond it the hill falls steeply to the tropics, and the gardens run down into the rich glens. Its height is some nine thousand feet above the sea, and its climate is always temperate; but three thousand feet beneath it is Equatoria, and on clear days a gleam can be caught of the great lakes. So the gardens, which begin with English flowers, fall in tiers through a dozen climates, till azalea gives place to hibiscus, and hibiscus to poinsettia, and below in the moist valley you end with orchids and palms.

Entering the house through the heavy brass-studded doors, you come first into a great panelled hall, floored with a mosaic of marble on which lie many skins and Karosses, and lit by a huge silver chandelier. In a corner is a stone fireplace like a cavern, where day and night in winter burns a great fire of logs. Round it are a number of low chairs and little tables, but otherwise the place is empty of furniture, save for the forest of horns and the grinning heads of lion and leopard on the walls. The second hall is more of a summer chamber, for it is panelled in lighter wood and hung with many old prints and pictures concerned with the great age of African adventure. There you will find quaint Dutch and Portuguese charts, and altar-pieces gifted by a de Silveira or a de Barros to some Mozambique church long since in ruins. Brass-bound sea-chests, tall copper vases of Arab workmanship, rare porcelain of the Indies, and rich lacquer cabinets line the walls, and the carpet is an exquisite old Persian fabric. Beyond, through the folding windows, lie the verandahs, whence one looks over a sea of mist to the trough of the lakes. To the right stretch more panelled chambers – dining-room, smoking-rooms, a library of many thousand volumes, and as fine a private museum as you will find in the world. To the left are the drawing-rooms, hung with flowered silks and curious Eastern brocades, opening on a cool verandah, and lit in the evening by the same wild fires of sunset. Upstairs the bedrooms are masterpieces of arrangement, all fresh and spacious, and yet all unmistakably of Africa and the Tropics. From any window there is a vision of a landscape which has the strange glamour of a dream. The place is embosomed in flowers, whether growing in brass-hooped mahogany tubs or cut and placed daily in the many silver bowls; but no heavy odours ever impair the virginal freshness of the house. Luxury has been carried to that extreme of art where it becomes a delicate simplicity. It is a place to work, to talk, to think, but not to idle in – a strenuous and stimulating habitation. For on every side seems to stretch an unknown world, calling upon the adventurous mind to take possession.

A Lodge in the Wilderness

A PLACE TO LIVE – AFRICA

XVIII

Hereabouts, when my ship comes home, I shall have my country house. There is a piece of flat land, perhaps six acres square, from which a long glen runs down to the Letaba. There I shall have my dwelling. In front there will be a park to put England to shame, miles of rolling green dotted with shapely woods, and in the centre a broad glade in which a salmon-river flows in shallows and falls among tree-ferns, arums and bracken. There may be a lake, but I am undecided. In front I shall have a flower-garden, where every temperate and tropical blossom will appear, and in a sheltered hollow an orchard of deciduous trees, and an orange plantation. Highland cattle, imported at incredible expense, will roam on the hillsides. My back windows will look down 4,000 feet on the tropics, my front on the long meadow vista with the Iron Crown mountain for the sun to set behind. My house will be long and low, with broad wings, built of good stone and white-washed, with a thatched roof and green shutters, so that it will resemble a *prazo* such as some Portuguese seigneur might have dwelt in in old times. Within it will be cool and fresh, with stone floors and big fireplaces, for the mists are chill and the winds can blow sharply on the mountains. There will be good pictures and books, and quantities of horns and skins. I shall grow my own supplies, and make my own wine and tobacco. Rides will be cut in the woods, and when my friends come to stay we shall drive bushbuck and pig, and stalk tiger-cats in the forest. There will be wildfowl on my lake, and Lochleven trout in my waters. And whoever cares to sail 5,000 miles, and travel 1,500 by train, and drive 50 over a rough road, will find at the end of his journey such a palace as Kubla Khan never dreamed of. The accomplishment is difficult, but not, I trust, impossible. Once upon a time, as the story goes, a Dutchman talked with a predikant about the welfare of his soul. "You will assuredly be damned," said the predikant, "and burn in hell." "Not so," said the Dutchman. "If I am so unfortunate as to get in there, I shall certainly get out again." "But that is folly and an impossibility," said the predikant. "Ah," said the other with confidence, "wait and see: I shall make a plan." *Ek sal'n plan maak* – this must be my motto, and I shall gratefully accept all honourable suggestions.

The African Colony

A PLACE TO DIE – THE CANADIAN ARCTIC

XIX

Late next afternoon they reached the Ghost River delta, striking in upon it at an angle from the south-west. The clear skies had gone, and the "ceiling" was not more than a thousand feet. Low hills rimmed the eastern side, but they were cloaked in a light fog, and the delta seemed to have no limits, but to be an immeasurable abscess of decay. Leithen had never imagined such an abomination of desolation. It was utterly silent, and the only colours were sickly greens and drabs. At first sight he thought he was looking down on a bit of provincial Surrey, broad tarmac roads lined with asphalt footpaths, and behind the trim hedges smooth suburban lawns. It took a little time to realize that the highways were channels of thick mud, and the lawns bottomless quagmires. He was now well inside the Circle, and had expected from the Arctic something cold, hard, and bleak, but also clean and tonic. Instead he found a horrid lushness – an infinity of mire and coarse vegetation, and a superfluity of obscene insect life. The place was one huge muskeg. It was like the no-man's-land between the trenches in the

War – a colossal no-man's-land created in some campaign of demons, pitted and pocked with shell-holes from some infernal artillery.

They skirted the delta and came down at its western horn on the edge of the sea. Here there was no mist, and he could look far into the North over still waters eerily lit by the thin pale evening sunlight. It was like no ocean he had ever seen, for it seemed to be without form or reason. The tide licked the shore without purpose. It was simply water filling a void, a treacherous deathly waste, pale like a snake's belly, a thing beyond humanity and beyond time. Delta and sea looked as if here the Demiurge had let His creative vigour slacken and ebb into nothingness. He had wearied of the world which He had made and left this end of it to ancient Chaos.

Leithen scarcely tasted supper and fell asleep in a stupor of depression. Already it seemed he was beginning to know death.

Next morning the scene had changed, and to his surprise he felt a lightening of both mind and body. Sky and sea were colourless, mere bowls of light. There seemed to be no tides, only a gentle ripple on the grey sand. Very far out there were blue gleams which he took to be ice. The sun was warm, but the body of the air was cold, and it had in it a tonic quality which seemed to make his breathing easier. He remembered hearing that there were no germs in the Arctic, that the place was one great sanatorium, but that did not concern one whose trouble was organic decay. Still he was grateful for a momentary comfort, and he found that he wanted to stretch his legs. He walked to the highest point of land at the end of a little promontory.

It was a place like a Hebridean cape. The peaty soil was matted with berries, though a foot or two beneath was eternal ice. The breeding season was over and the migration not begun, so there was no bird life on the shore; the wild fowl were all in the swamps of the delta, The dead level of land and sea made the arc of sky seem immense, the "intense inane" of Shelley's poem. The slight recovery of bodily vigour quickened his imagination. This was a world not built on the human scale, a world made without thought of mankind, a world colourless and formless, but also timeless; a kind of eternity. It would be a good place to die in, he thought, for already the clinging ties of life were loosened, and death would mean little since life had ceased.

Sick Heart River

CHAPTER VI

SPORT

There is in every man, deep down in his nature, something simple and primeval, a memory of an earlier and fresher life. Hence angling and hunting, travelling and sailing on the sea, are things of an enduring interest to human kind. All do not care for literature, not many for art, few indeed for metaphysics; but adventure and sport, "Crusoe" and "Walton," have always their legions of enthusiastic followers.

Musa Piscatrix

SPORT

I

...sport in itself is a good thing. It brings out all the virile and sterling qualities of a man; it leaves little room, it is true, for some virtues, but it keeps the ground against the more unmanly vices.

The Scholar Gypsies

II

...A sport, strictly speaking, I take to be a contest with wild Nature in some one of her forms, a contest in which there is commonly some risk; a game, a contest under agreed rules with other human beings. Big-game shooting, fox-hunting, and mountaineering are clearly in the first class; cricket, in the second...

Great Hours in Sport

III

It is a fair working rule of life that the behaviour of a man in his sports is a good index to his character in graver matters. With certain reservations the same holds true of a people. For on the lowest interpretation of the word "sport," the high qualities of courage, honour, and self-control are part of the essential equipment, and the mode in which such qualities appear is a reflex of the idiosyncrasies of national character. But this is true mainly of the old settled peoples, whose sports have long lost the grim reality in which they started. To a race which wages daily war with savage nature the refinements of conduct are unintelligible; sport becomes business; and unless there is a hereditary tradition in the matter the fine manners of the true hunter's craft are notable by their absence.

The African Colony

IV

...We have become naturalists, too, the best of us – naturalists first and sportsmen afterwards. If we have lost something from the wild life we have recovered something – the capercailzie, for instance, and the woodcock, which in the beginning of last century was as scarce as the ruff. On a profit and loss account, perhaps, our books would balance.

Great Hours in Sport

V

The naturalist sportsman is happily on the increase.

Great Hours in Sport

FISHING

VI

Agrippa Postumus is a puzzling figure. He seems to have been a case of arrested development, perhaps half an idiot... He was a keen fisherman, and few anglers are altogether vile.

Augustus

VII

The muse of fishing is not an introspective dame: she loves the crust of things better than the kernel.

Musa Piscatrix

VIII

It is possible, it would appear, for the man of letters, usually a duffer at sports, to be a good fisherman...

Great Hours in Sport

IX

The charm of fishing is that it is the pursuit of what is elusive but attainable, a perpetual series of occasions for hope.

Great Hours in Sport

X

If fishing, as I maintain, be not only a craft but a way of life, then a fisherman must begin young.

Memory Hold-the-Door

XI

...I have fished all my life, but I never caught a salmon heavier than 25 lbs, or more than six in a day; yet I can hear without chagrin of the 50-pounders of others, and contemplate with satisfaction such baskets as that once made by the late Lord Lovat, who, during five successive days on the Beauly, caught 156 fish.

Great Hours in Sport

XII

I was an expert "guddler," scooping up trout from below stones in the channel and under the deep-cut banks. These "lowland" burns could become degraded indeed, choked with rubbish in passing a farmyard, or at the outlet of a village. But sometimes, when they looped through a broad pasture-land, they afforded pools and streams from which trout could only be taken by casting fine and far. They had occasional big fish, too, for, though it was never my luck, I have seen trout of two pounds and more taken from them. I was ill-equipped for fly-fishing, since my rod was the two upper joints of my grandfather's salmon rod, my reel and line were indifferent, and my gut was far too coarse for slender waters and bright weather. But it was there and then that the possibilities of the art began to dawn on me, and fly-fishing became for me a necessity of life.

Memory Hold-the-Door

XIII

At the age of nine my only lure was the worm. I could not cast a fly properly, and on the lower waters I made myself too conspicuous. But in those little hill runlets rush and heather provided a natural cover, and the fish were innocent things. I would drop my worm in a pool and let it float down the hidden stream until there came a check and a small trout was swung high over my head. If it came off the hook it was as often as not lost in the thick herbage. Now and then it was too heavy for such treatment – half a pound in weight perhaps – in which case it was dragged clumsily ashore. This was the beggarly element of fishing, but both exciting and satisfying. I have had as many as four dozen in a day, to be fried for breakfast in oatmeal and eaten bones and all. To call such takings a "basket" would be a misnomer, for I did not possess a creel, but carried my catch in my pockets or threaded through the gills on rushes.

In April and May I never felt lonely, for the birds were cheerful companions. But when the summer quiet fell on them I used to have fits of panic in the silence and solitude. The worst places for this were the glens where there was no heather, but only moss and bent and turf, for heather, especially when charred in patches by moor-burn, was to me a half-human thing. Greenness, utter, absolute greenness, has all my life seemed to me uncanny, and the places which in my memory are invested with a certain awe are the green places.

Memory Hold-the-Door

XIV

...my 'prentice days were spent on streams which ran swift and open and very clear. It was wet-fly fishing, though, after I had been entered to the dry-fly, I often tried that mode with success on waters very unlike the Hampshire chalk streams. On two occasions only have I forsaken the artificial fly. In low water, fishing upstream. I have sometimes in my youth had good baskets with the red worm. In the may-fly season I followed the local practice, and in the small hours just before the dawn had considerable success dapping with the natural fly...in my attitude to the sport I am lamentably unscientific. I admire the shooter who has theories about the ballistics of his craft, but I have no wish to imitate him. Nor am I inclined to follow the angler who has elaborate views on optics – how the light strikes the fish's eye, and at what angle the fly is seen – or on entomology, for insects are a part of nature of which I have no taste – or on ichthyology – or on that mysterious subject, the working of a fish's mind. Some even connect the habits of fish with the phases of the moon; which seems to me a more promising line, for astrology may well be relevant, since the Fishes are a sign of the zodiac. I do not want to know too much about trout, for I like to leave some room for mystery. Indeed, I should prefer to keep science out of the business altogether... I am not interested either in the elaborate gadgets with which the angler is now fitted out. Indeed, my disinclination to fish with bait, natural or artificial, is largely due to my dislike of its complex apparatus. I have few theories, and I want only a modest equipment. For trout, wet-fly or dry-fly. I do not use more than a dozen patterns, though I believe in varying the size; for salmon about the same. I like old and well-tried rods and reels – everything old except the gut. When I see the bursting fly-books and tackle boxes of my friends I do not envy them;... I have few maxims, and they are all deductions from experience... I am very chary of dogmatising.

Memory Hold-the-Door

XV

What makes the difference between a successful and a less successful angler? Scarcely the length and delicacy of his casting. In salmon fishing the length of a cast may be important, and in certain Welsh, Devonian and Highland streams, where the banks are thickly wooded and one must wade up the channel, it may be necessary to cast fine and far. But generally speaking, most fishermen of experience attain to a fair level of expert casting. Nor is it the ability to select the appropriate fly. I do not believe there is ever any completely appropriate fly... Nor is it any extra skill in striking and playing a fish. The *differentia* in my view is knowledge of the particular water and the habits of the trout in it – where and at what season are the likeliest lies. In the bare pasturelands of my youth that was all-important. I have had a good basket on a stream where my companion not only caught no fish but saw none. If a man knows his stream, he will know that the haunts of fish will be different in April and in August, in low water and in full water. So, both for trout and salmon, I would maintain that, after a certain standard of technique has been attained, what makes the difference among anglers is just knowledge, local knowledge.

Memory Hold-the-Door

XVI

I have assisted in "burning the water," which was a favourite pursuit of Sir Walter Scott's, and apparently in his day not illegal.

It was an exciting business, for the shallows would be reddened by torches made of barrel staves dipped in tar, and wild figures with a three-pronged fork, called a leister, speared the fish as they blundered upstream. Once I was arrested by the bailiffs along with the others, but in consideration of my youth was released with a hearty kick! The story got about and was remembered many years after when I stood as parliamentary candidate for the county. I was assured that I had the poaching vote to a man.

Memory Hold-the-Door

FISHING IN THE MORNING

XVII

The true time of awakening is just before sunrise, as the real sleeping-time is a little before sunset. Then the world awakes, and in the activity of life around sleep is impossible. As we, scarce fully aroused, looked down from our perch on the valley, we felt the indefinable feeling of life returning. A rustle among the heather, a swaying and tossing of birches, a louder murmuring of streams, the first shrill pipe of a moorland bird – all told of a renewal of energy, an electric thrill passing through the earth. The air was cold and fresh, and over the opposite hills the grey foreglow of the dawn was spreading. A white mist clung to the low grounds, making the fields seem deep in snow; but above on the brown and purple shoulders the faint light fluttered among deep shadows. It was a strange and beautiful sight for any man to witness, as the early sun sent his first shafts through the spaces of the hills, waking chill splendours among pines and wildwood. In his train came the pomp of many-tinted clouds, of long vistas of light and shadow, an affluence of riotous imagery, tempered and chastened by the cold pallor which still held the uplands. The darkness of the sky changed imperceptibly to a lucid blue, which each new light flushed with rare colour. Then suddenly the distant fields and cornlands caught the sun, and the golden sheaves and green, shorn meadows were flooded with a dazzling brilliance. The remote distances became clear, and down the valley woodlands a score of miles away grew as vivid as the grass at our feet. But the grim hills still kept darkness in their nooks, though their summits were flaming like beacons.

The birds awoke, and a twittering and singing filled the glen. Larks with their high trills, desultory pipits, curlews, snipe, ill-fated grouse, lackadaisical plovers made the moor lively with their varied notes. A hawk sailed high bent on some morning foray, and so clear was the air that it was possible for us to see the motion of his wings. The whole hillside seemed alert with life; only the black ashes of our fire were left to remind us of the silent dark.

"Let's try a cast wi' your rod i' the burn," said the shepherd; "there's a great troot i' the pool below the brig. We micht grip him." So we went down by rocks and brackens and stunted trees to the green, lawn-like turf by the stream. Here we must needs walk with caution, for the rain had made the waters high, and in places a turbulent current had overpassed its banks and left treacherous marshes for unwary fishermen. Below the wooden foot-bridge a great pool was formed by a little fall – black and girt with masses of scented fern which dipped in the swirling eddies.

The shepherd went stealthily forwards, and dropped a fly in a space of still water. Twice he cast in the place, but still his lure remained unheeded; then in the whirl at the foot, but with no better success. Once again he cast in an eddy below the further bank, and now he had a mighty rise. His fly sank and darted down stream, then up again to the rough water, where he had much ado to keep the fish from grating his line on a jagged rock. For full ten minutes the contest lasted, until he drew it, spent and unresisting, to a patch of shingle, and brought it to the grass – a shapely trout of near a pound's weight, delicately marked and glittering in the cold sun.

"On my word, master," I said, "this is a gallant trout; what shall we do with him?"

"Dae wi' him?" quoth the shepherd, who was ignorant of Walton though he gave me the very answer which Piscator gave to Viator on that May morning long ago, "hae him to your breakfast. He'll cut red, and taste like a saumon."

The Scholar Gypsies

FISHING AT NIGHT

XVIII

There are certain days in August when the air is soft and lucid, and the pale skies have a delicate fragility which is unknown at other times. The Lammas floods have worked their boisterous will and clarified earth and air, and the drenched meadows and abundant waters sleep under sober heavens. This is the first warning of the autumn, the fore-hint of frost and decline, but as yet these things are not; and to all wearied men there is a subtle peace in the harmonious monotony. In the lowlands there may be torrid heat and all the sultriness which one associates with the harvest month; but in the hill country a cool greyness is on nature.

As if to make amends for the dearth of colour in the daytime, the evenings are extraordinarily splendid. Then the restraint is loosened and the colours of sunset are things for a man to remember with delight all his days. The world becomes jovial once more, and in the rich light all natural things grow hilarious. Birds sing with an unwonted fervour, as if they had entered on a second spring; flowers are fresher and more brilliant; the turf has a new elasticity; and in the streams the trout are on the alert for their evening meal. The earth dries quickly after the rains, and one may walk dryshod in the meadows by the great swollen waters, and find an enchanting union of spring and summer.

On such a night the angler who has tried in vain in the daytime to allure the sluggish trout, goes out to his fishing with some good hope of success. I have spent many an hour in the morning and afternoon casting across the stream when water and sky seemed alike favourable; but only when the bright evening came had I any great sport. But it is still better to fish in the hours about midnight, for then the largest trout come to feed; and if you are not town-bred and over-dainty to sleep on the heather, you may make a great basket and see something of the mysteries of night, and dawn, and the sleeping world.

One such evening I remember in the high glens about the source of Tweed, when I spent the night in the solemn fastnesses of the hills. Leaving a sleeping-rug in the shadow of a rock behind a belt of pines, with my rod and creel I went up a burn which loitered down a flat upland valley. The water was flooded and clear, and made a pleasant noise twining round the corner of a weather-stained rock or winding among odorous thickets of thyme. The quietness of the hills – so great that the most distant sounds fell distinctly on the ear and one heard the running of faraway waters – was enlivened by the gorgeous sunset light and the activity of bird and insect. The flash of brown bees, the wavering flight of snipe, the dart of water-ousels, gave liveliness to the quiet valley. The hills stood out against the saffron sky, great violet-coloured shoulders and peaks, looking remote in the evening air. The wholesome smell of the moorlands, which stirs a man's blood strangely, had a lowland luxury in it from the crushed summer flowers.

At every cast the flies, as they trailed on the surface, caught a glow from the sky and looked like dancing fireflies. The trout, when they rose or plashed in mere wantonness, made wide circles of light in the darkening water. The first fish I landed on a spit of green land came out so quivering with a thousand colours that it seemed almost a sacrilege to break his neck and put him in a common wicker creel. But the sport was good, and many gleaming trout, three or four to the pound, were brought dripping to the crisp heather. The gathering dusk made the stream the one vivid thing in the scene, inky in the shadow but living fire in the open places.

The Scholar Gypsies

THE MAY-FLY

XIX

The hall clock has scarce struck the hour of one when we tramp over the lawn through the thin, fleeting darkness. The earth is buried in shadow, but the sky above is lightening, and in the open spaces a sort of ghostly dusk prevails. The air is sharp, for there is a point of east in the wind, and at this hour in the towns on the east seaboard there will be a *haar*, chill and oppressive. But here there is midsummer weather, which will yield in two days' time to the grey desolation of a windy June. A bat flutters about, and as we strike the road a black shape glides into the hedge, which may be a weasel. Four miles of walking are before us ere we reach the bend of Tweed from which we would fish homewards. The slowly growing dawn comes flitting through the branches, revealing kine in the meadows and sheep on the hilly pasture, and now and then a glimmer of water or a sleeping cottage. Through thick woods and between straight hedges and over a ridge of stiff moorland we go, till at length we come to the little wicket whence runs the bypath to the river.

It is still dusky, though the sun has now risen, and the bank on the other side is hazy. The waters are grey as glass, with little films of fog rising from the surface. We choose the smallest and reddest of brandlings, fixed on the nicest of hooks dressed on the finest of gut. We can only cast by faith, for the eye cannot see where the line meets the water, or mark its downward progress. But this is the feeding-time of the fish, and in two casts there is a dead pull on the line, and a fish sulks at the bottom. From this we infer that he is no trout, for such churlish conduct is unworthy of that delicate creature. Sure enough, in ten minutes' time there comes tumbling on the shingle a stranger grayling, a pound and a half in weight, by the god of fishermen. For in these latter days some of the family have found their way into the Tweed, and work havoc among the little troutlings and break the fine gut of unsuspecting anglers.

So master grayling finds his place in the basket, and as the light on the water is now clearer the May-fly box is produced, and an elegant winged creature succeeds the sorely battered worm. Now is the time for sport, and as the thin rod bends to each throw, and the plash and gurgle of great trout rising strike on our ears, we swear that the world is a good one and life well worth living. But, alas, for the rarity of consistency, for in a trice we hook a trout, a violent half-pound fellow, and by gross stupidity our line fouls the branch of a tree and breaks short. Then we call down the vengeance of heaven on fish and rivers, and mournfully decide that the time is out of joint.

But soon we are successful, and with a little eddy our fly is sucked under, and another trout is hooked. This time we are less foolish, for with all the art we know we strive to keep him from the perils of reeds and dipping boughs, and guide his errant course to the kindly gravel. A little struggle, a moment of breathless anxiety, and there lies on the grass a well-bred yellow trout, scarlet-spotted, shapely, and shining like polished mail. Our hearts are cheered, and we fall to fishing warily, circumspectly, eyeing every likely nook, every hole and current, and casting as if our lives depended on the fly alighting like a stray petal of hawthorn. Soon we have secured another, and yet another, till the open water is past, and the entanglements of wood and shrub begin.

It is a charming morning, fresh, clear as crystal, and bright as only June can make it. Birds are twittering all round. The dipper is already flashing up stream, the moorhen is darting below her friendly bank, and the solemn heron is fishing up at yonder pool...

Fishermen! Whatever lie-abeds may say of their craft they can afford to smile. For it takes them out to the greenest spots on

God's earth at the time when man, in spite of an absurd custom of civilization, should be most active. It shows him much of the ways of bird and beast and flower, and if he be not the better for every minute he spends in its practice, then I take it there is something radically unwholesome in his whole nature. The man who fishes Tweed with the May-fly of a morning in June has the cream of the sport, and it is an experience which he will never forget...

What is the charm of May-fly fishing above all others? *Imprimis*, the trout, the big trout, love it especially and take it greedily. *Item*, it is a clean bait, easily handled, pleasant to use, and demanding much skill in the presentation. *Item*, it comes at the very sweet o' the year, when the heart of nature bursts into song, and morning, noon, and night are one substantial Elysium. One can fish with it in clear water, when all other lures, save that of the small worm, are worse than useless. And, truly, one fish out of the pellucid pool is, to the mind of the writer, better than five out of a turbid, muddy torrent. It is free from any taint of amateurishness, for though the novice may land a big fish with a lobworm, from a swollen stream, only one who has been much at the trade can hope to succeed with this.

The Scholar Gypsies

THE AMATEUR

XX

We were within some half-dozen miles, I think, of the head of the glen, when Sandy bethought himself of fishing. I laughed him to scorn, for, what with the bright day and the clear shallow water, I thought that no fish would rise to the fly. But I little knew the resources of my friend. He declined the offer of my fly-book, and produced from the mysterious depths of his pocket some lengths of gut and a few hooks of differing sizes, wrapped up in a dirty cloth. I watched him with an indolent interest.

From a willow bush he cut a long, ten-foot wand, thin and pliable at the top but solid at the butt. To the end he tied a piece of line, a yard or so of gut, and a finely dressed hook. He searched below stones and tufts of grass until he found a number of small white worms. Then he baited his hook, scrambled cautiously down to the river-side and began. Keeping well in the shade of the bank, he cast far upstream in a stretch of swift, shallow water. I have seen many fishers but never one so keen as Sandy. With his head down and his fragment of a hat all awry on his head and the water rippling over his boots, he watched his line as it floated down. He twitched it gently whenever it seemed to halt, but he must have made a dozen casts before he hooked a fish. Then began a battle royal. Upstream and down stream he went, for there was no reel on his home-made rod; and when at last he landed it, a trout of nearly a pound's weight on a patch of gravel on the other side, he was dripping with water and furiously warm – a strange spectacle for gods and men.

For some time we kept the stream side, which, as a path, was more varied and natural than the highway. Four other fish were caught, comely brown trout, with the exception of one great, black fellow which Sandy had out of a deep pool. We strung them on twisted rushes for ease in carrying. The tussocks of rough grass were diversified with crisp, green stretches of turf, which had all the elastic buoyancy peculiar to the hills. Sandpipers were busy by the water, and their plaintive, twittering cries mingled with the music of the running stream. All around us we heard an assiduous murmuring of bees – not the humble brown bee of the lowlands but a dashing cavalier fellow, splendidly habited in orange-tawny. Now and then a saffron butterfly or a gaudy blue moth fluttered past. There was something of a dearth of flowers, for we saw little else than thyme and half-opened heathbells; but we knew that in a month the glen would be one flaming expanse of blossoming heather.

The Scholar Gypsies

XXI

The charm of fishing is that it is the pursuit of what is elusive but attainable, a perpetual series of occasions for hope. Any hour may bring to the most humble practitioner the capture of the monster of his dreams. But with hope goes regret, and the more ardent the expectations of the fisherman the bitterer will be his sense of loss when achievement fails him by the breadth of the finest hair. It is a bitterness which is commonly soon forgotten, for the same chance may occur tomorrow or next week; but every angler has in his memory one or two disasters, the pangs of which are unforgettable. He knows in his soul that Fortune on that one day offered him something which will not come again. I confess that these heart-rending tales of lost monsters have for me a morbid fascination, when veraciously chronicled. I say "veraciously," for the whole point is that they should be strictly true. Human nature is apt to magnify the unknown and unassessable, and cynics ask why lost fish should be always the biggest ones. The habit of romance no doubt partly accounts for it; but it has a basis in solid fact. The bigger the fish the more difficult he must be to land, and there must be better salmon in the waters than ever came out of them. Here we are dealing with a problem quite different from that of other sports, such as big-game hunting. A stag with a record head falls as easily to the rifle as an ill-grown little switch-horn. But in fishing the difficulty of capture is roughly proportioned to the size and strength of the quarry, and the best must often be the lost.

Great Hours in Sport

XXII

But the epic of salmon fishing remains to be written, the story which will be for the sport what Mr Kipling's "Maltese Cat" is for polo. It should be romance, but true romance, with a fierce reality behind it. Andrew Lang tried his hand in *The Lady and the Salmon*, and Mr Hartley has written a stirring tale about a fish in the Awe. But, good as these are, they are not the thing we are waiting for. The story of our dreams should not deal with a record basket; it should tell of the capture or loss of a single monster. The tale will have all the elements of Aristotelian tragedy – *anagnorisis*, when you recognize the monster of your dreams, *peripeteia* when he breaks you in the gaffing, and a constant *katharsis* of the emotions by pity and fear. The scene may be the Awe in high water some autumn morning when the mist is on the prongs of Cruachan, or, better still, a dub of the lower Tweed on a lowering November afternoon. The end must be tragedy, for the river gods will not yield such a prize without exacting some sacrifice. The fish may be landed, but the fisher will fall dead from joy, or tumble in, leaving an immortal name. The motto for the tale may be taken from the Book of Job: "Canst thou draw out Leviathan with an hook?... Behold, the hope of him is in vain."

Great Hours in Sport

XXIII

Why is the one undisputed classic of British sport, *The Compleat Angler*, a fishing book? For such is the fact. Not Beckford, or Whyte-Melville, or Scrope, or St John can vie in assured immortality with Walton. The reason, perhaps, is that our sport in itself is scarcely adequate to the demands of literature; in our homely pastimes there is too little of the high adventure which gives high drama; and we must eke it out, as in Walton, with meditations and the literary graces. Fishing permits of such pleasing excursions, for the angler has a better chance to be a philosopher and observer than the anxious mortal in a butt or the man who crawls breathlessly in the lee of a morose gillie. For the future, now that sports are standardized and these islands somewhat crowded, we must go for the literature of sport to those who see more in wild life than the raw material of a bag or a basket, to the men who are naturalists and poets as well as sportsmen, and, like Piscator, have ears for Coridon's song as well as for the plash of trout below the willows. Let us by all means have the expert treatise and the reminiscences of enthusiasts who have been specially favoured of Heaven. But the enduring book will be something more – the revelation of the inner heart of nature or of a man's own soul.

Great Hours in Sport

XXIV

I prepared my tackle on the grass, making a casting-line of fine horse-hair which I had plucked from the tail of our own grey gelding. I had no such fine hooks as folk nowadays bring from Edinburgh, sharpened and barbed ready to their hand; but rough homemade ones, which Tam Todd, the land Grieve, had fashioned out of old needles. My line was of thin, stout whipcord to which I had made the casting firm with a knot of my own invention. I had out my bag of worms and, choosing a fine red one, made it fast on the hook. Then I crept gently to the alder and climbed on the branch which hung far out over the stream. Here I sat like an owl in the shade, and dropped my line in the pool below me, where it caught a glint of the sun and looked like a shining cord let down, like Jacob's ladder, from heaven to the darkness of earth.

I had not sat many minutes before my rod was wrenched violently downwards, then athwart the stream, nearly swinging me from my perch. I have got a monstrous trout, I thought, and with a fluttering heart stood up on the branch to be more ready for the struggle. He ran up the water and down; then far below the tree roots, whence I had much difficulty in forcing him; then he thought to break my line by rapid jerks, but he did not know the strength of my horse-hair. By-and-by he grew wearied, and I landed him comfortably on a spit of land – a great red-spotted fellow with a black back. I made sure that he was two pounds weight if he was an ounce.

I hid him in a cool bed of leaves and rushes on the bank, and crawled back to my seat on the tree. I baited my hook as before, and dropped it in; and then leaned back lazily on the branches behind to meditate on the pleasantness of fishing...

John Burnet of Barns

SHOOTING

XXV

"I am not a great performer with the gun, and you will not find me often in the first flight in the hunting-field, but, busy as I was, I made time now for an occasional day's shooting or hunting, for I had fallen in love with the English country, and it is sport that takes you close to the heart of it. Is there anything in the world like the corner of a great pasture hemmed in with smoky-brown woods in an autumn twilight: or the jogging home after a good run when the moist air is quickening to frost and the wet ruts are lemon-coloured in the sunset; or a morning in November when, on some upland, the wind tosses the driven partridges like leaves over tall hedges, through the gaps of which the steel-blue horizons shine? It is the English winter that intoxicates me more even than the English May, for the noble bones of the land are bare, and you get the essential savour of earth and wood and water."

Sir Edward Leithen in *The Dancing Floor*

XXVI

...Grouse shooting comes first among northern sports in the popular mind, and it has been amply treated in series like the *Badminton* and the *Fur and Feather*. But it has attracted little in the way of adventitious literature, because it is a tame business after all, a matter of skill rather than of enterprise. There is drama in a 40 lb salmon or a big stag, but none in a bag which by a dozen brace or so eclipses a past record. Besides the circumstances of the sport today are unfriendly to the muses. In other times there might have been inspiration in the tramping of the heather wet with the morning dew, the spectacle of dogs working well, with long hours on some purple shoulder of hill, and the weary legs turned homeward in the gloaming. But to stand in a butt while birds come down wind like bullets is another matter. Grouse driving is a great game, but no more than pigeon shooting at Monte Carlo is it likely to kindle the imagination.

Great Hours in Sport

XXVII

One suggestion I would make the writer in search of a subject. The life-story of a blackcock – from birth till he is slain, an insolent patriarch, by a rook-rifle – done after the manner of Mr Fortescue's *Story of a Red Deer*, would be an engrossing work. No bird that flies is so complex in its psychology, so profound in its intelligence, and so clearly in league with the Enemy of man- kind.

Great Hours in Sport

DEER STALKING

XXVIII

On my marriage I gave up mountaineering as scarcely a married man's game. I still fished whenever and wherever I got the chance, and I discovered a new sport in deer-stalking. About that time I ceased to shoot with a gun, for my love for birds was so great that I disliked killing them. I have never been much of a gun shot at my best, like the Ancient Mariner, "stopping one of three," but I was fairly good on my day with a rifle. Stalking supplied the hunting element and also took me to the high tops as much as in my old climbing days. In my time I have stalked in over twenty deer forests, and I have always had a clear view of how the game should be played. I like best those forests in which long experience gave me some knowledge of the ground, so that I was not the slave of the stalker. I was a professed scavenger, and shot only for the sake of the forest. I wanted to kill freaks like hummels and switch-horns and old back-going beasts that would perish in the next winter. I would gladly stalk a young royal, but when I got my sights behind his shoulder I would take off my cap to him and go home – a habit popular with owners but not so popular with stalkers and gillies. Then I was in terror of wounding, and in the days of my pride, when I could trust myself, I generally took neck shots, which meant a dead kill or a clean miss. I only once wounded a stag, and after a sleepless night I got him the following day.

Memory Hold-the-Door

XXIX

The red deer is by nature a woodland animal, but in Scotland he inhabits mountains which are for the most part treeless, and he has had to develop a new technique of defence. Living under conditions which are more or less artificial, he has become far more wary than, say, the African kudu or the Canadian wapiti. His sense of smell and hearing are acute; but his eyesight is indifferent, for though he can see things far off he is not clever at recognising them. I found endless interest in devising new ways of circumventing him, devices which every professional stalker knows, but which he does not usually communicate to his "gentlemen." For example, if you are looking down on a glen with stags in the bottom and the wind is wrong, it is often possible to have your scent carried by the wind so that it ricochets off the opposite wall of the glen, and, coming up behind the stags, makes them move towards you. Camouflage, too, is important. I always believed in breaking up my costume, for, whatever the forest, its colour will not be uniform, and I would wear, say, a checked jacket, grey flannel knickerbockers and grey-blue stockings. The ground often consists of a ribbon of turf bounded by heather and shingle, and by crawling along the border-line between the green and the rough, keeping half of the body in each, if the wind is right it is possible to get within shot, though you are in full view of the deer.

Memory Hold-the-Door

XXX

When we turn to deer stalking we find a different case... We know more about the habits of deer; we have improved the average of head and weight by the introduction of fresh blood; and the limits of forests are jealously circumscribed, even to the erection of deer fences. The sport is more artificial than it was, but no "improvements" can wholly rob it of its wildness. It is "hunting" in a different sense from any other form of British shooting. Though a man may be confined to two corries, yet within these limits he must use the same art to circumvent his quarry as if he were pursuing wapiti in the Selkirks. If he returns of an evening to a villa-like lodge instead of to a hunter's tent, he has yet spent some hours in the primeval world. It may be complained that the sport with modern weapons is too easy, but it should be answered that the very circumscribing of the area creates its own special difficulties, if, for example, the wind be wrong. So it is reasonable to hope that deer stalking will never lose its literature.

Great Hours in Sport

XXXI

...a rifle was out on the Correi na Sidhe beat, and a thin spire of smoke had risen from the top of Sgurr Dearg to show that a stag had been killed at the burn-head. The lumpish hill pony with its deer-saddle had gone up the Correi in a gillie's charge, while we followed at leisure, picking our way among the loose granite rocks and the patches of wet bogland. The track climbed high on one of the ridges of Sgurr Dearg, till it hung over a cauldron of green glen with the Alt-na-Sidhe churning in its linn a thousand feet below. It was a breathless evening, I remember, with a pale-blue sky just clearing from the haze of the day. West-wind weather may make the North, even in September, no bad imitation of the Tropics, and I sincerely pitied the man who all these stifling hours had been toiling on the screes of Sgurr Dearg. By and by we sat down on a bank of heather, and idly watched the trough swimming at our feet. The clatter of the pony's hoofs grew fainter, the drone of bees had gone, even the midges seemed to have forgotten their calling. No place on earth can be so deathly still as a deer-forest early in the season before the stags have begun roaring, for there are no sheep with their homely noises, and only the rare croak of a raven breaks the silence. The hillside was far from sheer – one could have walked down with a little care – but something in the shape of the hollow and the remote gleam of white water gave it an air of extraordinary depth and space. There was a shimmer left from the day's heat, which invested bracken and rock and scree with a curious airy unreality.

The Moon Endureth: Space

DEATH OF A SPORTSMAN

(Sir Edward Leithen)

XXXII

"The last time he was able to go abroad, Galliard and I assisted him down to the edge of the lake. There was still a broad selvedge of ice – what the Canadian French call *batture* – but in the middle the ice was cracking, and there were lanes of water to reflect the pale blue sky. Also the streams were being loosed from their winter stricture. One could hear them talking under their bonds, and in one or two places the force of water had cleared the boulders and made pools and cascades... A wonderful thing happened. A bull moose, very shaggy and lean, came out of the forest and stood in an open shallow at a stream's mouth. It drank its fill, and then raised its ugly head, shook it, and stared into the sunset. Crystal drops fell from its mouth, and the setting sun transfigured the beast into something magical, a beneficent dragon out of a fairy-tale. I shall never forget Leithen's delight. It was as if he had his last sight of the beauty of the earth, and found in it a pledge of the beauty of Paradise, though I doubt if there will be anything like a bull moose in the Heavenly City..."

Father Jean-Marie Duplessis in *Sick Heart River*

MOUNTAINEERING

XXXIII

Just as sailing a small boat brings one close to the sea so mountaineering lays one alongside the bones of mother earth. One meets her on equal terms and matches one's skill and endurance against something which has no care for human life. There is also the joy of technical accomplishment. I never took kindly to snow and ice work but I found a strong fascination in rock climbing, whether on the granite slabs of the Chamonix *Aiguilles*, or the sheer fissured precipices of the Dolomites, or the gabbro of the Coolins. A long rock climb is a series of problems each one different from the rest, which have to be solved by ingenuity of mind and versatility of body. I was fortunate to have the opposite of vertigo, for I found a physical comfort in looking down from great heights. Bodily fitness is essential, for there are always courses which you must have the strength to complete or court disaster. In any mountaineering holiday there are miserable days when the muscles are being got in order by training walks; but when these are over I know no physical well-being so perfect as that enjoyed by the mountaineer.

Memory Hold-the-Door

XXXIV

Another of my consolations was mountaineering. In South Africa I had scrambled among the kloofs of the Drakensberg and the ranges of the Northern Transvaal, and long before I had climbed in the Highlands, but it was not until 1904 that I paid my first visit to the Alps. There I did a number of the usual courses, my chief resorts being Chamonix and Zermutt, and in 1906 I became a member of the Alpine Club. But my favourite ground was the Scots hills, especially Skye and the Coolins. In them it was still possible to make first ascents, and I came to know every stack and cranny from Garbsheinn to Sgurr-nan-Gillian. It was my ambition to be the first to traverse the whole range in a summer's day, but I put off the enterprise too long and others got in before me.

Memory Hold-the-Door

GOLF

XXXV

As for golf, I utterly failed to excel; and indeed it seems to me that golf is like the divine art of poetry, the gift for which is implanted in man at his birth or not at all. Be that as it may, I never struck a golf ball fairly in my life, and I misdoubt I never shall.

John Burnet of Barns

CHAPTER VII

REFLECTIONS AND JUDGMENTS

REFLECTIONS
LITERATURE
STYLE
THE FALLIBILTY OF MORTAL JUDGMENT
AFTERMATH OF WAR
THE MENTALITY OF THE GERMAN PEOPLE
DEMOCRACY
PURITANISM
THE MODERATE MAN
PAST AND FUTURE

The wheel of birth and death moves inexorably in that sphere of man's activity which is concerned with government. Constitutions come into being, flourish, wither and descend to an unlamented grave only to be later revived, acclaimed and again rejected. Nothing lives continuously, but nothing wholly dies.

Multa renascentur quae jam cecidere, cadentque quae nunc sunt in honore.

Augustus

REFLECTIONS

I

...The great individuals – Alexander, Caesar, Mahomet, Charlemagne, Luther, Calvin, Peter the Great, Napoleon, Lenin – cannot be explained in the terms of any contemporary movement. They are in a sense the children of their age, but they bring to their age more than they draw from it; they seem to be like Melchizedek, without recognizable ancestry, and by the sheer force of personality and mind they lift the world to a new plane...

Men and Deeds: The Causal and the Casual in History

II

...Every man has a creed, but in his soul he knows that that creed has another side, possibly not less logical, which it does not suit him to produce. Our most honest convictions are not the children of pure reason, but of temperament, environment, necessity, and interest. Most of us take sides in life and forget the one we reject. But our conscience tells us it is there and we can on occasion state it with a fairness and fullness which proves that it is not wholly repellent to our reason.

The Moon Endureth: The Lucid Interval

III

...Let us by all means accept the doctrine of predestination, whether in its metaphysical or theological form, so long as we do not try to show in detail how it works.

Men and Deeds: The Causal and the Casual in History

IV

Criticism is primarily judgment, and judgment is a matter of perspective, and perspective is a matter of knowledge.

Homilies and Recreations: The Old and the New in Literature

V

...common-sense, the sense of reality, a rare and more valuable gift even than the power of nice interpretation.

Homilies and Recreations: The Judicial Temperament

VI

...there is nothing to be said against the retention of prejudices. I believe in every man having a good stock of them, for otherwise we should be flimsy, ineffective creatures, and deadly dull at that.

Homilies and Recreations: The Judicial Temperament

VII

...without optimism there can be no vitality...

The Novel and the Fairy Tale

VIII

"How if Space is really full of things we cannot see and as yet do not know? How if all animals and some savages have a cell in their brain or a nerve which responds to the invisible world? How if all Space be full of these landmarks, not material in our sense, but quite real? A dog barks at nothing, a wild beast makes an aimless circuit. Why? Perhaps because Space is made up of corridors and alleys, ways to travel and things to shun? For all we know to a greater intelligence than ours the top of Mont Blanc may be as crowded as Piccadilly Circus."

The Moon Endureth: Space

IX

"What would you call the highest happiness?"... Wratislaw asked.

"The sense of competence," was the answer, given without hesitation.

"Right. And what do we mean by competence? Not success! God knows it is something very different from success! Any fool may be successful, if the gods wish to hurt him. Competence means that splendid joy in your own powers and the approval of your own heart which great men feel always and lesser men now and again at favoured intervals. There are a certain number of things in the world to be done, and we have got to do them. We may fail – it doesn't in the least matter. We may get killed in the attempt – it matters still less. The things may not altogether be worth doing – it is of very little importance. It is ourselves we have got to judge by. If we are playing our part well, and know it, then we can thank God and go on. That is what I call happiness."

"... And how are you to get happiness? Not by thinking about it. The great things of the world have all been done by men who didn't stop to reflect on them. If a man comes to a halt and analyses his motives and distrusts the value of the thing he strives for, then the odds are that his halt is final. You strive to strive and not to attain. A man must have that direct practical virtue which forgets itself and sees only its work. Parsons will tell you that all virtue is self-sacrifice, and they are right, though not in the way they mean. It may all seem to you a tissue of contradictions. You must not pitch on too fanciful a goal, nor, on the other hand, must you think on yourself. And it is a contradiction which only resolves itself in practice, one of those anomalies on which the world is built.

"... And the moral of it all is that there are two sorts of people who will never do any good on this planet. One is the class which makes formulae and shallow little ideals its gods and has no glimpse of human needs and the plain issues of life. The other is the egotist whose eye is always filled with his own figure, who investigates his motives, and hesitates and finicks, till Death knocks him on the head and there is an end of him. Of the two give me the second, for even a narrow little egotistical self is better than a formula. But I pray to be delivered from both."

"... There are two men only who will not be ashamed to look their work in the face in the end – the brazen opportunist and the rigid Puritan."

The Half-hearted

X

The essence of civilization lies in man's defiance of an impersonal universe. It makes no difference that a mechanised universe may be his own creation if he allows his handiwork to enslave him. Not for the first time in history have the idols that humanity has shaped for its own ends become its master.

Memory Hold-the-Door

XI

The thought of death even to the more valiant has in it something of affright and natural terror. Or if this be wanting, as is the case with the more high and valorous natures, there is a certain repugnance, shyness, strangeness, as of one entering upon a difficult and scarcely discerned path. But if one accustoms himself to it, this shrinking departs, and the one fear left is that of the trappings and unseemly attendants of the last scene. Indeed, but for these loathly surroundings, the great enemy has few terrors for the better half of mankind.

The Scholar Gypsies

XII

...Man can face up to anything the universe can pit against him if his nerve doesn't crack.

A Prince of the Captivity

XIII

The race must have a goal, or it would be no race; some day man must take his wages and go bravely home.

A Prince of the Captivity

LITERATURE

XIV

...A poet like Milton or Dante brings cosmic sublimities within hail of our common life; a great novelist makes our common life itself cosmic and sublime.

The Novel and the Fairy Tale

XV

...The trouble about cleverness is that it is so rarely greatness. The clever person is much more interested in himself than in anything else, and in whatever he does he is always looking at his own face in the mirror. It is a curious fact that since the War, which meant for all the world such a noble renunciation of self, most of our poetry and fiction should be so egocentric. The writers are perpetually wrestling with their own moods and tinkering with their own emotions, and they rarely rise to the self-forgetfulness of the greater art.

The Novel and the Fairy Tale

XVI

...the folk tale is a profound thing, for it is based upon a very clear and candid view of life. The folk tale knows only too well the stubborn brutality of things; and, knowing this, it is still prepared to hope. Such optimism is far more merciless than any pessimism. Also it is far closer to reality. A tale which describes any aspect of life and makes of it nothing but a pathological study in meanness and vice is more fantastic than any fairy tale.

The Novel and the Fairy Tale

XVII

The folk tale belongs to no one country or age. Many go back to the ancientry of our race. They are part of the common stock of humanity and are closer to mankind than any written word. They are the delight of our childhood and they are part of our unconscious thought. I have a notion that things so long descended and prepotent are not likely to be forgotten. I have a notion, too, that any form of literature related to them, inspired by the same creed, close to the earth and yet kin to the upper air, will have the same immortality...

The Novel and the Fairy Tale

XVIII

...The true hero in all the folk tales and fairy tales is not the younger son, or the younger daughter, or the stolen princess, or the ugly duckling, but the soul of man. It was a world where a great deal of discomfort and sorrow had to be borne, and where the most useful virtue was the passive virtue of fortitude; but in the folk tales it is not this passive virtue that is exalted, but daring, boldness, originality, brains – because the people who made them realized that the hope of humanity lay not in passivity but in action.

The Novel and the Fairy Tale

XIX

...It has always been my secret view that the English novelists of the eighteenth century were a little over-praised – even Defoe and Fielding. But I think that the nineteenth-century novel in England is one of the main achievements in our literature, comparable with the Elizabethan drama. I should rank without hesitation Sir Walter Scott and Charles Dickens among the greatest of the world's novelists, and I should class at least two novels of Thackeray, one of George Eliot's, and three of Thomas Hardy's, among the world's greatest works of fiction.

The Novel and the Fairy Tale

XX

...It is hard to say what is the special gift of our people in literature. Sometimes I think it is for a kind of lyric; sometimes I think it lies in the writing of history; but on the whole I believe it is for fiction. The Victorian novel is the most typical product of our national genius.

The Novel and the Fairy Tale

STYLE

XXI

Style in the verbal sense is indispensable if only to make the narrative easy and compact. In sheer mastery of words Thucydides still ranks first in the literature of the world; Gibbon stands high; and among the moderns Froude is unsurpassed. Style such as these men possessed has both colour and light in it. Macaulay and Carlyle are a little weighted by their mannerisms, and Michelet, who had far more balance and scrupulosity of mind than he is usually credited with, is at the mercy of his effervescing rhetoric. Style, indeed, is a somewhat double-edged gift, which too often cuts the hand of the user. If the historian be a hot partisan, then his writing will have fire and speed, whatever its other vices; whereas, if he be detached and passionless like Ranke, his use of words will be apt to be flat and chilly. To get the best results as literature it is unfortunately true that the narrative must generally fail a little as history. That is why a flavour of partisanship seems almost essential in the historian, for a perfect bloodless urbanity will almost inevitably desiccate the style. Provided the bias be reasonable and not too violent, it is perhaps to be welcomed. Let the historian present his facts with the impartiality of a judge, and there is no harm in his stating his view with the fervour of an advocate, for then the reader has the material for forming his own opinion and is not bound to agree with the advocate.

Homilies and Recreations: The Muse of History

XXII

There is only one rule for good prose, the rule which Newman and Huxley in their different ways enunciated and followed – to set down your exact, full and precise meaning so lucidly and simply that no man can mistake it... I am ready to assert that almost the best prose has been written by men who are not professional men of letters, and who therefore escape the faded and weary mannerisms of the self-conscious litterateur. As an example I would point to the prose of Cromwell, of Abraham Lincoln, and of a dozen explorers like Captain Scott and Captain Boyd Alexander, and of soldiers...like the Canadian general Sir Arthur Currie.

Homilies and Recreations: The Judicial Temperament

THE FALLIBILITY OF MORTAL JUDGMENT

XXIII

I should like to see an anthology compiled of critical dicta, the work of wise men, which time has made ridiculous. Thomas Hobbes, who had a mind of remarkable range and vigour, thought that Sir John Davenant's *Gondibert*, which we do not now greatly admire, "would last as long as the *Æneid* or the *Iliad*." Byron thought Samuel Rogers a good poet and Mr Hayley's *Triumphs of Temper* an enduring work. Lord Jeffrey, after disparaging some of the noblest things in Scott and Wordsworth, praised Felicia Hemans in language which would be extravagant if applied to Sappho. The *Quarterly Review* considered Milman's unreadable epic *The Fall of Jerusalem* certain "of whatever immortality the English language can bestow." These, be it noted, are instances, not of insensitiveness to a new and strange voice, which is natural enough in human nature – an ear attuned to Pope would take some time to get accustomed to Blake – but of preposterous praise given to contemporaries. They are examples, which might be indefinitely multiplied, of the fallibility of mortal judgment, and they are due to a bias, which may now be conservative and now revolutionary – a distortion caused by temperament or circumstance. Hobbes praised *Gondibert* because there was a touch of the new rationalism in it; Jeffrey, who was a conservative at heart, liked Mrs Hemans because he liked the familiar sentimental conventions.

... But behind all these accidental biases there seems to me to be a broad distinction between minds, which gives reality and dignity to the eternal dispute. There is the mind which loves law and order, and which exults in the continuity of things, and there is the mind which craves adventure and change and likes to think of the world as each morning a new birth. It is the distinction (shall we say?) not so much between age and youth, as between the conformist temper and the non-conformist; between the static and the dynamic; between Apollo and Dionysos; between ordered power and disordered ecstasy; between the paean and the dithyramb; or in the words of the Book of Isaiah, between those who say "In returning and in rest shall we be saved; in quietness and in confidence shall be our strength," and those whose cry is "We will flee upon horses, we will ride upon the swift." Define these two moods by their virtues, and it is the opposition between learning, discipline, tradition, service, the slow labour of art, and freedom and originality; define them by their vices, and it is reaction, ossification, convention, set against revolution, slovenliness, wilfulness, impatience. It is cool blood against hot blood, sobriety against enthusiasm. As a matter of fact, of course, the opposition is never complete; for the most fiery voluntary is not independent of tradition, and the most stubborn conservatism has its odd romantic moments; but we can fairly place the two schools by their predominant qualities. Not schools, indeed – the word is a misnomer; let us rather say moods and attitudes and inclinations of mind.

Homilies and Recreations: The Old and the New in Literature

AFTERMATH OF WAR

XXIV

Those who believed that victory would mean a fresh start with high hearts and girded loins and clear eyes in a new world were strangely forgetful of the lessons of history. For war clogs the brain and weakens the nerve, and the heavy burden of settlement falls upon shoulders already wearied and bowed. The task had to be undertaken by statesmen all of whom were tired, and many of whom were unfit for the work, since the qualities which made them eminent in war were often a handicap in the very different duties of peace. As with the leaders, so with the peoples. Little assistance could be got from the rank and file, who were as bewildered as their masters. When Michelet after the writing of his history fell ill and sought rest, he excused himself on the plea, "J'ai abattu tant de rois." Like the historian, the world desired above all things leisure and ease, dazed with the long effort and the clattering about its ears of so many landmarks. Men's minds were relaxed and surfeited, when they were not disillusioned. After the strain of the distant vision they were apt to seek the immediate advantage; after so much altruism they asked leave to attend to private interests; after their unremitting labours they claimed the right of apathy. In short, problems of a magnitude unknown in history had to be faced by jaded statesmen and listless, confused peoples. There was yet another bequest of war, its natural offspring –

> "*Discordia demens,*
> *Vipereum crinem vittis innexa cruentis.*"

A lurking madness was abroad in the world. Human life had been shorn of its sacredness, death and misery and torture had become too familiar, the old decorums and sanctions had lost something of their power. The passions of many millions cannot be stirred for four years without leaving a hideous legacy... The crust which we call civilization had worn thin, and beneath could be heard the muttering of the primordial fires.

Therefore those who looked forward to peace with happy dreams were fated to be disillusioned. It was very certain that high hopes would be dashed, and that generous souls would cry out in bitterness that the battles had been fought in vain, and that what began as a crusade had ended in a cynical huckstering. But this pessimism was as unreasonable as the earlier illusions and as blind to the teaching of the past. Peace does not follow naturally upon victory. It is itself a construction, a slow and difficult effort to bridge the chasm between two worlds, and it is inevitably a time of discouragement. It is like a season of thaw. The frosts of January are cruel things, but for the strong they tauten the sinews and stir the blood, whereas in a thaw there is nothing but grey skies and muddy roads and plashing fields. Yet that is the course of nature, and summer cannot follow winter without the depressing stage of early spring. If the winter wheat has been truly sown, there will come in due season the time of harvest.

The gains and losses are not yet to be assessed, but there is ground for humble confidence that that sowing in unimaginable sacrifice and pain will yet quicken and bear fruit to the bettering of the world. The war was a vindication of the essential greatness of our common nature, for victory was won less by genius in the few than by faithfulness in the many. Every class had its share, and the plain man, born in these latter days of doubt and divided purpose, marched to heights of the heroic unsurpassed in simpler ages. In this revelation democracy found its final justification, and civilization its truest hope. Mankind may console itself in its hour of depression and failure, and steel itself to new labours with the knowledge that once it has been great.

The sacrifice was chiefly of innocence and youth, and in computing it there can be no distinction between friend and enemy. *Hanc ex diverso sedem veniemus in unam.* That Country of the Young knows no frontiers of race or creed. Most men who fell died for honourable things, and perversities of national policy were changed into the eternal sanctities – love of country and home, comradeship, loyalty to manly virtues, the indomitable questing of youth. Innocence does not perish in vain, against such a spirit the gates of death cannot prevail, and the endurance of their work is more certain than the coming of spring. The world is poor indeed without them, for they were the flower of their race, the straightest of limb, the keenest of brain, the most eager of spirit. In such a mourning each man thinks first of his friends; for each of us has seen his crowded circle become like the stalls at an unpopular play; each has suddenly found the world of time strangely empty and eternity strangely thronged. Yet to look back upon the gallant procession of those who offered their all and had the gift accepted, is to know exultation as well as sorrow. The youth which died almost before it had gazed on the world, the poets with their songs unsung, the makers and the doers who left their tasks unfinished, found immortal achievement in their death. Their memory will abide so long as men are found to set honour before ease and a nation lives not for its ledgers alone but for some purpose of virtue. They have become, in the fancy of Henry Vaughan, the shining spires of that City to which we travel.

A History of the Great War, Vol. IV

THE MENTALITY OF THE GERMAN PEOPLE

XXV

As for the ordinary German he was of an obedient temper, and the Government had drawn him so wholly into its net that the thought of opposing its will did not enter his head. The intricate system of minor decorations with which his good conduct was rewarded, and the surveillance by the State over every part of his daily life, had deprived him of all political individuality. Lastly the bulk of the "intellectuals," the teachers in the schools, the professors at the universities, the clergy, and the men of letters, were in questions of politics little more than officials, speaking from a brief. The educational hierarchy was as much a branch of the bureaucracy as the management of the post office, and the class which in Germany's dark days had roused the people by dwelling upon her ancient strength and the hope of the future, now taught the same creed in coarser accents to the greater glory of the Hohenzollerns.

But our picture of Germany is not completed when we have analyzed the elements of power in her community and sketched the formal nature of her Government. For behind everything lay an impulse to a certain view of life, a conscious creed – explicitly formulated by the few and present as a temperament in the many – to which Germans gave the name of "kultur" or civilization.

More important than Emperor or General Staff or the kings of commerce was this German soul, this *Deutschtum*, the sum of subtle prepossessions, hopes and fears which the world only guessed at in 1914, but which in four years of war it came to know with bitter precision.

We have seen that Germany had made steady progress in most departments of life. But there was one conspicuous exception. In art and literature, in pure thought and in political science she had declined since 1870. The simple bourgeois Germany of the early nineteenth century produced some of the greatest of the world's thinkers, poets, and musicians; Imperial Germany was content with mediocrities. In thought the great constructive epoch was over; philosophy had become applied and pragmatic, the handmaid of the practical world. Thinkers were unfashionable unless they could preach a topical gospel. The German equivalent of the *Wealth of Nations* was Clausewitz's classic *On War*, which explored the foundations of statecraft, and showed the intimate connection between principles and facts, a manual alike for the politician and the soldier. A thousand teachers spread his views, taken for the most part at second hand, throughout the nation, and among his disciples had been Moltke and Bismarck. The passion for deeds took the place of the old passion for truth, and history was taught as the text-book of the man of action. The preference was always for the scorner of formulas, the iron opportunist, the man who had succeeded. We can see the trait in Mommsen's *Roman History*, and in Sybel's *History of the French Revolution*, both the work of professed Liberals – a reaction against all idealism which had not its "cash value." The materialism of writers such as Mach and Haeckel produced a fruitful ground for the political seed sown by Treitschke, the historian of Prussia, by Droysen, and by soldiers such as von der Goltz and von Bernhardi, who pointed a contemporary moral. Gradually *Deutschtum* was formulated as a creed, a creed which must conquer because of its inherent vitality and which had the right to use any weapons for this lofty end. If the world was to advance, the higher must crush the lower. War to Treitschke was the "drastic medicine of the human race," and the dream of banishing it from the earth not only meaningless but immoral. "It has always been the weary, spiritless, and exhausted ages which have played with the vision of perpetual peace." The megalomania grew like a fungus. Swollen with complacency and drunk with success the exponents of Germanism came to set themselves above the human family, to regard their divine mission as freeing them from all obligations of morality and law, to demand that their altar-fires should be fed with the rights and ideals of every other people, to claim for themselves the only freedom, and to seek to make all nations dependent upon their good pleasure.

This doctrine had its roots far back in German literature and deep down in the German temperament. A craze for large syntheses had characterized the great days of German philosophy. There had always been a tendency to racial arrogance, which, contemplating the stately progress of the Absolute Will, found its final expression up to date in modern Germany. The seeds of the new Machiavellianism – which in essence was simply an abstraction of man as a politician from the rest of his aspects, a fallacy on the same plane as "economic man" of the Benthamites – had been sown in the earliest days of German culture. The intense specialization of German scholarship and science did not tend to produce minds with an acute sense of perspective, and sedentary folk have at all times been inclined to blow a louder trumpet than men of affairs. What Senancour has called "le vulgaire des sages" – the narrow absorption to which pedants are prone – had long been a characteristic of German "intellectuals." Had the thing been confined to the professors and theorists it would have undergone a steady disintegration by criticism.

"*Sapping a solemn creed with solemn sneer*,"

till it lost its power to hurt. As a literary fashion it was so preposterous as to be innocent, an essay in provincialism which was pardonable because of its absurdity. But exalt this mannerism into a faith, base on it a thousand material interests, and give it great armies to make it real, and you are confronted with a dangerous mania. Self-worshippers are harmless till they compel the rest of mankind to make the same obeisance.

The danger came from the alliance of the pedant with the practical man. German statesmen from Metternich to Prince Bülow had praised the German intellect but denied their countrymen political capacity. But now that Germany was no longer content to be a "kultur-staat" only, the politician could join hands with the doctrinaire. It was an easy and natural union, for in the classic philosophy of Germany there were elements akin to the temperament of its new supporters. German idealism, as I have said, had always been noted for its love of vast unification, its devotion to a cosmic grandiosity. But the philosopher, beating his wings in the void, could never hope to see his dream come true till the practical Prussian, himself cast crudely in the same mould, offered his aid. Now the ideal could be made the actual, spirit and matter were become one, the City of Cecrops could be amalgamated on business lines with the City of God. In both philosopher and politician there was that *naïveté* which Renan found in the tissue of the German mind, the desire to canalize the free currents of life and reduce the stubborn complex of the organic to an artificial simplicity. Both sides in the compact gave and received. The Prussian had his material ambitions invested with a spiritual glamour; the dreamer saw the enigma of life solved at last and the dream about to become the reality. Plato's vision had come to pass, and the philosophers were kings and the kings philosophers, but it was a perverse philosophy and a sinister kingship.

But there was more than a mere marriage of fact and theory. To glorify the union came a tempestuous poetry welling from the deeps of the Teutonic soul. Behind all the arguments of the learned and the calculations of the practical we can discern a kind of barbaric imagination akin to the grandiosity of Wagner's music.

"Thinking," wrote Madame de Staël, "calms men of other nations; it inflames the Germans." Something untamed and primeval came out of the centuries to invest a prudential policy with the glamour of a crusade. If a man stands on the left bank of the Rhine facing the Taunus hills, he is looking away from Roman Germany to a land which was never settled by Rome. The eagles marched through the forests beyond the river, but they did not remain there, and that strong civilization which is the fibre of the Western world never took root and flourished. The thickets and plains running to the northern seas remained the home of aboriginal gods. It is long since the woods were thinned and the plains tilled, but the healing and illuminating and formative forces of the great Mediterranean culture, though their aspect might be simulated, were never reborn in the hearts of the people. The North remained a thing incalculable and unreclaimed, and its ancient deities might sleep but did not die. Some day, as Heine in 1834 told France, they would rise from their graves to the undoing of Europe.

...This "religion of valour" was not without its magnificence. In its essentials it was such a creed as might have been preached by some Old Testament warrior or some English Ironside. Like all doctrines which have moved the hearts of men, it was based not on whole falsehoods but on half truths. To many of its devotees it seemed the salt needed to save the world from putrefaction. As against the slack-lipped individualism of the West it set man's supreme duty to the State; instead of a barren freedom it offered that richer life which comes from service. It demanded immense vitality, immense discipline, immense self-sacrifice. The poetry in it seemed to some the necessary antidote to the materialism of Germany's success. "Technical science and inward culture, or even human happiness, have little connection with each other. In the midst of vast technical achievements, it is possible for humanity to sink back into complete barbarism." It embodied the longing of a race to express its national exaltation in heroic deeds. Its weakness lay in the fact that this expression of national self-consciousness was conceived as possible only at the expense of other people. Sacrifice and discipline were enjoined upon the German citizen as duties to his State, hut the attitude of the German State towards its neighbours was one of brigandage and licence. The respect for law, which was laid down as the first virtue of the individual, was banished from the intercourse of nations. It may be true that "la petite morale" is the enemy of "la grande"; but the higher ethics of Germany turned out on inquiry to be merely the higher selfishness. Race pride, a noble thing in its way, degenerated fast into a kind of mania. The Germans were God's chosen people and dare not refuse their destiny. All that was good in other lands derived from Teutonic culture. The nations who cavilled at Germany's just pretensions must be made to kiss her feet. She was unpopular throughout the globe because of her greatness, but that mattered nothing, for she would conquer her ill-wishers. *Oderint dum metuant.*

There is no sentence in Burke more often quoted than that which forbids us to draw an indictment against a nation. But the dictum must not be pressed too far. A nation can have national vices; it can blunder as a community; and it is permitted now and then to fasten guilt upon the corporate existence which we call a people. Very notably a people may go mad, when its governing elements fall into a pathological state and see strange visions. A malign spirit broods over the waters. Something which cannot be put into exact words flits at the back of men's minds. Perspective goes, exultation fires the fancy, the old decencies of common sense are repudiated, men speak with tongues not their own. That viewless thing which we call national spirit is tainted with insanity. The mania which now afflicted Germany can be best described by the French phrase, *folie de grandeur.* As such it must be distinguished from that other vice of success, *la gloire.* The great leaders of history – Julius Caesar, Charlemagne, Cromwell, Gustavus Adolphus, Washington – have as a rule striven for a political or religious ideal which made mere fame of no account in their eyes. Others, like Alexander, have been possessed by a passion for glory, and have blazed like comets athwart the world. The perfect example is Charles XII of Sweden, who in his short career of nineteen years followed glory alone, and drew no material benefit from his conquests. In his old clothes he shook down monarchies and won thrones for other men. Glory may be a futile quest, but it has a splendour and a generosity which raise it beyond the level of low and earthy things. Its creed is Napoleon's: "J'avais le goût de la fondation et non celui de la propriété. Ma propriété à moi était dans la gloire et la célebrité"; and to the end of time it will be an infirmity of minds which are not ignoble. But *grandeur* is a perversion, an offence against our essential humanity. It may be the degeneration of a genius like Napoleon, but more often it is the illusion of excited mediocrities. It is of the earth earthy, intoxicating itself with flamboyant material dreams. Its heroics are mercantile, and the cloud palaces which it builds have the vulgarity of a fashionable hotel. It seeks a city made with hands and heavily upholstered. Its classic exponents were those leaden vulgarians, the early Roman Emperors, of the worst of whom Renan wrote: "He resembled what a modern tradesman of the middle class would be whose good sense was perverted by reading modern poets, and who deemed it necessary to make his conduct resemble that of Han of Iceland or the Burgraves." *Grandeur* has always vulgarity in its fibre, vulgarity and madness.

It would be an error to regard this obsession as universal among the German people. There were millions of plain men to whom the word "kultur" was unknown, and to whom *Deutschtum* stood only for homely and honourable things. They had no hankering after conquest and would accept no war except one of self-defence. Before such it was necessary for any bellicose government to pose as the aggrieved and not as the aggressor. There were some, too, in all classes who had diagnosed the national madness and suffered a disillusion, like Caliban's:

> "*What a thrice-double ass*
> *Was I, to take this drunkard for a god,*
> *And worship this dull fool!*"

But the perversion had the governing classes in its grip; specious arguments, consonant to the German temper, could be found to rally the waverers; and even those who would have shrunk from a bald statement of the creed had their minds subconsciously attuned to it. The thing was in the intellectual air, men absorbed it through every pore, and it was certain that once the barques of war were launched it would rise like a mighty wind to speed them on their way.

A History of the Great War, Vol. I

XXVI

Let us deal first with the vandalism which was proven and admitted – the destruction of old and beautiful cities. Louvain was the chief university town of Belgium, and one of the intellectual centres of Catholic Europe. Even more than Oxford it whispered from its spires "the last enchantments of the Middle Age." Its town hall was the most miraculous of the many miracles of Gothic architecture which adorned the Belgian plain. Its university was one of the oldest in Europe, and contained in its library riches of *incunabula* and manuscripts befitting a city which was associated with More and Erasmus. Its Church of St Peter was full of treasures of painting and carving, and the fabric itself in its solemn simplicity rose majestically above the cluster of ancient dusky streets. On the evening of 25th August, while the Belgian front was about ten miles distant, there was an outburst of rifle fire in the town, and several Germans were hit. The Germans announced that it was the outcome of a plot among the civilian populace, instigated by the Belgian Government; the Belgians declared that a detachment of Germans, driven back from Malines, was fired upon in mistake by the German troops of occupation. Such were the two tales; we need only add that the first was weakened by the fact that the Civic Guard of Louvain had already been disarmed, and the rifles in the town hunted out and confiscated; while the probability of the second was heightened by the proven circumstance that many of the German garrison were drunk. A certain Major von Manteuffel, an unworthy bearer of a famous name – was in command, and he gave the order for the destruction of the city. It was done as systematically as the condition of the soldiers allowed. Small incendiary tablets and faggots soaked in paraffin were flung in through the broken windows. Houses were entered and assiduously looted, what could not be carried away being smashed and flung into the streets. Presently much of the city was ablaze. The university disappeared, and with it the great library...

A History of the Great War, Vol. I

XXVII

Termonde, which Marlborough had captured in his wars, was another historic town lying between Ghent and Malines, on the banks of the Scheldt. Unhappily it too had treasures in stone and lime – the Church of Notre Dame, with its paintings by Vandyck and Rubens, and its exquisite town hall. It was the theatre of desperate fighting during the first fortnight of September, but its destruction was not due to any battle. It was deliberately smashed to pieces during the German occupation because the fine levied upon it was not immediately forthcoming. Of all the Belgian cities, its fate perhaps was the direst, for almost literally it was levelled with the ground. Small wonder, for the burning was most scientifically managed. The houses were first sprayed with paraffin by soldiers, who perambulated the streets with oil-carts and hoses.

To cite Louvain, Malines, and Termonde is only to mention the most famous instances of destruction. Hundreds of little villages were laid waste, towns like Alost and Dinant were wantonly bombarded, and scarcely any part of this vandalism was imposed upon the invaders by military needs. Let us be very clear on this subject. War is a stern taskmistress, and will not be denied. If a famous church happens to be in the field of fire of an army in battle, the church must go. No aesthetic compunction can be allowed to interfere with strategical necessities. But only a small part of the demolition of Belgian cities was done for the purposes of military operations. Louvain was destroyed by the Germans at their leisure, while they were the force in occupation. Malines and Termonde were bombarded apparently out of pique, for the Belgians did not defend them. As for Dinant, it is hard to see what purpose was served by the ruin of its pleasant streets and the quaint church which lay in the nook of its cliffs. The Saxon army, who did the work, crossed the Meuse without difficulty, and did all their fighting on the farther bank. The only apparent motive was the inspiration of terror in the conquered, that the task of the future masters might be easy. Civilized war respects non-combatants, and not less those inanimate non-combatants, the great fabrics of the past. But this was not civilized war.

We come next to the subject of looting. Every town which was shelled or burned, and many which were not, were made the object of a comprehensive robbery. Little places were plundered down to the last sheet and florin. Now, looting was once the perquisite of the victors, but it had long been interdicted in civilized warfare. Soldiers, of course, break out occasionally and loot; but they are disobeying orders, and suffer for it. But the German soldier did not break loose and disobey; he was too well drilled by the machine. The looting of the Belgian cities would have been impossible had it not been permitted and instigated by the officers in command. They turned their men free, and human nature, which is eternally acquisitive, did the rest.

Last comes the subject which made of this war a nightmare, and recalled the days of Tilly and Wallenstein – the murder and outrage done upon civilian non-combatants. Even after all doubtful cases are discarded – and the world for months was full of wild legends – there remains a long catalogue of proven outrages, many of which Germany admitted by the nature of her defence. She did not deny; she justified, and apparently believed sincerely in the justice of her plea. The bare facts – whatever the condonation – were, roughly, these. At Louvain there was a great deal of wholesale shooting of civilians – men, women, and children. At Aerschot there was something not unlike a massacre.

A History of the Great War, Vol. I

XXVIII

There have been various pleas in extenuation. One is that the Germans did not choose to treat armed civilians according to the ordinary laws of war, and they included the Belgian Civic Guard in this category. They simply did not accept the findings of the Hague Conventions on the subject. What their theory of war was we shall presently consider; but – difficult as it is to understand – it allowed them to do things which other nations chose to regard as monstrous. This is, of course, not a defence, but it affords a partial explanation on other grounds than mere inherent brutality. A second is that there was a great deal of heavy drinking among the troops – an explanation again, not an excuse. German peasants swilled heavy red wine with the same freedom with which they were used to drink light beer, and the results were disastrous. Having said so much, the fact remains that in many cases there was a carnival of sheer murder which excelled the sack of Magdeburg and other seventeenth-century horrors. Let us accept for a moment the German explanation of Louvain and Aerschot, and admit that they were treacherously shot at by one or more of the inhabitants. Did the punishment – the burning and looting of the town and wholesale murder and outrage – show any reasonable proportion to the crime? The plea is preposterous. It may be expedient that one man die for the people, but not that the people die for one or two men. The doctrine of collective responsibility might conceivably, if modestly interpreted, be used in war. The Roman penalty of "decimation" was such a use. It is barbarous and, to modern eyes, unjust, but it might be defended. But a holocaust by way of atonement has no sort of relation to any civilized code of justice. In barbarous armies, like Timour's or Attila's, we see how it happens. There you are dealing with elementary beings, savages inflamed and maddened by conquest. But this was the most modern of armies springing from the most modern of fatherlands, which had long vaunted to the world its civilization. Louvain and Aerschot were the fruit not of sudden passion but of a long-accepted doctrine.

A doctrine, let it be remembered, an "armed dogma" of the kind against which Burke warned the world. The ordinary German is not naturally cruel or brutal. He behaved badly in 1815, as we know from Wellington; but he conducted himself well on the whole in 1870. The authors of the atrocities were mostly Landwehr troops, many of them decent fathers of families and respectable *bourgeois*. There are blackguards in every army who now and then get out of hand, but it is impossible to think of the majority of these German troops as naturally blackguards. They carried in their knapsacks letters from their own Gretchens and Gertruds, and had set out with high notions about warring for their land and its "kultur." Yet the result of their campaigning was Louvain. How is it to be explained? Partly, no doubt, by panic – the fear of nervous, excitable folk in the midst of a hostile country; but mainly by the German doctrine of war. Their leaders had evolved an inhuman creed which they practised with the rigidity of Brahmins, and the disciplined troops acted as they were bid. Presently drink and bloodshed did their work, and what began as obedience to orders ended as a debauch.

The unhappy consequence of those deeds in France and Belgium was to destroy among the Allies the chivalrous respect for their opponents which is one of the antiseptics of war – that feeling which found expression in Whitman's cry, "My enemy is dead, a man divine as myself is dead." It is necessary to be very precise in our charges. Every nation at war believes evil things about its opponents, and takes for premeditated crimes what are merely the incidents of campaigning. Therefore we must confine ourselves to the outrages which are fully substantiated and incapable of being explained away as mistakes. Germany, again, broke many of the conventions of international law which she herself had formally accepted, but on these more abstract questions it is not worth while to argue. It matters little how many of the Hague rules she violated, since she altogether repudiated the bondage of international obligations. What is vital is the German breaches of laws, written and unwritten, which lie at the very root of civilized warfare. It is possible to imagine a Power, with Machiavellian notions about public conduct, and loose ideas about the rights of neutrals, who in the greater matters would fight with reasonable decency. But it is a different thing if she offends against those elementary human conventions which are observed by many savages and by all who claim the title of civilized. It is indubitable that Germany so offended, not once or twice, but with a consistency which argued a reasoned policy. The tradition of the German machine did not frown upon outrages; it favoured them.

A History of the Great War, Vol. 1

XXIX

...The German answer – always implied and often explicitly stated – was that they did not accept any laws of war which were against their interests. In the pride of those early days all classes, from the ordinary junker to intellectuals like Maximillian Harden, laughed and shrugged their shoulders at tales of outrage, even when they suspected that they might be true. Such things, they said, would be forgotten when they had conquered. They claimed to be a law to themselves, and if other people did not like it it was their business to show themselves stronger than the Germans. To this it might be replied that such anarchism was, to say the least of it, bad policy. Clausewitz long ago warned his countrymen that it was "inexpedient" to do anything to outrage the general moral sense of other peoples, and the great men who made the German Empire, Bismarck and Moltke, were tireless in their efforts to keep right with European opinion. For if no law is acknowledged, no conventions and codes of honour, then this lawlessness will certainly be turned some day against the law-breakers themselves. No land will make an alliance with them or a treaty if their views on the duty of obligations are so notoriously lax. But the main point is that this crude lawlessness illustrated an interesting characteristic of what was then in Germany the governing mind – its curious immaturity. That mind was like a child's which simplifies too much. As we grow up we advance in complexity; we see half-tones where before we saw only harsh blacks and whites; we realize that nothing is quite alone, that everything is interrelated, and we become shy of bold simplicities. The mechanical may be simple; the organic must be complex and manifold. It sounds so easy to say, like the villain in melodrama, that you will own no code except what you make yourself; but it really cannot be done. It was not that the rejection of half a dozen of the diffuse findings of the Hague Tribunal mattered much; what signified was the disregard of the unformulated creed which penetrates every part of our modern life – Germany's too, in her sober, non-martial moments. To massacre a hundred unarmed people because one man has fired off a rifle may be enjoined by some half-witted military theorist, but it is fundamentally inhuman and silly. It offends not only the heart of mankind, but against their common sense. It is not even virilely wicked. It lacks intelligence. It is merely childish.

A History of the Great War, Vol. I

XXX

The impression left by the spectacle of the wonderful machine, the proudest achievement of the modern German spirit, with its astonishing efficiency up to a point, its evidence of unwearied care and endless industry, remained oddly childish, like a toy on the making of which a passion of affection has been lavished. It was a perversion, an aberration, not a healthy development from the great Germany of the past. The man who can devise the campaign of Trafalgar is not the man who is always busy about the brasswork. Undue care is, not less than slovenliness, a sign of the immature and unbalanced mind. And the profession of a morality above all humble conventions, so far from impressing the world as godlike, seemed nothing but the swagger of a hobbledehoy. It was not barbarism, which is an honest and respectable thing; it was decivilization, which stands to civilization as a man's decay stands to his prime.

A History of the Great War, Vol. I

DEMOCRACY

XXXI

Lincoln fought to prevent Democracy making a fool of itself, and if that noble but most brittle type of polity is to be preserved to the world, we have not done with the fight. To most of his colleagues it seemed a mere debating issue, an absurdly narrow ground on which to plunge the nation into war; but I am inclined to think that every great decision in history has been taken on a fine point. The foothold may be narrow, but if it be of granite it will suffice.

Homilies and Recreations: Two Ordeals of Democracy

XXXII

...Democracy as a form of government is subject to a perpetual challenge, not from foreign enemies alone, but from foes within its own household. Liberty demands a close and unremitting guardianship. The leaders of a democracy must be prepared to do battle with false causes which profess to fight under the democratic banner. They must be prepared to speak the truth unflinchingly to their peoples, and shun that shallow sentiment and confidence in loud formulas which is their special temptation. They must be ready to make decisions far more difficult than any which can confront an oligarchy or a tyrant. They must be willing for the sake of true liberty to wage war upon licence. America faced the ordeal, and because she faced it manfully and clear-sightedly she emerged triumphant. It is an ordeal with which at any time the world may be again confronted. If it should be our fate to meet anew that fiery trial, may God send us the same clearness of vision and stalwartness of purpose.

Homilies and Recreations: Two Ordeals of Democracy

PURITANISM

XXXIII

Puritanism was neither an ecclesiastical system nor a theological creed. Calvinism, with its doctrine of "exclusive salvation," was, at first, the belief of Anglican and Presbyterian alike, and it remained the prevailing creed of the Puritan party as of the bulk of their opponents – rejected only by Laud's Arminian school, and by sects like the Baptists and the Quakers. The most powerful statement of Puritan theology will be found in Anglican divines like Donne; no Scottish Covenanter ever dwelt more terribly upon original sin, the torments of hell, and the awe of eternity. Nor was the Puritan either a very learned and subtle theologian, or a profound expositor of his own ecclesiastical tastes. When a man of

Milton's genius embarks upon doctrinal questions he is "in wandering mazes lost," like the evil spirits in *Paradise Lost,* who sat on a hill and debated predestination. For wisdom, breadth of knowledge, and logical acumen, no Puritan champion can vie with Hooker, Chillingworth, John Hales, and Jeremy Taylor – few even reach the standard of Laud.

Puritanism was above all things the result of a profound spiritual experience in the Puritan. It is to John Bunyan and George Fox that we must go if we would learn the strength of the faith. The questioning of the epoch resulted for such men in an overwhelming sense of sin and an overpowering consciousness of God; their knowledge, in Cromwell's famous words, was not "literal and speculative, but inward and transforming the mind to it." Unless we realize this primary fact we cannot explain why so many diverse creeds were ultimately conjoined to form one conquering temperament. Inevitably the faith and the practice narrowed and hardened. Sunday, the day on which Calvin played bowls and John Knox gave supper parties, became the Jewish Sabbath, and the Mosaic law in many of its most irrelevent details was incorporated with the Christian creed. Toleration was impossible for men who saw life as a narrow path through a land shaken by the fires of hell; only kindred communions were tolerated, save by those few sects who, from hard experience, had learned a gentler rule. A limited number inclined to a complete separation of Church and State, but the majority desired a purified State, which would be the ally and the servant of the Church. They rejected the world of sense, for there could be no innocency in what had been corrupted by Adam's sin, and their eyes were fixed austerely upon their own souls. The strength of Puritanism lay in its view of the direct relation of God and man; its weakness in the fact that this relation was narrowly and often shallowly construed. The Puritan became, by his severe abstraction, a dangerous element in society and the State, since human institutions are built upon half-truths, opportunisms, and compromises. He was pre-eminently a destructive force, for he was without the historical sense, and sought less to erect and unite than to pull down and separate. Milton's words might be taken as his creed: "By His divorcing command the world first rose out of chaos; nor can be renewed again out of confusion but by the separating of unmeet consorts."

With the Puritans, as with the Cavaliers, many streams from remote wells were in the end canalized into a single channel. The mood of those who accepted the natural world as the gift of God was set against that which saw that world as conceived in sin and shapen in iniquity; the ancient institutions of the realm, which to the mind of the Cavalier should be reformed, but in substance retained, were opposed to a clean page on which men could write what they pleased; the conception of the State as a thing of balances and adjustments was met by a theory of government as an abstract ideal to be determined mainly by the half-understood words of an old book; the free exercise of men's conscience in religion was confronted with a denial of freedom except to those of a certain way of thinking. The truth is that the Puritan was hampered both in civil and ecclesiastical statesmanship by that intense individualism which was also his strength. His creed was not social or readily communicable –

> "*...a dark lanthorn of the spirit,*
> *Which none see by but those who bear it.*"

To him, as to Newman in his youth, the world was narrowed to "two and two only, supreme and luminously self-evident beings" – himself and his Creator.

If we put the contrast thus, it would seem that generosity and enlightenment were predominantly on the side of the Cavaliers. But it must not be forgotten that, owing to the spiritual atmosphere of the age and the tendency in such a conflict to narrower and yet narrower definition, the common creed of Puritanism did not fairly represent the best men in its ranks. Had Hampden and Falkland ever argued on fundamentals they might well have found themselves in substantial agreement. The difference, as the struggle progressed, came to lie far less in creeds than in the moods behind them, and the Puritan mood, solemn under the Almighty's eye, austere, self-centred, unhumorous, unbending, was more formidable and more valuable than their crude apologetics. Its spiritual profundity was as rich a bequest to the future as the saner and sunnier temper of the Cavalier. The difference between the best men of the two parties was a fine one – the exact border-line between the king's prerogative and popular liberties in Church and State; but most great contests in the world's history have been fought on narrow margins. And in practice the narrowness disappeared, and the divergence was glaring. For the Cavalier, with his reasoned doctrine of a central authority based on historical sanctions, had to define that authority as the king, and that king not an ideal monarch, but an actual person then living in Whitehall. The Puritan, who might have dissented reluctantly from the abstract argument, was very ready to differ about Charles.

Montrose

XXXIV

Thank God, we shall always have both conservatives and radicals among us, for they represent eternally the two sides of the human head. Both defend a truth which is not all the truth.

Homilies and Recreations: The Old and the New Literature

XXXV

...At certain stages in the world's history destruction, wholesale and single-hearted destruction, has been the one thing needful. In certain crises, when something evil has to be rooted out, moderation and toleration may be synonyms for moral apathy and spiritual sloth. Men cannot be led to a worthy purpose by one who has his flag firmly nailed to the fence. Yet – and this rule has no exception – the extremist will only be a constructive as well as a destroying force if his extremism is based upon reason, and not upon the surrender of reason – upon a clear facing of facts, and not upon their emotional simplification. We dare not underrate the power of fanaticism, even of the craziest kind. Its strength comes from its narrowness, since its spiritual force has been canalized and brought to a mighty head of water. It has done great things in history, but these things have been principally negative – necessary negations often, but still negations. Moreover, there is no finality about its work, for there is always the certainty that it will produce a counter-fanaticism, since it is based upon a half-truth, and the world will find this out. An arbitrary conception of the Divine will induce a blind denial of its existence at all. A fanatic glorification of the State will produce as its corrective a fanatic individualism. Therefore I suggest to you that the moderate is the more valuable type of leader, for, while the other type may do wonderful work in pulling down a crazy structure, it is he who has the constructive task and builds a new home for mankind. The Beatitude of the Meek, in the Sermon on the Mount, is true in the most literal and practical sense. It is the meek, the moderates, who inherit the earth.

Men and Deeds: Essay on Montrose and Leadership

THE MODERATE MAN

XXXVI

The moderate man is slow to appeal to arms. He sees too clearly the values on both sides to commit himself readily to that desperate hazard. But in a revolution it may be the only way. If men's passions are deeply stirred there must be recourse to the last and sternest arbitrament. In such a crisis it is the soldier who turns the scale, whether it be Caesar's army of Gaul, or the Puritan New Model, or Washington's militia, or Napoleon's Grande Armée, or

Garibaldi's Thousand, or Lincoln's citizen levies. A Holles or a Vane may dream his dreams, but it is Cromwell who brings his into being. Montrose both courted and warred against revolution. He desired to preserve the monarchy as against its anarchical assailants, but he was as ardent a revolutionary as Lilburne in his crusade against the existing régime in Scotland, with its dull tyranny of kirk and nobles. For there is a moderation which is in itself a fire, where enthusiasm burns as fiercely for the whole truth as it commonly does for half-truths, where toleration becomes not a policy but an act of religion. Such inspired moderation is usually found in an age of violent contraries. Henri IV of France possessed it, as did William the Silent. Montrose, like Henri, was the supreme moderate of his age; and, like Henri, he realized that it needs a fiery soul to enforce moderation in a rabble of fanatics and debauchees. In such a strife, the ultimate word can only be spoken by one who is willing to make the ultimate sacrifice. To enter into the kingdom of the spirit a man must take his life in his hands, as martyr or as soldier.

XXXVII

...The moderate can never be a barren dogmatist. He does not spend his time, like Sir Walter Scott's Old Mortality, in deepening the inscriptions on tombstones. He realizes that there are eternal truths, but that they require a frequent restatement; and he knows that most of our rules of life are not eternal truths, but working conventions, which must often be drastically overhauled to make certain that they have not survived their usefulness. But at the same time he will not underrate the value of the inscriptions on tombstones, and he will treat reverently whatever has been an inspiration to mankind, till the last dregs of inspiration have departed.

Men and Deeds: Montrose and Leadership

PAST AND FUTURE

VXXXVIII

...In the disordered crowd of a boy's dreams, we may discern, I fancy, two notable features. He is all for the past, the bond slave of associations, hustled about by every vagrant memory. It is indeed curious to mark how lovingly a child will think on his bygones, recalling every feature of the way he has travelled, and seeking aids to memory in every circumstance of life. Then, again, he is cognisant of the present in an eager, wondering fashion; always on the alert for new experience; a seeker after hid treasure, confident of the issue and flushed with hope. These are, it seems to me, the twin and kindred graces of childhood – bondage to the past, and high expectation for the future.

For, to be the slave of yesterday is, not to speak it flippantly, to be the lord of today and master of tomorrow. To be tenderly affectioned to the past is the surest way of becoming tolerant of the present, and he who has reached this height is not wont to be despondent about the rest of the journey.

The Scholar Gypsies

XXXIX

"*Nevermore the deep fern...or the bell of the dun deer, for my castle is wind-blown sands, and my homelands are a stranger's.* And the air brought back in a flash my own little house on the grey hill-sides of Douglasdale, the cluck of hens about the doors on a hot summer morn, the crying of plovers in the windy Aprils, the smell of peat-smoke when the snow drifted over Cairntable. Homesickness has never been my failing, but all at once I had a vision of my own land, the cradle of my race, well-beloved and unforgotten over the leagues of seas. Somehow the thought strengthened me... If all hell laid hold on me, I must stand fast for the honour of my own folk.

Salute to Adventurers

CHAPTER VIII

POEMS

FRATRI DILECTISSIMO
FROM THE PENTLANDS, LOOKING NORTH AND SOUTH
THE GIPSY'S SONG TO THE LADY CASSILIS
AVIGNON, 1759
WOOD MAGIC
AN ECHO OF MELAEAGER
THE MAGIC WALKING-STICK
THINGS TO REMEMBER
THE FORERUNNERS
QU'APPELLE?
HOME THOUGHTS FROM ABROAD
FISHER JAMIE

I

FRATRI DILECTISSIMO
W H B

When we were little wandering boys,
  And every hill was blue and high,
On ballad ways and martial joys
  We fed our fancies, you and I.
With Bruce we crouched in bracken shade,
  With Douglas charged the Paynim foes;
And oft in moorland noons I played
  Colkitto to your grave Montrose.

The obliterating seasons flow –
  They cannot kill our boyish game.
Though creeds may change and kings may go,
  Yet burns undimmed the ancient flame.
While young men in their pride make haste
  The wrong to right, the bond to free,
And plant a garden in the waste,
  Still rides our Scottish chivalry.

Another end had held your dream –
  To die fulfilled of hope and might,
To pass in one swift rapturous gleam
  From mortal to immortal light –

But through long hours of labouring breath
  You watched the world grow small and far,
And met the constant eyes of Death,
  And haply knew how kind they are.
One boon the Fates relenting gave –
  Not where the scented hill-wind blows
From cedar thickets lies your grave,
  Nor 'mid the steep Himālayan snows.
Night calls the stragglers to the nest,
  And at long last, 'tis home indeed
For your far-wandering feet to rest
  Forever by the crooks of Tweed.

In perfect honour, perfect truth,
  And gentleness to all mankind,
You trod the golden paths of youth,
  Then left the world and youth behind.
Ah no! 'Tis we who fade and fail –
  And you from Time's slow torments free
Shall pass from strength to strength and scale
  The steeps of immortality.

Dear heart, in that serener air,
  If blessed souls may backward gaze,
Some slender nook of memory spare
  For our old happy moorland days.
I sit alone, and musing fills
  My breast with pain that shall not die,
Till once again o'er greener hills
  We ride together, you and I.

The Marquis of Montrose (1912)

II

FROM THE PENTLANDS, LOOKING NORTH AND SOUTH

Around my feet the clouds are drawn
  In the cold mystery of the dawn;
No breezes cheer, no guests intrude
  My mossy, mist-clad solitude;
When sudden down the steeps of sky
  Flames a long, lightening wind. On high
The steel-blue arch shines clear, and far,
  In the low lands where cattle are,
Towns smoke. And swift, a haze, a gleam, –
  The Firth lies like a frozen stream,
Reddening with morn. Tall spires of ships,
  Like thorns about the harbour's lips,
Now shake faint canvas, now, asleep,
  Their salt, uneasy slumbers keep;
While golden-grey o'er kirk and wall
  Day wakes in the ancient capital.
Before me lie the lists of strife,
  The caravanserai of life,
Whence from the gates the merchants go
  On the world's highways; to and fro
Sail laden ships; and in the street
  The lone foot-traveller shakes his feet,
And in some corner by the fire
  Tells the old tale of heart's desire.
Thither from alien seas and skies
  Comes the far-quested merchandise: –
Wrought silks of Broussa, Mocha's ware
  Brown-tinted, fragrant, and the rare
Thin perfumes that the rose's breath
  Has sought, immortal in her death:

Gold, gems, and spice, and haply still
  The red rough largesse of the hill
Which takes the sun and bears the vines
  Among the haunted Apennines.
And he who treads the cobbled street
  Today in the cold North may meet,
Come month, come year, the dusky East,
  And share the Caliph's secret feast;
Or in the toil of wind and sun
  Bear pilgrim-staff, forlorn, fordone,
Till o'er the steppe, athwart the sand,
  Gleam the far gates of Samarkand.
The ringing quay, the weathered face,
  Fair skies, dusk hands, the ocean race,
The palm-girt isle, the frosty shore,
  Gales and hot suns the wide world o'er,
Grey North, red South, and burnished West,
  The goals of the old tireless quest,
Leap in the smoke, immortal free,
  Where shines yon morning fringe of sea.

I turn; – how still the moorlands lie,
  Sleep-locked beneath the awakening sky!
The film of morn is silver-grey
  On the young heather, and away,
Dim, distant, set in ribs of hill,
  Green glens are shining, stream and mill,
Clachan and kirk and garden-ground,
  All silent in the hush profound
Which haunts alone the hills' recess,
  The antique home of quietness.
Nor to the folk can piper play
  The tune of "Hills and Far Away,"
For they are with them. Morn can fire
  No peaks of weary heart's desire,

Nor the red sunset flame behind
  Some ancient ridge of longing mind.
For Arcady is here, around,
  In lilt of stream, in the clear sound
Of lark and moorbird, in the bold
  Gay glamour of the evening gold.
And so the wheel of seasons moves
  To kirk and market, to mild loves
And modest hates, and still the sight
  Of brown kind faces, and when night
Draws dark around with age and fear
  Theirs is the simple hope to cheer.
A land of peace where lost romance
  And ghostly shine of helm and lance
Still dwell by castled scarp and lea
  And the lost homes of chivalry,
And the good fairy folk, my dear,
  Who speak for cunning souls to hear,
In crook of glen and bower of hill
  Sing of the Happy Ages still.

O Thou to whom man's heart is known,
  Grant me my morning orison.
Grant me the rover's path – to see
  The dawn arise, the daylight flee,
In the far wastes of sand and sun!
  Grant me with venturous heart to run
On the old highway, where in pain
  And ecstasy man strives amain,
Outstrips his fellows, or, too weak,
  Finds the great rest that wanderers seek!
Grant me the joy of wind and brine,
  The zest of food, the taste of wine,
The fighter's strength, the echoing strife,
  The high tumultuous lists of life –

May I ne'er lag, nor hapless fall,
  Nor weary at the battle-call!...
And when the even brings surcease,
  Grant me the happy moorland peace;
That in my heart's depth ever lie
  That ancient land of heath and sky,
Where the old rhymes and stories fall
  In kindly, soothing pastoral.
There in the hills grave silence lies,
  And Death himself wears friendly guise;
There be my lot, my twilight stage,
  Dear city of my pilgrimage.

Poems, Scots and English (1898)

III

THE GIPSY'S SONG TO THE LADY CASSILIS

"Whereupon the Faas, coming down from the Gates of Galloway, did so bewitch my lady that she forgat husband and kin, and followed the tinkler's piping." –

Chap-book of the *Raid of Cassilis.*

The door is open to the wall,
  The air is bright and free;
Adown the stair, across the hall,
  And then – the world and me;
The bare grey bent, the running stream,
  The fire beside the shore;
And we will bid the hearth farewell,
  And never seek it more,
My love,
  And never seek it more.

And you shall wear no silken gown,
  No maid shall bind your hair;

The yellow broom shall be your gem,
  Your braid the heather rare.
Athwart the moor, adown the hill,
  Across the world away;
The path is long for happy hearts
  That sing to greet the day,
My love,
  That sing to greet the day.
When morning cleaves the eastern grey,
  And the lone hills are red;
When sunsets light the evening way
  And birds are quieted;
In autumn noon and springtide dawn
  By hill and dale and sea,
The world shall sing its ancient song
  Of hope and joy for thee,
My love,
  Of hope and joy for thee.

And at the last no solemn stole
  Shall on thy breast be laid;
No mumbling priest shall speed thy soul,
  No charnel vault thee shade.
But by the shadowed hazel copse,
  Aneath the greenwood tree,
Where airs are soft and waters sing,
  Thou'lt ever sleep by me,
My love,
  Thou'lt ever sleep by me.

Poems, Scots and English (1898)

IV
AVIGNON
1759

Hearts to break but nane to sell,
Gear to tine but nane to hain; –
We maun dree a weary spell
Ere our lad comes back again.

I walk abroad on winter days,
When storms have stripped the wide champaign,
For northern winds have norland ways,
And scents of Badenoch haunt the rain.
And by the lipping river path,
When in the fog the Rhone runs grey,
I see the heather of the strath,
And watch the salmon leap in Spey.

The hills are feathered with young trees, –
I set them for my children's boys.
I made a garden deep in ease,
A pleasance for my lady's joys.
Strangers have heired them. Long ago
She died – kind fortune thus to die;
And my one son by Beauly flow
Gave up the soul that could not lie.

Old, elbow-worn, and pinched I bide
The final toll the gods may take,
The laggard years have quenched my pride;
They cannot kill the ache, the ache.
Weep not the dead, for they have sleep
Who lie at home; but ah, for me
In the deep grave my heart will weep
With longing for my lost countrie.

Hearts to break but nane to sell,
Gear to tine but nane to hain; –
We maun dree a weary spell
Ere our lad comes back again.

Poems, Scots and English (1911)

V

WOOD MAGIC
(Ninth Century)

I will walk warily in the wise woods on the fringes of eventide,
For the covert is full of noises and the stir of nameless things.
I have seen in the dusk of the beeches the shapes of the lords that ride,
And down in the marish hollow I have heard the lady who sings.
And once in an April gloaming I met a maid on the sward,
All marble-white and gleaming and tender and wild of eye; –
I, Jehan the hunter, who speak am a grown man, middling hard
But I dreamt a month of the maid, and wept I knew not why.

Down by the edge of the firs, in a coppice of heath and vine,
Is an old moss-grown altar, shaded by briar and bloom,
Denys, the priest, hath told me 'twas the lord Apollo's shrine
In the days ere Christ came down from God to the Virgin's womb.
I never go past but I doff my cap and avert my eyes –
(Were Denys to catch me I trow I'd do penance for half a year) –
For once I saw a flame there and the smoke of a sacrifice,
And a voice spake out of the thicket that froze my soul with fear.

Wherefore to God the Father, the Son, and the Holy Ghost,
Mary the Blessed Mother, and the kindly Saints as well,

I will give glory and praise, and them I cherish the most,
For they have the keys of Heaven, and save the soul from Hell.
But likewise I will spare for the lord Apollo a grace,
And a bow for the Lady Venus – as a friend but not as a thrall.
'Tis true they are out of Heaven, but some day they may win the place;
For gods are kittle cattle, and a wise man honours them all.

Poems, Scots and English (1911)

VI
AN ECHO OF MELAEAGER

Scorn not my love, proud child. The summers wane.
Long ere the topmost mountain snows have gone
The Spring is fleeting; 'neath the April rain
For one brief day flowers laugh on Helicon.
The breeze that fans thy honeyed cheek this noon
Tomorrow will be blasts that scourge the main,
And youth and joy and laughter fleet too soon. –
Scorn not my love, proud child. The summers wane.

Today the rose blooms by the garden plot,
The swallows twitter 'neath the Parian dome;
But soon the roses fall and lie forgot,
And soon the swallows will be turning home.
Tempt not the arrows of the Cyprian's eye,
Vex not the god that will not brook disdain; –
Love is the port to which the wise barks fly.
Scorn not my love, proud child. The summers wane.

Poems, Scots and English (1910)

VII
THE MAGIC WALKING-STICK

"Magic," gasped the dull of mind,
  When the harnessed earth and skies
Drew the nomads of their kind
  To uncharted emperies –
Whispers round the globe were sped,
  Construed was the planets' song.

But the little boy playing in the orchard said,
  Conning his tale in the orchard said,
  "*I knew it all along.*"
Power deduced from powerless dust,
  Nurture from the infertile grave;
Much the years may hold in trust,
  Space a thrall and Time a slave.
Hark the boasting of the wise:
  "First are we of those that know!"

But the little boy playing by the roadside cries,
  Trundling his hoop by the roadside cries,
  "*I said it long ago.*"

The Magic Walking-Stick

VIII
THINGS TO REMEMBER

Child, if you would live at ease
  Learn these few philosophies.
If you fear a bully's frown,
  Smite him briskly on the crown.
If you're frightened of the dark,
  Go to bed without a spark

To light up the nursery stairs,
  And be sure to say your prayers.
If your pony's raw and new,
  Show that you can stick like glue.
If the fence seems castle-high,
  Throw your heart across and try.
Whatsoever risk portends,
  Face it and you'll soon be friends.

But though many perils you dare
  Mingle fortitude with care.
Do not tempt the torrent's brim
  Till you've really learned to swim.
Do not climb the mountain snow
  If inclined to vertigo.
Do not let yourself be seen
  Mother bear and cubs between;
Or essay your marksman's skill
  On a grizzly couched uphill, –
Else this mortal stage you'll leave
  And your parents fond will grieve.

The Long Traverse

IX
THE FORERUNNERS

You may follow far in the blue-goose track
  To the lands where spring is in mid-July;
You may cross to the unmapped mountains' back,
  To lakes unscanned by the trapper's eye.
You may trace to its lair the soft Chinook,
  And the North Wind trail to the Barrens' floor;
But you'll always find, or I'm much mistook,
  That some old Frenchman's done it before.

You may spirit wealth from despisèd dust,
  Gold from the refuse and gems from the spoil;
You may draw new power from the torrent's thrust,
  And bend to your use the Ocean's toil;
You may pierce to Nature's innermost nook,
  And pluck the heart of her secret lore;
But you'll always find, or I'm much mistook,
  That some old Frenchman's done it before.

You may hunt all day for the fitting word,
  The aptest phrase and the rightful tune,
Beating the wood for the magic bird,
  Dredging the pond to find the moon.
And when you escape (in the perfect book)
  From the little less and the little more,
You're sure to find, or I'm much mistook,
  That some old Frenchman's done it before.

The Long Traverse

X

QU'APPELLE?

Qu'appelle?
A whisper steals through the sunburnt grasses;
  Faint as a twilight wind it passes,
Broken and slow,
  Soft and low,
And the heart responds like a beaten bell;
  For the voice comes out of the ancient deeps
Where the blind, primordial Terror sleeps,
  And hark! It is followed by soft footfalls!
Who calls?

Qu'appelle?
What is it stirs the cedars high,
  When there is no wind in all the sky,
And plays queer tunes
  On the saskatoons,
Subtler airs than the ear can tell?
  The evening breeze? But wise men warn
That the tune and the wind are elfin-born,
  And lure the soul to uncanny things,
Who sings?

Qu'appelle?
The world is empty of stir and sound,
  Not a white fox barks in the void profound;
On the Elder Ice
  Old Silence lies,
Older than Time and deep as Hell.
  Yet a whisper creeps as a mist from a fen
Which is not the speech of articulate men,
  And the hunter flees like a startled bird.
Whose word?

The Long Traverse

XI
HOME THOUGHTS FROM ABROAD

Aifter the war, says the papers, they'll no be content at hame,
The lads that hae feucht wi' death twae 'ear i' the mud and the rain and the snaw;
For aifter a sodger's life the shop will be unco tame;
They'll ettle at fortune and freedom in the new lands far awa'.

No me!
  By God! No me!
Aince we hae hickit oor faes
  And aince I get oot o' this hell,
For the rest o' my leevin' days
  I'll make a pet o' mysel'.
I'll haste me back wi' an eident fit
  And settle again in the same auld bit.
And oh! the comfort to snowk again
  The reek o' my mither's but-and-ben,
The wee box-bed and the ingle neuk
  And the kail-pat hung frae the chimley-heuk!
I'll gang back to the shop like a laddie to play,
  Tak doun the shutters at skreigh o' day,
And weigh oot floor wi' a carefu' pride,
  And hear the clash o' the countraside.
I'll wear for ordinar' a round hard hat,
  A collar and dickey and black cravat.
If the weather's wat I'll no stir ootbye
  Wi'oot an umbrella to keep me dry.
I think I'd better no tak a wife –
  I've had a' the adventure I want in life. –
But at nicht, when the doors are steeked, I'll sit,
  While the bleeze loups high frae the aiken ruit,
And smoke my pipe aside the crook.
  And read in some douce auld-farrant book;
Or crack wi' Davie and mix a rummer,
  While the auld wife's pow nid-nods in slum'er;
And hark to the winds gaun tearin' bye
  And thank the Lord I'm sae warm and dry.

When simmer brings the lang bricht e'en,
  I'll daunder doun to the bowling-green,
Or delve my yaird and my roses tend
  For the big floo'er-show in the next back-end.

Whiles, when the sun blinks aifter rain,
  I'll tak my rod and gang up the glen;
Me and Davie, we ken the püles
  Whaur the troot grow great in the howes o' the hills;
And, wanderin' back when the gloamin' fa's
  And the midges dance in the hazel shaws,
We'll stop at the yett ayont the hicht
  And drink great wauchts o' the scented nicht,
While the hoose lamps kin'le raw by raw
  And a yellow star hings ower the law.
Davie will lauch like a wean at a fair
  And nip my airm to mak certain shüre
That we're back frae yon place o' dule and dreid,
  To oor ain kind warld –
But Davie's deid!
  Nae mair gude nor ill can betide him.
We happit him doun by Beaumont toun,
  And the half o' my heart's in the mools aside him.

Poems, Scots and English (1917)

XII
FISHER JAMIE

Puir Jamie's killed. A better lad
  Ye wadna find to husk a flee
Or burn a püle or wield a gad
  Frae Berwick to the Clints o' Dee.

And noo he's in a happier land. –
  It's Gospel truith and Gospel law
That Heaven's yett maun open stand
  To folk that for their country fa'.

But Jamie will be ill to mate;
He lo'ed nae müsic, kenned nae tünes
Except the sang o' Tweed in spate,
Or Talla loupin' ower its linns.

I sair misdoot that Jamie's heid
A croun o' gowd will never please;
He liked a kep o' decent tweed
Whaur he could stick his casts o' flees.

If Heaven is a' that man can dream
And a' that honest herts can wish,
It maun provide some muirland stream,
For Jamie dreamed o' nocht but fish.

And weel I wot he'll up and speir
In his bit blate and canty way,
Wi' kind Apostles standin' near
Whae in their time were fishers tae.

He'll offer back his gowden croun
And in its place a rod he'll seek,
And bashfu'-like his herp lay doun
And speir a leister and a cleek.

For Jim's had aye a poachin' whim;
He'll sun grow tired, wi' lawfu' flee
Made frae the wings o' cherubim,
O' castin' ower the Crystal Sea...

I picter him at gloamin' tide
Steekin' the backdoor o' his hame
And hastin' to the waterside
To play again the auld auld game,

And syne wi' saumon on his back,
  Catch't clean against the Heavenly law,
And Heavenly byliffs on his track,
  Gaun linkin' doun some Heavenly shaw.

Poems, Scots and English (1916)

CHAPTER IX

SCENES FROM NOVELS

SALUTE TO ADVENTURERS
THE BLANKET OF THE DARK
THE PATH OF THE KING
MR STANDFAST

SALUTE TO ADVENTURERS

I

A man stood out from the others, a tall savage with a hard face, who looked at me with eyes of hate. I recognized my opponent, whom the chief called by some name like Mayoga.

Before us on the hill-side across the stream was a wood, with its limits cut as clear on the meadow as a coppice in a nobleman's park. 'Twas maybe half a mile long as it stretched up the slope, and about the same at its greatest width. The shape was like a stout bean with a hollow on one side, and down the middle ran the gorge of a mountain stream.

Onotawah pointed to the wood. "Hearken, brother, to the customs of our race in such combats. In that thicket the twain of you fight. Mayoga will enter at one end and you at the other, and once among the trees it is his business to slay you as he pleases and as he can."

"What are the weapons?" I asked.

"What you please. You have a sword and your little guns."

Mayoga laughed loud. "My bow is sufficient," he cried. "See, I leave knife and tomahawk behind," and he cast them on the grass.

Not to be outdone, I took off my sword, though that was more an encumbrance than a weapon.

"I have but the two shots," I said.

"Then I will take but the two arrows," cried my opponent, shaking the rest out of his quiver; and at this there was a murmur of applause. There were some notions of decency among these Western Indians.

I bade him take a quiverful. "You will need them," said I, looking as truculent as my chicken heart would permit me.

They took me to the eastern side of the wood, and there we waited for the signal, which was a musket shot, telling me that Mayoga was ready to enter at the opposite end. My companions were friendly enough, and seemed to look on the duel as a kind of sport. I could not understand their tongue, but I fancy that they wagered among themselves on the issue, if, indeed, that was in doubt, or, at any rate, on the time before I should fall. They had forgotten that they had tortured me the night before, and one clapped me on the shoulder and seemed to encourage me. Another pointed to my raw shins, and wound some kind of soft healing fibre round my feet and ankles. I did my best to keep a stout face, and when the shot came, I waved my hand to them and plunged boldly into the leafy darkness.

But out of the presence of men my courage departed, and I became the prey of dismal fear. How was I, with my babyish woodcraft, to contend for a moment against an Indian who was as subtle and velvet-footed as a wild beast? The wood was mostly of great oaks and chestnuts, with a dense scrub of vines and undergrowth, and in the steepest parts of the hill-side many moss-grown rocks. I found every movement painful in that rough and matted place. For one thing, I made an unholy noise. My tender limbs shrank from every stone and twig, and again and again I rolled over with the pain of it. Sweat blinded my eyes, and the fatigues of yesterday made my breath labour like a foundered horse.

My first plan – if the instinct of blind terror can be called a plan – was to lie hid in some thick place and trust to getting the first shot at my enemy when he found me. But I realized that I could not do this. My broken nerves would not suffer me to lie hidden. Better the torture of movement than such terrible patience. So I groped my way on, starting at every movement in the thicket.

Once I roused a deer, which broke off in front of me towards my adversary. That would tell him my whereabouts, I thought, and for some time I lay still with a palpitating heart. But soon the silence resumed its sway, a deathlike silence, with far off the faint tinkle of water.

By and by I reached the stream, the course of which made an open space a few yards wide in the trees. The sight of its cool foaming current made me reckless. I dipped my face in it, drank deep of it, and let it flow over my burning legs. Then I scrambled up the other bank and entered my enemy's half of the wood. He had missed a fine chance, I thought, in not killing me by the water's edge; and this escape, and the momentary refreshment of the stream, heartened me enough to carry me some way into his territory.

The wood was thinner here, and the ground less cumbered. I moved from tree to tree, crawling in the open bits, and scanning each circle of green dusk before I moved. A reel bird fluttered on my right, and I lay long watching its flight. Something moved ahead of me, but 'twas only a squirrel.

Then came a mocking laugh behind me. I turned sharply, but saw nothing. Far up in the branches there sounded the slow flap of an owl's flight. Many noises succeeded, and suddenly came one which froze my blood – the harsh scream of a hawk. My enemy was playing with me, and calling the wild things to mock me.

I went on a little, and then turned up the hill to where a clump of pines made a darker patch in the woodland. All was quiet again, and my eyes searched the dusk for the sign of human life. Then suddenly I saw something which stiffened me against a trunk.

Forty paces off in the dusk a face was looking from behind a tree. It was to the west of me, and was looking downhill towards a patch of undergrowth. I noted the long feather, the black forelock, the red skin of the forehead.

At the sight for the first time the zest of the pursuit filled me, and I forgot my pain. Had I outwitted my wily foe, and by some miracle stolen a march on him? I dared not believe it; but yet, as

I rubbed my eyes, I could not doubt it. I had got my chance, and had taken him unawares. The face still peered intently downhill. I lifted a pistol, took careful aim, and fired at the patch of red skin.

A thousand echoes rang through the wood. The bullet had grazed the tree trunk, and the face was gone. But whither? Did a dead man lie behind the trunk, or had a wounded man crawled into cover?

I waited breathlessly for a minute or two, and then went forward, with my second pistol at the cock.

There was nothing behind the tree. Only a piece of red bark with a bullet-hole through it, some greasy horsehair, and a feather. And then from many quarters seemed to come a wicked laughter. I leaned against the trunk, with a deadly nausea clutching at my heart. Poor fool, I had rejoiced for a second, only to be dashed into utter despair!

I do not think I had ever had much hope, but now I was convinced that all was over. The water had made my burns worse, and disappointment had sapped the little remnants of my strength. My one desire was to get out of this ghoulish thicket and die by the stream side. The cool sound of it would be a fitting dirge for a foolish fellow who had wandered far from his home.

I could hear the plunge of it, and struggled towards it. I was long past taking any care. I stumbled and slipped along the hillside, my breath labouring, and a moaning at my lips from sheer agony and weakness. If an arrow sped between my ribs I would still reach the water, for I was determined to die with my legs in its flow.

Suddenly it was before me. I came out on a mossy rock above a deep, clear pool, into which a cascade tumbled. I knelt feebly on the stone, gazing at the blue depths, and then I lifted my eyes.

There on a rock on the other side stood my enemy.

He had an arrow fitted to his bow, and as I looked he shot. It struck me on the right arm, pinning it just above the elbow. The pistol, which I had been carrying aimlessly, slipped from my nerveless hand to the moss on which I kneeled.

That sudden shock cleared my wits. I was at his mercy and he knew it. I could see every detail of him twenty yards off across the water. He stood there as calm and light as if he had just arisen from rest, his polished limbs shining in the glow of the sun, the muscles on his right arm rippling as he moved his bow. Madman that I was, ever to hope to contend with such dauntless youth, such tireless vigour! There was a cruel, thin-lipped smile on his face. He had me in his clutches like a cat with a mouse, and he was going to get the full zest of it. I kneeled before him, with my strength gone, my right arm crippled. He could choose his target at his leisure, for I could not resist. I saw the gloating joy in his eyes. He knew his power, and meant to miss nothing of its savour.

Yet in that fell predicament God gave me back my courage. But I took a queer way of showing it.

I began to whimper as if in abject fear. Every limb was relaxed in terror, and I grovelled on my knees before him. I made feeble plucks at the arrow in my right arm, and my shoulder drooped almost to the sod. But all the time my other hand was behind my back, edging its way to the pistol. My fingers clutched at the butt, and slowly I began to withdraw it till I had it safe in the shadow of my pocket.

My enemy did not know that I was left-handed.

He fitted a second arrow to his bow, while his lips curved maliciously. All the demoniac, panther-like cruelty of his race looked at me out of his deep eyes. He was taking his time about it, unwilling to lose the slightest flavour of his vengeance. I played up to him nobly, squirming as if in an agony of terror. But by this time I had got a comfortable posture on the rock, and my left shoulder was towards him.

At last he made his choice, and so did I. I never thought that I could miss, for if I had had any doubt I should have failed. I was as confident in my sureness as any saint in the mercy of God.

He raised his bow, but it never reached his shoulder. My left arm shot out, and my last bullet went through his brain.

He toppled forward and plunged into the pool. The grease from his body floated up, and made a scum on the surface.

Then I broke off the arrow and pulled it out of my arm, putting the pieces in my pocket. The water cleared, and I could see him lying in the cool blue depths, his eyes staring, his mouth open, and a little dark eddy about his forehead.

I came out of the wood a new being. My wounded arm and my torn and inflamed limbs were forgotten. I held my head high, and walked like a free man. It was not that I had slain my enemy and been delivered from deadly peril, nor had I any clearer light on my next step. But I had suddenly got the conviction that God was on my side, and that I need not fear what man could do unto me. You may call it the madness of a lad whose body and spirit had been tried to breaking-point. But, madness or no, it gave me infinite courage, and in that hour I would have dared every savage on earth.

I found some Indians at the edge of the wood, and told one who spoke Powhatan the issue of the fight. I flung the broken arrow on the ground. "That is my token," I said. "You will find the other in the pool below the cascade."

Then I strode towards the tents, looking every man I passed squarely in the eyes. No one spoke, no one hindered me; every face was like a graven image.

I reached the teepee in which I had spent the night, and flung myself down on the rude couch. In a minute I was sunk in a heavy sleep.

THE BLANKET OF THE DARK

XX

...The King grumbled. (Henry VIII)

"I am no fox to kennel in a hole. Whence came those women? Have they no dwelling near where I may bed me?"

"A mile and more of rough ground distant. And miserable cabins at that, with a plague of rats and the stars shining through the thatch. You will be better in Lovell's cell."

"Let me lie by the fire."

"It is already dying and there is no more fuel. There will be frost ere morning and you will get a chill at the heart."

"But I will stick in that hole, and you who have dragged me from water may have no power to drag me from earth."

"The place is wide enough. Two months back I made the passage with a brother of Oseney."

"A holy man has entered it! That gives a flavour of grace to as graceless a spot as ever my eyes beheld. It looks like some werewolf's lair... But lead on, sir. Maybe you are right, and I shall be warmer if I have some yards of stone and earth for blanket."

Peter led the way down the slimy steps and over the prostrate outer door. The first part of the passage was narrow, and in bending the King had some trouble with his leg. When he jarred it on a knuckle of stone he would bellow with pain, and Peter, turning the lantern, saw the great face flushed and furious. Then the roof rose, and Peter's arm could give him support. At the subsidence it was hard to get the King through, and Peter had to clear away much rubble, Then came the sound of falling water.

"Have we escaped one flood to drown in another?" the King asked tartly.

The corridor broadened, and at last came the iron-bound door. It had been left unlocked on the last visit, and a pull set it creaking on its hinges. The little chamber smelt dry and fresh, and it had the chill neither of the water-logged outer air nor of the mildewed passage.

Peter set the lantern on the floor and dropped his burden.

"Behold your majesty's lodging for the night," he said, while Henry sat himself heavily in the chair which had once been Lovell's.

Peter flung the rotting bedclothes from the pallet, and laid on it Mother Sweetbread's blankets. He helped the King to strip off his soaked doublet and hose – a task of delicacy owing to the ulcer on his leg, and wrapped his great body in one of the deerskin cloaks.

"Get you among the blankets, sire," he said, "and I will serve your supper."

He fed him with Mother Sweetbread's provender, and he gave him to drink of Mother Sweetbread's sloeberry cordial. The King made an ample meal and the strong liquor warmed his blood. "Ha!" he cried, "I begin to thaw, and the ice has gone from my belly. This is a rough inn, but the entertainment might be worse. Give me another cup, and I will compose myself to sleep. What mountain is above me?"

"Lovell's castle," said Peter. "The abode of the last lord of that house."

The King cried out and crossed himself.

"It has an ill name," he murmured. "You say you came here with a brother of Oseney? Did the holy man lustrate this chamber, for wherever Lovell trod Sathanas walked in his tracks?"

"Set your mind at ease, sire. It was lustrated by prayer and tears, and the bones of Lovell were laid in hallowed earth."

But the King was not at ease. Some notion had arisen to vex him. He watched Peter strip off his clothes, wrap himself in the other cloak and make a bed beside the door.

"Oseney," he muttered, "what have I heard of a brother of Oseney?" and he raised himself on his elbow, and stared at his companion.

Peter, ever since he had dragged the King ashore, had had a mind empty of thought. He saw the clear hand of God, and let himself follow blindly as it guided... There could be no failure now, for events had turned miraculously in his favour. Before dawn Darking and his men would be at Minster Lovell, and by noon the King would be safe at Avelard. The household at Woodstock would be hunting high and low for its lord and master, but here in this dungeon of Lovell's he was hidden more securely than if he were in the heart of Wales with all Neville's pickets to guard him... He had not troubled to think of Henry. The man with his gross body and his ulcerated leg was no more to him than a derelict log plucked from the water.

"Compose yourself to sleep, sire," he said. "On the morrow I can promise you better fare and a softer bed."

He was himself very weary, but before he lay down he raised the lantern to see to the candle within. Then he set it and the tinder-box on the floor beside him, blew out the light, and turned to sleep.

But in the moment when his face had been clear in the lantern's glow, Henry had seen in it something which made his cheek, now ruddy with the cordial, grow mottled and pale again. "By God, it is he," he whispered. "The Oseney clerk! He is Buckingham's get, for he has the Bohun lip..." There was no drowsiness now for the King.

Peter slept lightly, as was his custom, for one trained in the Oseney services, which broke the night into short stages, was not likely to be a sluggard. He was awakened to sudden consciousness by the sound of a creaking pallet. The King was restless; nay, the King was rising.

He lay and listened. He heard Henry fumbling among his discarded clothes, and the clink of something hard – metal or stone. Then he heard the stealthy movements of the heavy body, which seemed to be coming towards him. He had that consciousness of imminence which comes neither from touch, nor sight, nor hearing, but from some subtler sense. He slipped from under the blanket, and rolled very softly a few feet to his left.

The King was approaching the bed. He was close on it, leaning above it... And then there was a rapid movement, the sound of an arm descending, a sudden jar of metal driven through woollen on to stone.

Peter's brain worked fast. The King had recognized him, had hoped to rid himself of a rival by the speediest way. Had he been sleeping heavily where he had laid himself down, the King's hunting-knife would now be in his heart.

Wrath plucked him to his feet and hurled him on his enemy. He felt the kneeling King topple over under his impact, and found himself grappling with something as soft and unresisting as a bolster. He wrested the knife from his grasp and sent it spinning into a corner. His hand found the thick throat, but there was no need to choke it, for the man was without strength… Instead he felt along the floor for the tinder-box and relit the lantern.

The King sprawled on his side, almost black in the face, his lips contorted with pain, while one hand groped at his leg. Peter dragged him back to his pallet, and set the lantern on the chair. In the struggle the deerskin had half fallen from Henry, and revealed his misshapen limbs and huge paunch and unwholesome elderly flesh. Peter looked down on him with a shiver of disgust. Then he filled a cup of cordial and put it to his lips, which greedily drained it. The King lay panting for a little while, while the darkness passed from his face, leaving it mottled and pale again. The pain in his leg seemed to have gone, for he opened his eyes, and they were bright and wary with fear.

"That was a foolish enterprise, sire," said Peter. "We two are alone here in this cell. One is old and one is young, one is sick and one is hale. If two such contend there can be but the one issue… He whom you would have slain had a few hours back saved you from death… I would remind you likewise that murder is a deed on which Heaven frowns."

The King had recovered his bodily ease, and with it his wits. He lay with the blanket drawn up to his chin and his little eyes as sharp as a bird's. There was still panic in them, but also cunning.

"*Peccavi*," he said. " 'Twas a sudden tempting of the Devil. May God and His saints have mercy on me! I ask your forgiveness, young sir – I, the King of England, abase myself before you."

"You would have slain me. Why?"

"A sudden madness. I feared you… I took you for one who was plotting my hurt."

"Whom do I favour? I, a nameless man of the forest! What enemy of your majesty's have I the ill fortune to recall?"

"None that lives," said the King, "but one that died long ago."

"Even so. It seems I bear on my face the proof of my begetting. Your majesty is right. I am the son of Edward of Buckingham."

The King's face did not change, but his lips moved.

"You have come into the west to seek me. I, too, sought you, and God has prepared a meeting. I deserve some favour at your majesty's hands for this night's work. First, I saved you from the floods, and second, when your majesty would have knifed me, I forbore to strike back."

There was a new light in Henry's eyes. His panic was now under command, and he was back in a world which he understood.

"You talk reason, my lord. I bear no ill will to your house – I have ever admitted its splendour. Your father stood in my way, and I had to thrust him aside, but I have no malice towards his son. You speak truth – I am most deeply beholden to you for what has befallen this night... I will make you the second man in the kingdom. The lands and dukedom of Buckingham shall be yours again, and you shall ride by the King's bridle and sit high in his Council."

Henry's eye was alert and watchful, but his smile was that grave and kindly smile that had often beguiled men's hearts.

Peter lifted his hand.

"Let me tell you of this cell where we now lie," he said. "Hither after Stoke battle came one who had been the second man in the kingdom, who had ridden by the King's bridle, and had sat high in his Council. He was a fugitive, but in this place he was safe. Here he could lie till the hunt had passed, and he could get himself and his wealth abroad. But only one other knew the secret of the place, and that other fell sick and died. So the great lord Lovell was left to starve like a rat whose hole had been stopped. Two months back I entered this place, and stumbled over his bones. I came seeking treasure and I found it."

The King pulled the blanket from his chin. "'Fore God, I knew it," he said. " 'Twas not Neville nor Avelard that paid for this mischief in the west… "

"You mistake me. I said I found treasure, but it was not Lovell's gold. I found the philosopher's stone, the touch of which dissolves earth's ambitions. I no longer seek what Lovell sought."

The King sat up, and as he moved his leg he squealed with pain.

"That is an honest thought," he cried. "You would go back to Holy Church? I commend you, my lord. I will rejoice to further your purpose. You may have the choice of any abbey in this land. Nay, you will be bishop as soon as I can make room for you. I… "

"Your majesty misreads me. I will never be clerk again. But I will not rest till there is a new England, for I am a fighter on God's side. I would save my soul."

"By the rood so would I!" The King's face had a serious bewilderment. "I am the devoutest man that ever wore ermine. If I have broken with the Pope, I will defend the faith better than he. No heretic shall breathe freely in this land while I sit on the throne. I have confuted in argument Luterano and Sacramentary alike. My chief study in my closet is holy learning. Every day I serve the priest at mass, every Sunday I receive the holy bread, every Good Friday I creep on my knees to the Cross."

There was a strong passion in the King's voice. This man, who a little before had been a murderer in intent, believed devoutly that he was on the side of virtue.

"You would serve God by putting yourself in God's place?" Peter said quietly.

The King looked puzzled.

"I am God's vicegerent on earth," he said, "therefore I sit in God's place. But the creature abaseth itself before the Creator."

"Is it God's purpose that you burn honest folk for a little deviation of faith, and likewise send to death those who hold in trust God's estates because they will not surrender them to your minions?"

The King's face lit up. Here was ground with which he was familiar.

"*Distinguo*," he cried. "No man suffers under me save for denying the catholic faith in which is alone found salvation. You are a strange clerk if you contemn that duty. I am the guardian under God of my people's hopes of Heaven. I am determined to make this realm one in faith as it is one in law. If I have shouldered his Holiness of Rome from the headship of Christ's Church in England, the more need that I perform the task in which his Holiness was somewhat negligent. Listen, my lord. Law is above all men, king and peasant alike. Of that law there are two branches, the law of God and the law of England, and both are in my care. The first is based upon God's Word and that inherited practice of God's Church which, being inspired by the Holy Ghost, is likewise canonical. I would make the Scriptures free to all in the vulgar tongue – you may have heard of my efforts thereto – but I would not permit ignorant men to interpret them as they please. The interpretation is laid down by Holy Church, and he who rebels against it will burn, be he bishop or noble, clerk or cotter."

There was no fear now in the small bright eyes. Henry spoke with a fierce authority, and his broad low brow had set in weighty lines.

"As to the second law, the law of England, I am its most devout and humble servant. I have never acted save in obedience to that law. 'Twas that law that shook off the Pope's burden. 'Tis under that law that I have taken order with certain religious houses. I have made it my care that the blessing of law shall be free to all, the poorest as well as the greatest, and that all shall stand equal before the royal tribunals. That law is not my private will, but the approved judgment of the wisest men. Maybe I have guided it into new channels, but the flow is that which came down through six centuries. I have sworn before God, that if any man, be he never so great, outrage that law I will make his head fly for it, and by God's help I will keep that vow so long as there is breath in my nostrils."

"Yet you have made an England," said Peter, "which is in some sort a stye and in some sort a desert."

"In what respect, sir!" the King asked sharply. "I have given it peace."

"That peace which is a desert," was the answer. "Your loans and benevolences have bled it white. There is as much suffering as in the days of the Black Death. The rich grow richer, and the poor die by thousands in the ditches."

"Ay," said the King. "No doubt there is much misery abroad. But mark you, young sir, 'tis a shallow philosophy which judges on what exists but takes no account of what has been prevented... I have had to steer a difficult course among the plots of the Emperor and the French King. Had I steered less skilfully a new Duke William might have landed on English earth. To defeat my enemies cost money, and that my people have cheerfully paid, for they knew it was for them that I fought... For the rest, I say again that I have given them peace. But for my strong hand the nobles would have been at each other's throats, and at mine, as in the old Wars of the Roses. I have shed blood, doubtless, but had I been weak, every drop of that blood would have been a river. *Quicquid delirant reges*, says the poet, *plectuntur Achivi.* By curbing the madness of the kings I have saved the commons from stripes. Think you that is a small thing? By God, I am the man in all England best loved by the commonalty."

"I read it otherwise. What know you of the true commonalty of England? Your counsellors are the new men who have risen to power by the oppression of the poor."

To Peter's surprise the King assented.

"I do not altogether deny that. Hark you, my lord. These be strange and perilous times in which we live. Men's minds everywhere and in all things are in a confusion. Europe is a whirlpool because of the ambition of kings and the unsettlement of the Church. Here in England is the same strife in lesser degree.

Not in things religious only, but in the things of Mammon, for it would appear that a new world is coming to birth. It is a hard world for many, a kind world to a few, but it needs must come as spring must follow winter. Everywhere in the land men are following new trades, and old customs are passing away. We grow rich, and in growing rich we doubtless grow hard, but that hardness is needful in the narrow portals of a new world. Had I been a slack-mouthed king, this England of mine would have been booty to the proud. Had I summoned to my councils only the ancient nobles, a promising growth would have been nipped in the bud. In a time of unsettlement one thing is needful above all others, and that is a strong hand and an iron law. That law I will give to England, though every shire be in flames against me!"

The man was great. It was borne in on Peter that this vast being, wallowing among Mother Sweetbread's homespun blankets, had the greatness of some elemental force. He hated him, for he saw the cunning behind the frank smile, the ruthlessness in the small eyes; but he could not blind himself to his power. Power of Mammon, power of Antichrist, power of the Devil, maybe, but something born to work mightily in the world.

The King was speaking again.

"I will have no treason in this land," he said, "for it is treason not against my person – which matters less – but against the realm of England. In Europe there is Cæsar who has empire over men's bodies, and the Pope who has empire over men's souls. I have sworn that I too shall be imperial, and England an empire. No foreign Cæsar or foreign Pope will issue edicts over this English soil. There will be one rule within these isles, not of Henry or Henry's son, but of English law. The Church will acknowledge its headship. Even now I am bringing my turbulent kinsmen of Wales inside its pale. There is not a noble but will be made to bow his stiff neck to it. Before I die I hope with God's help to make Scotland my vassal, so that the writ of England shall run from Thule and the Ebudes to the Narrow Seas. Only thus shall my people have peace, and as a peacemaker I shall be called the child of God."

"It will be a peace without God. You may preserve men's bodies, but you will damn their souls."

"Not so. In time the new wealth which this land is getting will spread itself so that the poor will benefit. Some day there will be an England prosperous and content, and what better soil for the flourishing of true religion and sound learning?"

Peter shook his head.

"There may be nobleness in your dreams, but in the meantime you are burdening your soul with evil deeds. Can piety and graciousness spring from what is evil? You are imperilling your salvation in a proud venture."

The King laughed – a low rumbling laugh, with mirth in it.

"I am willing to run the hazard. Listen, my lord. There is an old tale of a mighty Emperor who died and came to Peter's Gate. The devil's advocate had much to say against him – sackings and burnings and politic lies and politic slayings. 'But,' said the Emperor, 'I have had a hard task, fighting all my days with desperate men to put a little decency and order into my world. It is not fair to judge me by the canons of the cloister.' And the Lord God, who knows how difficult is the labour of government, admitted the plea, and the Emperor passed into Paradise. I am content to leave my own judging to the same wise God."

"You walk in Lovell's path," said Peter. "Would you had been with me when I first came to this place, and had seen the end of Lovell's glory."

"Tush, man, I have made account of that. All earthly splendour ends in rottenness. This body of mine is half-rotten already. But the flaming spirit of man outlasts his dust, and till God send for me I will rule England."

He yawned.

"I am weary and would sleep, for my leg is now at peace. Take you that knife into your bed, if it comfort you... You are an honest lad, but you are a monk in bone. Return to Oseney and I will make you its abbot."

THE PATH OF THE KING
III

Two years passed, and once again it was spring in Washington – about half-past ten of the evening of the 14th April – Good Friday – the first Eastertide of peace. The streets had been illuminated for victory, and the gas jets were still blazing, while a young moon, climbing the sky, was dimming their murky yellow with its cold pure light. Tenth Street was packed from end to end by a silent mob. As a sponge cleans a slate, so exhilaration had been wiped off their souls. On the porch of Ford's Theatre some gaudy posters advertised Tom Taylor's comedy, *Our American Cousin*, and the steps were littered with paper and orange peel and torn fragments of women's clothes, for the exit of the audience had been hasty. Lights still blazed in the building, for there was nobody to put them out. In front, on the side-walk, was a cordon of soldiers.

Stanton elbowed his way through the throng to the little house, Mr Peterson's, across the street. The messenger from the War Department had poured wild news into his ear – wholesale murder, everybody – the President – Seward – Grant. Incredulous he had hurried forth, and the sight of that huge still crowd woke fear in him. The guards at Mr Peterson's door recognized him and he was admitted. As he crossed the threshold he saw ominous dark stains.

A kitchen candle burned below the hat-rack in the narrow hall, and showed further stains on the oilcloth. From a narrow room on the left hand came the sound of women weeping.

The door at the end of the passage was ajar. It opened on a bare little place, once perhaps the surgery of some doctor in small practice, but now a bedroom. A door gave at the farther side on a tiny veranda, and this and the one window were wide open. An oil lamp stood on a table by the bed and revealed a crowd of people. A man lay on a camp bed, lying aslant, for he was too long for it. A sheet covered his lower limbs, but his breast and shoulders had been bared. The head was nearest to the entrance, propped on an out-jutting bolster.

A man was leaving whom Stanton recognized as Dr Stone, the Lincoln family physician. The doctor answered his unspoken question. "Dying," he said. "Through the brain. The bullet is now below the left eye. He may live for a few hours – scarcely the night."

Stanton moved to the foot of the bed like one in a dream. He saw that Barnes, the Surgeon-General, sat on a deal chair on the left side, holding the dying man's hand. Dr Gurley, the minister, sat beside the bed. He noted Sumner and Welles and General Halleck and Governor Dennison, and back in the gloom the young Robert Lincoln. But he observed them only as he would have observed figures in a picture. They were but shadows; the living man was he who was struggling on the bed with death.

Lincoln's great arms and chest were naked, and Stanton, who had thought of him as meagre and shrunken, was amazed at their sinewy strength. He remembered that he had once heard of him as a village Hercules. The President was unconscious, but some tortured nerve made him moan like an animal in pain. It was a strange sound to hear from one who had been wont to suffer with tight lips. To Stanton it heightened the spectral unreality of the scene. He seemed to be looking at death in a stage tragedy.

The trivial voice of Welles broke the silence. He had to give voice to the emotion which choked him.

"His dream has come true," he said – "the dream he told us about at the Cabinet this morning. His ship is nearing the dark shore. He thought it signified good news from Sherman."

Stanton did not reply. To save his life he could not have uttered a word.

Then Gurley, the minister, spoke very gently, for he was a simple man sorely moved.

"He has looked so tired for so long. He will have rest now, the deep rest of the people of God... He has died for us all... Today nineteen hundred years ago the Son of Man gave His life for the world... The President has followed in his Master's steps."

Sumner was repeating softly to himself, like a litany, that sentence from the second Inaugural – "With malice toward none, with charity for all."

But Stanton was in no mood for words. He was looking at the figure on the bed, the great chest heaving with the laboured but regular breath, and living again the years of colleagueship and conflict. He had been loyal to him; yes, thank God! he had been loyal. He had quarrelled, thwarted, criticized, but he had never failed him in a crisis. He had held up his hands as Aaron and Hur held up the hands of Moses...

The Secretary for War was not in the habit of under-rating his own talents, and achievements. But in that moment they seemed less than nothing. Humility shook him like a passion. Till his dying day his one boast must be that he had served that figure on the camp bed. It had been his high fortune to have his lot cast in the vicinity of supreme genius. With awe he realized that he was looking upon the passing of the very great... There had never been such a man. There never could be such an one again. So patient and enduring, so wise in all great matters, so potent to inspire a multitude, so secure in his own soul... Fools would chatter about his being a son of the people and his career a triumph of the average man. Average! Great God, he was a ruler of princes, a master, a compeller of men... He could imagine what noble nonsense Sumner would talk... He looked with disfavour at the classic face of the Bostonian.

But Sumner for once seemed to share his feelings. He, too, was looking with reverent eyes towards the bed, and as he caught Stanton's gaze he whispered words which the Secretary for War did not condemn: "The beauty of Israel is slain upon thy high places."

The night hours crawled on with an intolerable slowness. Some of the watchers sat, but Stanton remained rigid at the bed foot. He had not been well of late and had been ordered a long rest by his doctor, but he was not conscious of fatigue. He would not have left his post for a king's ransom, for he felt himself communing with the dying, sharing the last stage in his journey as he had shared all the rough marches. His proud spirit found a certain solace in the abasement of its humbleness.

A little before six the morning light began to pale the lamps. The window showed a square of grey cloudy sky, and outside on the porch there was a drip of rain. The faces revealed by the cold dawn were as haggard and yellow as that of the dying man. Wafts of the outer air began to freshen the stuffiness of the little room.

The city was waking up. There came the sound of far-away carts and horses, and a boy in the lane behind the house began to whistle, and then to sing. "When I was young," he sang –

"*When I was young I used to Wait*
At Massa's table, 'n' hand de plate,
An' pass de bottle when he was dry,
An' brush away de blue-tailed fly."

"It's his song," Stanton said to himself, and with the air came a rush of strange feelings. He remembered a thousand things, which before had been only a background of which he had been scarcely conscious. The constant kindliness, the gentle healing sympathy, the homely humour which he once thought had irritated but which he now knew had soothed him... This man had been twined round the roots of every heart. All night he had been in an ecstasy of admiration, but now that was forgotten in a yearning love. The President had been part of his being, closer to him than wife or child. The boy sang –

"*But I can't forget, until I die,*
Ole Massa an' de blue-tailed fly."

Stanton's eyes filled with hot tears. He had not wept since his daughter died.

The breathing from the bed was growing faint. Suddenly the Surgeon-General held up his hand. He felt the heart and shook his head. "Fetch your mother," he said to Robert Lincoln. The minister had dropped on his knees by the bedside and was praying.

"The President is dead," said the Surgeon-General, and at the words it seemed that every head in the room was bowed on the breast.

Stanton took a step forward with a strange, appealing motion of the arms. It was noted by more than one that his pale face was transfigured.

"Yesterday he was America's," he cried. "Our very own. Now he is all the world's... Now he belongs to the ages."

THE SUMMONS COMES FOR MR STANDFAST
IV

...There was no morning *strafe*, such as had been our usual fortune in the past week. I went out-of-doors and found a noiseless world under the lowering sky. The rain had stopped falling, the wind of dawn had lessened, and I feared that the storm would be delayed. I wanted it at once to help us through the next hours of tension. Was it in six hours that the French were coming? No, it must be four. It couldn't be more than four, unless somebody had made an infernal muddle. I wondered why everything was so quiet. It would be breakfast time on both sides, but there seemed no stir of man's presence in that ugly strip half a mile off. Only far back in the German hinterland I seemed to hear the rumour of traffic.

An unslept and unshaven figure stood beside me which revealed itself as Archie Roylance.

"Been up all night," he said cheerfully, lighting a cigarette. "No, I haven't had breakfast. The skipper thought we'd better get another anti-aircraft battery up this way, and I was superintendin' the job. He's afraid of the Hun gettin' over your lines and spying out the nakedness of the land. For, you know, we're uncommon naked, sir. Also," and Archie's face became grave, "the Hun's pourin' divisions down on this sector. As I judge, he's blowin' up for a thunderin' big drive on both sides of the river. Our lads yesterday said all the country back of Peronne was lousy with new troops. And he's gettin' his big guns forward, too. You haven't been troubled with them yet, but he has got the roads mended and the devil of a lot of new light railways, and any moment we'll have the five-point-nines sayin' Good mornin'... Pray Heaven you get relieved in time, sir. I take it there's not much risk of another push this mornin'?"

"I don't think so. The Boche took a nasty knock yesterday, and he must fancy we're pretty strong after that counter-attack. I don't think he'll strike till he can work both sides of the river, and that'll take time to prepare. That's what his fresh divisions are for... But remember, he can attack now, if he likes. If he knew how weak we were he's strong enough to send us all to glory in the next three hours. It's just that knowledge that you fellows have got to prevent his getting. If a single Hun plane crosses our lines and returns, we're wholly and utterly done. You've given us splendid help since the show began, Archie. For God's sake keep it up to the finish and put every machine you can spare in this sector."

"We're doin' our best," he said. "We got some more fightin' scouts down from the north, and we're keepin' our eyes skinned. But you know as well as I do, sir, that it's never an ab-so-lute certainty. If the Hun sent over a squadron we might beat 'em all down but one, and that one might do the trick. It's a matter of luck. The Hun's got the wind up all right in the air just now and I don't blame the poor devil. But I'm inclined to think we haven't had the pick of his push here. Jennings says he's doin' good work in Flanders, and they reckon there's the deuce of a thrust comin' there pretty soon. I think we can manage the kind of footler he's been sendin' over here lately, but if Lensch or some lad like that were to choose to turn up I wouldn't say what might happen. The air's a big lottery," and Archie turned a dirty face skyward where two of our planes were moving very high towards the east.

The mention of Lensch brought Peter Pienaar to my mind, and I asked if he had gone back.

"He won't go," said Archie, "and we haven't the heart to make him. He's very happy, and plays about with the Gladas single-seater. He's always speakin' about you, sir, and it'd break his heart if we shifted him."

I asked about his health, and was told that he didn't seem to have much pain.

"But he's a bit queer," and Archie shook a sage head. "One of the reasons why he won't budge is because he says God has some work for him to do. He's quite serious about it, and ever since he got the notion he has perked up amazin'. He's always askin' about Lensch, too – not vindictive-like, you understand, but quite friendly. Seems to take a sort of proprietary interest in him. I told him Lensch had had a far longer spell of first-class fightin' than anybody else and was bound by the law of averages to be downed soon, and he was quite sad about it."

I had no time to worry about Peter. Archie and I swallowed breakfast and I had a pow-wow with my brigadiers. By this time I had got through to Corps HQ and got news of the French, It was worse than I expected. General Péguy would arrive about ten o'clock, but his men couldn't take over till well after midday. The Corps gave me their whereabouts and I found it on the map. They had a long way to cover yet, and then there would be the slow business of relieving. I looked at my watch. There were still six hours before us when the Boche might knock us to blazes, six hours of maddening anxiety... Lefroy announced that all was quiet on the front, and that the new wiring at the Bois de la Bruyère had been completed. Patrols had reported that during the night a fresh German division seemed to have relieved that which we had punished so stoutly yesterday. I asked him if he could stick it out against another attack. "No," he said without hesitation.

"We're too few and too shaky on our pins to stand any more. I've only a man to every three yards." That impressed me, for Lefroy was usually the most devil-may-care optimist.

"Curse it, there's the sun," I heard Archie cry. It was true, for the clouds were rolling back and the centre of the heavens was a patch of blue. The storm was coming – I could smell it in the air – but probably it wouldn't break till the evening. Where, I wondered, would we be by that time?

It was now nine o'clock, and I was keeping tight hold on myself, for I saw that I was going to have hell for the next hours. I am a pretty stolid fellow in some ways, but I have always found patience and standing still the most difficult job to tackle, and my nerves were all tattered from the long strain of the retreat. I went up to the line and saw the battalion commanders. Everything was unwholesomely quiet there. Then I came back to my headquarters to study the reports that were coming in from the air patrols. They all said the same thing – abnormal activity in the German back areas. Things seemed shaping for a new 21st of March, and, if our luck were out, my poor little remnant would have to take the shock. I telephoned to the Corps and found them as nervous as me. I gave them the details of my strength and heard an agonized whistle at the other end of the line. I was rather glad I had companions in the same purgatory.

I found I couldn't sit still. If there had been any work to do I would have buried myself in it, but there was none. Only this fearsome job of waiting. I hardly ever feel cold, but now my blood seemed to be getting thin, and I astonished my staff by putting on a British warm and buttoning up the collar. Round that derelict farm I ranged like a hungry wolf, cold at the feet, queasy in the stomach, and mortally edgy in the mind.

Then suddenly the cloud lifted from me, and the blood seemed to run naturally in my veins. I experienced the change of mood which a man feels sometimes when his whole being is fined down and clarified by long endurance. The fight of yesterday revealed itself as something rather splendid. What risks we had run and how gallantly we had met them! My heart warmed as I thought of that old division of mine, those ragged veterans that were never beaten as long as breath was left them. And the Americans and the boys from the machine-gun school and all the oddments we had commandeered! And old Blenkiron raging like a good-tempered lion! It was against reason that such fortitude shouldn't win out. We had snarled round and bitten the Boche so badly that he wanted no more for a little. He would come again, but presently we should be relieved and the gallant blue-coats, fresh as paint and burning for revenge, would be there to worry him,

I had no new facts on which to base my optimism, only a changed point of view. And with it came a recollection of other things. Wake's death had left me numb before, but now the thought of it gave me a sharp pang. He was the first of our little confederacy to go. But what an ending he had made, and how happy he had been in that mad time when he had come down from his pedestal and become one of the crowd! He had found himself at the last, and who could grudge him such happiness? If the best were to be taken, he would be chosen first, for he was a big man, before whom I uncovered my head. The thought of him made me very humble. I had never had his troubles to face, but he had come clean through them, and reached a courage which was for ever beyond me. He was the Faithful among us pilgrims, who had finished his journey before the rest. Mary had foreseen it. "There is a price to be paid," she had said – "the best of us."

And at the thought of Mary a flight of warm and happy hopes seemed to settle on my mind. I was looking again beyond the war to that peace which she and I would some day inherit. I had a vision of a green English landscape, with its far-flung scents of wood and meadow and garden... And that face of all my dreams, with the eyes so childlike and brave and honest, as if they, too, saw beyond the dark to a radiant country. A line of an old song, which had been a favourite of my father's, sang itself in my ears:

"There's an eye that ever weeps and a fair face will be fain
When I ride through Annan Water wi' my bonny bands again!"

We were standing by the crumbling rails of what had once been the farm sheepfold. I looked at Archie and he smiled back at me, for he saw that my face had changed. Then he turned his eyes to the billowing clouds.

I felt my arm clutched.

"Look there!" said a fierce voice, and his glasses were turned upward.

I looked, and far up in the sky saw a thing like a wedge of wild geese flying towards us from the enemy's country. I made out the small dots which composed it, and my glasses told me they were planes. But only Archie's practised eye knew that they were enemy.

"Boche?" I asked.

"Boche," he said. "My God, we're for it now."

My heart had sunk like a stone, but I was fairly cool. I looked at my watch and saw that it was ten minutes to eleven.

"How many?"

"Five," said Archie. "Or there may be six – not more."

"Listen!" I said. "Get on to your headquarters. Tell them that it's all up with us if a single plane gets back. Let them get well over the line, the deeper in the better, and tell them to send up every machine they possess and down them all. Tell them it's life or death. Not one single plane goes back. Quick!"

Archie disappeared, and as he went our anti-aircraft guns broke out. The formation above opened and zigzagged, but they were too high to be in much danger. But they were not too high to see that which we must keep hidden or perish.

The roar of our batteries died down as the invaders passed westwards. As I watched their progress they seemed to be dropping lower. Then they rose again and a bank of cloud concealed them.

I had a horrid certainty that they must beat us, that some at any rate would get back. They had seen our thin lines and the roads behind us empty of supports. They would see, as they advanced, the blue columns of the French coming up from the south-west, and they would return and tell the enemy that a blow now would open the road to Amiens and the sea. He had plenty of strength for it, and presently he would have overwhelming strength. It only needed a spear-point to burst the jerry-built dam and let the flood through… They would return in twenty minutes, and by noon we would be broken. Unless – unless the miracle of miracles happened, and they never returned.

Archie reported that his skipper would do his damnedest and that our machines were now going up. "We've a chance, sir," he said, "a good sportin' chance." It was a new Archie, with a hard voice, a lean face, and very old eyes.

Behind the jagged walls of the farm buildings was a knoll which had once formed part of the highroad. I went up there alone, for I didn't want anybody near me. I wanted a view-point, and I wanted quiet, for I had a grim time before me. From that knoll I had a big prospect of country. I looked east to our lines on which an occasional shell was falling, and where I could hear the chatter of machine-guns. West there was peace, for the woods closed down on the landscape. Up to the north, I remember, there was a big glare as from a burning dump, and heavy guns seemed to be at work in the Ancre valley. Down in the south there was the dull murmur of a great battle. But just around me, in the gap, the deadliest place of all, there was an odd quiet. I could pick out clearly the different sounds. Somebody down at the farm had made a joke and there was a short burst of laughter. I envied the humorist his composure. There was a clatter and jingle from a battery changing position. On the road a tractor was jolting along – I could hear its driver shout and the screech of its unoiled axle.

My eyes were glued to my glasses, but they shook in my hands so that I could scarcely see. I bit my lip to steady myself, but they still wavered. From time to time I glanced at my wrist-watch.

Eight minutes gone – ten – seventeen. If only the planes would come into sight! Even the certainty of failure would be better than this harrowing doubt. They should be back by now unless they had swung north across the salient, or unless the miracle of miracles –

Then came the distant yapping of an anti-aircraft gun, caught up the next second by others, while smoke patches studded the distant blue of the sky. The clouds were banking in mid-heaven, but to the west there was a big clear space now woolly with shrapnel bursts. I counted them mechanically – one – three – five – nine – with despair beginning to take the place of my anxiety. My hands were steady now, and through the glasses I saw the enemy.

Five attenuated shapes rode high above the bombardment, now sharp against the blue, now lost in a film of vapour. They were coming back, serenely, contemptuously, having seen all they wanted.

The quiet had gone now and the din was monstrous. Anti-aircraft guns, singly and in groups, were firing from every side. As I watched it seemed a futile waste of ammunition. The enemy didn't give a tinker's curse for it... But surely there was one down. I could only count four now. No, there was the fifth coming out of a cloud. In ten minutes they would be all over the line. I fairly stamped in my vexation. Those guns were no more use than a sick headache. Oh, where in God's name were our own planes?

At that moment they came, streaking down into sight, four fighting scouts with the sun glinting on their wings and burnishing their metal cowls. I saw clearly the rings of red, white, and blue. Before their downward drive the enemy instantly spread out.

I was watching with bare eyes now, and I wanted companionship, for the time of waiting was over. Automatically I must have run down the knoll, for the next I knew I was staring at the heavens with Archie by my side. The combatants seemed to couple instinctively. Diving, wheeling, climbing, a pair would drop out of the melée or disappear behind a cloud. Even at that height I could hear the methodical rat-tat-tat of the machine-guns. Then there was a sudden flare and wisp of smoke. A plane sank, turning and twisting, to earth.

"Hun!" said Archie, who had his glasses on it.

Almost immediately another followed. This time the pilot recovered himself, while still a thousand feet from the ground, and started gliding for the enemy lines. Then he wavered, plunged sickeningly, and fell headlong into the wood behind La Bruyère.

Farther east, almost over the front trenches, a two-seater Albatross and a British pilot were having a desperate tussle. The bombardment had stopped, and from where we stood every movement could be followed. First one, then another, climbed uppermost and dived back, swooped out and wheeled in again, so that the two planes seemed to clear each other only by inches. Then it looked as if they closed and interlocked. I expected to see both go crashing, when suddenly the wings of one seemed to shrivel up, and the machine dropped like a stone.

"Hun," said Archie. "That makes three. Oh, good lads! Good lads!"

Then I saw something which took away my breath. Sloping down in wide circles came a German machine, and, following, a little behind and a little above, a British. It was the first surrender in mid-air I had seen. In my amazement I watched the couple right down to the ground, till the enemy landed in a big meadow across the highroad and our own man in a field nearer the river.

When I looked back into the sky, it was bare. North, south, east, and west, there was not a sign of aircraft, British or German.

A violent trembling took me. Archie was sweeping the heavens with his glasses and muttering to himself. Where was the fifth man? He must have fought his way through, and it was too late.

But was it? From the toe of a great rolling cloud-bank a flame shot earthwards, followed by a V-shaped trail of smoke. British or Boche? British or Boche? I didn't wait long for an answer. For, riding over the far end of the cloud, came two of our fighting scouts.

I tried to be cool, and snapped my glasses into their case, though the reaction made me want to shout. Archie turned to me with a nervous smile and a quivering mouth. "I think we have won on the post," he said.

He reached out a hand for mine, his eyes still on the sky, and I was grasping it when it was torn away. He was staring upwards with a white face.

We were looking at the sixth enemy plane.

It had been behind the others and much lower, and was making straight at a great speed for the east. The glasses showed me a different type of machine – a big machine with short wings, which looked menacing as a hawk in a covey of grouse. It was under the cloud bank, and above, satisfied, easing down after their fight, and unwitting of this enemy, rode the two British craft.

A neighbouring anti-aircraft gun broke out into a sudden burst, and I thanked Heaven for its inspiration. Curious as to this new development, the two British turned, caught sight of the Boche, and dived for him.

What happened in the next minutes I cannot tell. The three seemed to be mixed up in a dog-fight, so that I could not distinguish friend from foe. My hands no longer trembled; I was too desperate. The patter of machine-guns came down to us, and then one of the three broke clear and began to climb. The others strained to follow, but in a second he had risen beyond their fire, for he had easily the pace of them. Was it the Hun?

Archie's dry lips were talking.

"It's Lensch," he said.

"How d'you know?" I gasped angrily.

"Can't mistake him. Look at the way he slipped out as he banked. That's his patent trick."

In that agonizing moment hope died in me. I was perfectly calm now, for the time for anxiety had gone. Farther and farther drifted the British pilots behind, while Lensch in the completeness of his triumph looped more than once as if to cry an insulting farewell. In less than three minutes he would be safe inside his own lines, and he carried the knowledge which for us was death.

Someone was bawling in my ear, and pointing upward. It was Archie, and his face was wild. I looked and gasped – seized my glasses and looked again.

A second before Lensch had been alone; now there were two machines.

I heard Archie's voice. "My God, it's the Gladas – the little Gladas." His fingers were digging into my arm and his face was against my shoulder. And then his excitement sobered into an awe which choked his speech, as he stammered – "It's old – "

But I did not need him to tell me the name, for I had divined it when I first saw the new plane drop from the clouds. I had that queer sense that comes sometimes to a man that a friend is present when he cannot see him. Somewhere up in the void two heroes were fighting their last battle – and one of them had a crippled leg.

I had never any doubt about the result, though Archie told me later that he went crazy with suspense. Lensch was not aware of his opponent till he was almost upon him, and I wonder if by any freak of instinct he recognized his greatest antagonist. He never fired a shot, nor did Peter... I saw the German twist and side-slip as if to baffle the fate descending upon him. I saw Peter veer over vertically and I knew that the end had come. He was there to make certain of victory, and he took the only way... The machines closed, there was a crash which I felt though I could not hear it, and next second both were hurtling down, over and over, to the earth.

They fell in the river just short of the enemy lines, but I did not see them, for my eyes were blinded and I was on my knees.

After that it was all a dream. I found myself being embraced by a French General of Division, and saw the first companies of the cheerful blue-coats whom I had longed for. With them came the rain, and it was under a weeping April sky that early in the night I marched what was left of my division away from the battle-field. The enemy guns were starting to speak behind us, but I did not heed them. I knew that now there were warders at the gate, and I believed that by the grace of God that gate was barred forever.

They took Peter from the wreckage with scarcely a scar except his twisted leg. Death had smoothed out some of the age in him, and left his face much as I remembered it long ago in the Mashonaland hills. In his pocket was his old battered *Pilgrim's Progress.* It lies before me as I write, and beside it – for I was his only legatee – the little case which came to him weeks later, containing the highest honour that can be bestowed upon a soldier of Britain.

It was from the *Pilgrim's Progress* that I read next morning, when in the lee of an apple-orchard Mary and Blenkiron and I stood in the soft spring rain beside his grave. And what I read was the tale of the end not of Mr Standfast, whom he had singled out for his counterpart, but of Mr Valiant-for-Truth whom he had not hoped to emulate. I set down the words as a salute and a farewell:

"*Then said he, 'I am going to my Father's; and though with great difficulty I am got hither, yet now I do not repent me of all the trouble I have been at to arrive where I am. My sword I give to him that shall succeed me in my pilgrimage, and my courage and skill to him that can get it. My marks and scars I carry with me, to be a witness for me that I have fought His battles who now will be my rewarder.'*

"*So he passed over, and all the trumpets sounded for him on the other side.*"

JOHN BUCHAN'S BOOKS FROM WHICH QUOTATIONS ARE TAKEN

African Colony, The (1903),
Augustus (1937),
Blanket of the Dark, The (1931),
Dancing Floor, The (1926),
Gap in the Curtain, The (1932),
Great Hours in Sport (1921),
Half-Hearted, The (1900),
History of the Great War, A, Vols I, II, IV
Homilies and Recreations (1926),
John Burnet of Barns (1898),
Julius Caesar (1932),
Lodge in the Wilderness, A (1906),
*Long Traverse, The (1941),
Magic Walking-Stick, The (1932),
Marquess of Montrose, The (1928),
*Memory Hold-the-Door (1940),
Men and Deeds (1935)
Moon Endureth, The (1912),
Mr Standfast (1919),
Musa Piscatrix (1896),
Novel and the Fairy Tale, The (1931)
Oliver Cromwell (1934)

Path of the King, The (1921),
Poems, Scots and English (1917),
Prince of the Captivity, A (1933),
Salute to Adventurers (1915),
Scholar Gypsies, The (1896),
*Sick Heart River (1941),
Sir Walter Scott (1932),
Some Eighteenth-Century By-ways (1908),
Witch Wood (1927),

* Published after the author's death.

John Buchan

Gordon at Khartoum

The year is 1883 and Gladstone finds that the cutting of the Suez Canal has involved Britain irrevocably in Egypt's affairs. General Gordon, Governor of the Sudan, is sent on a mission to evacuate Khartoum. He is besieged there for ten months by the Mahdi's troops and is killed two days before a relief force arrives. This gripping historical account focuses on the bravery of this great man.

Grey Weather

Grey Weather is the first collection of sketches from John Buchan, author of *The Thirty-nine Steps.* The subtitle, Moorland Tales of My Own People, sets the theme of these fourteen stories. Shepherds, farmers, herdsmen and poachers are Buchan's subjects and his love for the hills and the lochs shines through.

John Buchan

Julius Caesar

John Buchan wrote of Caesar 'He performed the greatest constructive task ever achieved by human hands. He drew the habitable earth into an empire which lasted for five centuries, and he laid the foundations of a fabric of law and government which is still standing after two thousand years.'

In this romantic biography Buchan attempts to understand the hidden thoughts of the great soldier. He charts the tale of Caesar's youth, early political career, success, conquest of Gaul and of the world, ending with his murder at the hands of Brutus and the Republican-minded conspirators.

The King's Grace

This sympathetic portrait starts with the death of Edward VII and George V's succession. It was a reign that saw many changes including the Union of South Africa, the First World War and the General Strike of 1926.

John Buchan wrote that 'This book is not a biography of King George, but an attempt to provide a picture – and some slight interpretation – of his reign, with the Throne as the continuing thing through an epoch of unprecedented change.'

John Buchan

Montrose

This is a compassionate biography of the legendary Scottish commander, James Graham, Marquis of Montrose. John Buchan describes Montrose's command of the royalist forces during the 1644 to 1650 war with the Covenanters. Montrose's exceptional strength, leadership and military genius are brought to life. Buchan also illustrates an important period in Scottish history, adding his own measure of adventure to this study.

Oliver Cromwell

John Buchan sets out to redress popular opinion of this English soldier and statesman. His biography achieves that aim, starting with Cromwell's childhood and youth.

Born in 1599, Cromwell was a devout Puritan who, when war broke out, formed his Ironsides. He won the battles of Marston Moor and Naseby and brought Charles I to trial. After establishing the Commonwealth, he suppressed the Levellers, Ireland and the Scots. In 1653, five years before his death, he established a Protectorate.

John Buchan wrote of Cromwell 'He is a soldier now on the grand scale, strategist as well as tactician, statesman as well as fighting man, and it is by this new phase of his military career that his place is to be adjudged in the hierarchy of the great captains'.

TITLES BY JOHN BUCHAN AVAILABLE DIRECT FROM HOUSE OF STRATUS

Quantity		£	$(US)	$(CAN)	€
	FICTION				
☐	THE BLANKET OF THE DARK	6.99	12.95	19.95	13.50
☐	CASTLE GAY	6.99	12.95	19.95	13.50
☐	THE COURTS OF THE MORNING	6.99	12.95	19.95	13.50
☐	THE DANCING FLOOR	6.99	12.95	19.95	13.50
☐	THE FREE FISHERS	6.99	12.95	19.95	13.50
☐	THE GAP IN THE CURTAIN	6.99	12.95	19.95	13.50
☐	GREENMANTLE	6.99	12.95	19.95	13.50
☐	GREY WEATHER	6.99	12.95	19.95	13.50
☐	THE HALF-HEARTED	6.99	12.95	19.95	13.50
☐	THE HOUSE OF THE FOUR WINDS	6.99	12.95	19.95	13.50
☐	HUNTINGTOWER	6.99	12.95	19.95	13.50
☐	THE ISLAND OF SHEEP	6.99	12.95	19.95	13.50
☐	JOHN BURNET OF BARNS	6.99	12.95	19.95	13.50
☐	THE LONG TRAVERSE	6.99	12.95	19.95	13.50
☐	A LOST LADY OF OLD YEARS	6.99	12.95	19.95	13.50
☐	MIDWINTER	6.99	12.95	19.95	13.50
☐	THE PATH OF THE KING	6.99	12.95	19.95	13.50
☐	THE POWER-HOUSE	6.99	12.95	19.95	13.50
☐	PRESTER JOHN	6.99	12.95	19.95	13.50

PAYMENT

Please tick currency you wish to use:

☐ £ (Sterling) ☐ $ (US) ☐ $ (CAN) ☐ € (Euros)

Allow for shipping costs charged per order plus an amount per book as set out in the tables below:

CURRENCY/DESTINATION

	£(Sterling)	$(US)	$(CAN)	€(Euros)
Cost per order				
UK	1.50	2.25	3.50	2.50
Europe	3.00	4.50	6.75	5.00
North America	3.00	3.50	5.25	5.00
Rest of World	3.00	4.50	6.75	5.00
Additional cost per book				
UK	0.50	0.75	1.15	0.85
Europe	1.00	1.50	2.25	1.70
North America	1.00	1.00	1.50	1.70
Rest of World	1.50	2.25	3.50	3.00

PLEASE SEND CHEQUE OR INTERNATIONAL MONEY ORDER.
payable to: STRATUS HOLDINGS plc or HOUSE OF STRATUS INC. or card payment as indicated

STERLING EXAMPLE

Cost of book(s): .... Example: 3 x books at £6.99 each: £20.97
Cost of order: .... Example: £1.50 (Delivery to UK address)
Additional cost per book: .... Example: 3 x £0.50: £1.50
Order total including shipping: .... Example: £23.97

VISA, MASTERCARD, SWITCH, AMEX:

☐☐☐☐☐☐☐☐☐☐☐☐☐☐☐☐☐☐☐☐

Issue number (Switch only):

☐☐☐

Start Date: ☐☐/☐☐

Expiry Date: ☐☐/☐☐

Signature: ______________________

NAME: ______________________

ADDRESS: ______________________

COUNTRY: ______________________

ZIP/POSTCODE: ______________________

Please allow 28 days for delivery. Despatch normally within 48 hours.

Prices subject to change without notice.
Please tick box if you do not wish to receive any additional information. ☐